# Everybody's Children

William T. Gormley, Jr.

# Everybody's Children

*Child Care as a
Public Problem*

The Brookings Institution
*Washington, D.C.*

About Brookings

The Brookings Institution is a private nonprofit organization devoted to research, education, and publication on important issues of domestic and foreign policy. Its principal purpose is to bring knowledge to bear on current and emerging policy problems. The Institution was founded on December 8, 1927, to merge the activities of the Institute for Government Research, founded in 1916, the Institute of Economics, founded in 1922, and the Robert Brookings Graduate School of Economics, founded in 1924.

The Institution maintains a position of neutrality on issues of public policy. Interpretations or conclusions in Brookings publications should be understood to be solely those of the authors.

*Library of Congress Cataloging-in-Publication data:*

Gormley, William T., 1950–
    Everybody's children: child care as a public problem / William T. Gormley, Jr.
    p.    cm.
    Includes bibliographical references and index.
    ISBN 0-8157-3224-4 (alk. paper).—ISBN 0-8157-3223-6 (pbk. : alk. paper)
    1. Child care—United States.   2. Child care—Government policy—United States.   3. Child care services—Government policy—United States.   I. Title.
    HQ778.63.G674   1995
    362.7'0973—dc20                                                                95-18422
                                                                                          CIP

9 8 7 6 5 4 3 2 1

The paper used in this publication meets the minimum requirements of the American National Standard for Information Services—Permanence of Paper for Printed Library Materials, ANTI Z39.48-1984.

Typeset in Sabon and Gill Sans
Composition by Princeton Editorial Associates, Princeton, New Jersey
Printed by R. R. Donnelley and Sons Co., Harrisonburg, Virginia

*To my nieces and nephews*

# Acknowledgments

THIS RESEARCH WAS made possible by a grant from the Smith Richardson Foundation and by a sabbatical leave from Georgetown University. I am grateful to both for their support and to Cheryl Keller of the Smith Richardson Foundation for her encouragement.

Jennifer Bush did an outstanding job as my research assistant for this project. Her resourcefulness and persistence in ferreting out evidence and elusive documents were remarkable.

Several people read the manuscript and offered excellent suggestions. The critical commentary of Eugene Bardach, Donald Kettl, Stuart Kerachsky, and John Witte was extremely helpful.

A number of Georgetown University colleagues offered timely assistance on tricky questions relevant to their expertise. Gregg Bloche of the Law Center, Patty Fairchild and Catherine Langlois of the Business School, Tarhan Feyzioglu of the Economics Department, Jean Mitchell of the Public Policy Program, Diana Owen and Mark Warren of the Government Department all helped at critical junctures.

On legal issues, I received excellent advice from Ken Gormley and Chuck Tremper. On methodological issues, Jim Granato, Tim McDaniel, and Sandy Schneider were particularly helpful. On child care issues, I

learned a great deal from Lynn Kagan, Deborah Phillips, Sheila Kamerman, Gwen Morgan, Sandra Hofferth, Nancy Ebb, and Suzanne Helburn, among others. On diverse issues, Bob Katzmann and Kent Weaver
offered encouragement and support. On what it is like to be a child, I
have my nieces and nephews to thank.

It is not always easy to obtain access to databases gathered by other
analysts and organizations. Fortunately, Bill Chafetz of Deloitte and
Touche and Peg Keeler of the Springhouse Corporation shared their data
on hospitals' child care policies promptly and efficiently. Ellen Kisker of
Mathematica Policy Research Inc. supplied supplementary data to help
me understand the nuances of an unusually comprehensive survey of day
care centers in the United States. And Janet Mascia kindly furnished data
from a General Accounting Office study of regulatory enforcement.

Most of the data presented here were gathered from scratch. I am
particularly grateful to Coleman Baker for giving me access to Vermont's
child care licensing records over a five-year period. Donna Alexander
made a special contribution by helping me to interpret those records. I am
also grateful to several state licensing directors and supervisors who
granted me generous access to their child care staff: Prins Ella Anderson
of Oklahoma; Dana Andrews of Colorado; Katherine Holod of Pennsylvania; and Talitha Wright and Jan Keller of North Carolina. In addition,
I would like to thank Doug Sanders and Virginia Hancock of Texas, Bill
Henderson and Pat Wojchiehowski of Missouri, and Linda Nessen of
California for helping me to obtain data on family day care homes in their
states.

During the final stages, I was fortunate to work with my good friend
Alice Honeywell of Madison, Wisconsin, who deftly copyedited the
manuscript. David Bearce verified the references and Peggy Kim assisted
with the index. The staff of the Brookings Institution Publications Program pulled out all the stops to get the book out on schedule and to
present it effectively. Finally, Nancy Davidson of Brookings deserves
credit for prodding me to write the book.

# Contents

# 1 | Private Headaches, Public Dilemmas

D ESPITE OCCASIONAL BURSTS of attention, child care has not yet secured a firm niche on the public agenda. It captures headlines and triggers public policy debates when a Cabinet nominee who made hasty arrangements to care for a child is rejected, when a judge penalizes a mother for having placed her child in day care while earning a degree, or when child abuse at a day care center disrupts the tranquility of a small town. For the most part, though, child care remains a private headache, only fitfully addressed by public policies.

It is not as if people never think about child care. Parents of young children fret constantly about it. They ask whether they can afford child care or a particular child care arrangement. They wish they knew how to choose a good provider from a list of unfamiliar names and facilities. They dread the possibility that their favorite provider will quit. They worry about what will happen if relatives are not available to pinch-hit in an emergency. And they wonder if they are doing the best they can for their children.

Historically, child care in the United States has been a private issue, to be resolved within the family or community. When a problem arises, surely grandma will come to the rescue. And if grandma is not available,

1

how about the neighbor down the street? The fundamental premises used to be that (1) most young children would be cared for during the day by their mothers, with supplementary assistance from relatives, neighbors, and friends; (2) most families would remain intact over an extended period of time; (3) most wives would remain at home until their children reach the age of five or six; (4) most families would have close relatives nearby; and (5) most families would be firmly anchored in a supportive community.

These premises still hold for some people, but not for most Americans. Over time, young marrieds have moved away from grandma, and the neighbor down the street has gone off to work. In addition, a growing number of children have been born out of wedlock, while others have struggled with the consequences of divorce. The demand for child care has become more pervasive. At the same time, available, affordable, high-quality child care has become essential to meeting other public policy goals, such as welfare reform. Under such circumstances, it is difficult to think of child care as a purely private issue anymore. Institutions based on more accurate premises may be needed.

## Why Care about Child Care?

What is child care? For the purposes of this study, I define it as a regularly used arrangement for supervising young children that supplements care by one or both parents. It is usually provided outside the child's home but not always. It is usually for pay but not always. It is more frequent and more sustained than occasional babysitting but less sustained than around-the-clock care. It may or may not include a significant educational component; it may or may not be regulated by government.

In this book, I focus on child care for children who are under six years old, but I do devote some attention, in chapter 6, to school-age children. I place somewhat greater emphasis on poor children and their needs than other children, but I also discuss the needs of all children, because child care problems are not confined to one economic or social stratum.

With so many other problems to worry about, why should we care about child care in particular? First, unreliable child care contributes to family stress at a time when families are unusually fragile. Child care availability problems contribute to depression among employed mothers with young children.[1] And child care quality problems contribute to ill health among mothers who work.[2] The latter, incidentally, is true for both married and single mothers. Even fathers seem to suffer, though the effects are more muted.[3] Such pressures add to the heavy burdens that families already face.

Second, reliable child care is critical to the health of the economy. The percentage of women with children under the age of six who participate in the labor force has increased sharply in recent years, from 39 percent in 1975 to 60 percent in 1994 (see chapter 2). Women continue to shoulder a disproportionate share of child-rearing responsibilities, which has important implications for the American economy. Female employees distracted by unsuccessful child care arrangements are not good for business. Female employees who quit because their child care arrangements have collapsed are not good for business either. Men are distracted too when child care arrangements are uncertain or unsatisfactory. Overall, productivity suffers.

Third, reliable child care is indispensable to gender equity. In recent years, proponents of gender equity have made remarkable progress in providing equal opportunity to women who wish to experience the financial and psychological benefits of sustained employment outside the home. Legal changes and court decisions underscore a new commitment to gender equity. Women today enjoy choices that their mothers never had. But that freedom is often restricted by inadequate child care options.

A substantial percentage of working women have misgivings about their child care arrangements, and some have doubts about leaving their children in anyone else's hands. Among families with employed mothers, 30 percent of the parents who use child care report that they would switch to a different child care arrangement if they could.[4] Moreover, one-third of all women continue to believe that in an ideal world a woman should stay at home with her children until they enter school.[5]

At the same time, a substantial percentage of nonworking women wish that they were working and cite inadequate, inaccessible, or unaffordable child care as a key reason for their failure to do so. A Detroit-area study, for example, found that 24 percent of nonworking women would look for work or return to work if satisfactory child care were available at a reasonable cost.[6] And national studies demonstrate that as child care costs increase, women are less likely to work.[7]

Fourth, and most fundamental, children are more vulnerable and less articulate than the rest of society. They constitute the single largest disadvantaged group in America, and they are poorly equipped to deal with their disadvantages. They can smile and they can cry, but they cannot vote, lobby, contribute to political campaigns, run for office, give speeches, or drive to the capital for a demonstration. These limitations have taken their toll. Child poverty rates have increased to 22 percent in 1992.[8] Among children under the age of six, the poverty rate is even higher.[9] Children spend less time with parents. This need not be harmful if children enjoy continuous care with another responsible, caring adult, but continuity is unlikely in a profession with low pay and high turnover. As a result, many young children find themselves handed from one provider to the next. Numerous studies show that this adversely affects child development.[10]

## Why Should Government Act?

To argue that we as a society should care about child care is not necessarily to argue that the government should intervene to relieve every anxiety that parents of young children experience. Governments have other urgent responsibilities, and well-intentioned government interventions sometimes make matters worse. Although we must think carefully about how, when, and where government should act, several weaknesses of the child care market require government intervention.

Child care can strengthen or undermine children's cognitive and social development. If child care quality is high, children learn rapidly, develop strong attachments to adults, and behave sociably toward other children. If quality is low, children learn more slowly, develop less secure attachments, and demonstrate less sociability and consideration for others. These findings have held up in numerous settings, involving both group day care centers and family day care homes.[11] In short, child care quality affects how children grow up, for better or for worse.

When high-quality child care offers positive "externalities," or benefits that extend beyond the immediate beneficiaries, market mechanisms are inefficient. When individual children benefit from high-quality child care, other members of society may benefit as well. Under such circumstances, government has a responsibility to act. If children who have experienced high-quality child care arrive at the schoolhouse steps ready to learn, then education becomes easier, more rewarding, more effective. If schools succeed, then we can expect higher employment levels, higher wages, and better health, among other positive outcomes.[12] The alternative is sobering. As Fuchs puts it, "When children are stunted physically, mentally, or emotionally, we all pay a price, and we all ought to be willing to bear some of the cost of raising the potential of the next generation."[13]

Parents do not have easy access to good information on the relative merits of alternative child care arrangements, alternative child care facilities, or alternative child care providers. This is a classic example of "market failure." It means that parents cannot satisfy their preferences without investing significant time in search processes, time that parents of young children seldom have. Even if parents do invest significant time and effort in the quest for better information about child care options, they cannot effectively monitor child care facilities and providers. The result may be adverse selection, in which only low-quality providers enter the market, or hidden action, in which providers defraud consumers who cannot perfectly monitor them. As Walker has argued, both adverse selection and hidden action are very real possibilities in child care, because of the relatively low attractiveness of the field and the practical difficulties of monitoring so many facilities.[14] Approximately 80,000 day care centers and at least 668,000 family day care homes operated in 1990.[15] To monitor such an industry is a formidable task.

The private sector cannot be counted upon to remedy these problems. Private firms and private charities are limited as to what they can and will contribute. This also illustrates market failure. Take, for example, the cost of child care. Day care centers receive only 6 percent of their total income from community organizations, religious organizations, and cash donations from nongovernment sources.[16] Because government support is fairly limited (only 22 percent), parents foot the rest of the bill. One-third of all day care centers do receive some significant in-kind contributions, but only 15 percent of day care centers receive free or discounted space.[17] Other contributions (such as supplies or toys) help but are not usually significant. And hidden subsidies from providers, though well intentioned, may actually make matters worse. By accepting extraordinarily low wages, in an effort to accommodate tight parental budgets, providers help parents to pay their bills in the short run but also guarantee that child care will remain a low-paying, relatively unattractive profession in the long run.

Government also has special responsibilities to care for poor children who need high-quality child care if they are to overcome their economic disadvantages. Markets are indifferent to income distributions, but governments should not be. Indeed, one of the basic functions of government is to care for the least fortunate members of society. Transfer payments to poor children to achieve equality of opportunity are justifiable whether buttressed by cost-benefit analyses or not. Transfer payments to achieve greater equality of result are also justifiable, especially in a society where the gap between the rich and the poor is enormous. The case is even stronger when one considers the effects of past and current discrimination on certain disadvantaged groups in society.

Because other programs depend on the success of child care, government also cannot be indifferent to it. For example, a well-functioning child care system is essential to welfare reform. If AFDC recipients with young children are to participate in job training and education programs, they need stable, secure child care arrangements. Otherwise they will not participate or they will participate half-heartedly and then fail.[18] That would be unfortunate because studies show that welfare-to-work programs usually offer net benefits to society.[19] In recognition of these needs, President Clinton's welfare reform proposal would have allocated nearly half of the total package for child care. Welfare reform initiatives offered by Republicans have also stressed the vital importance of child care subsidies. For example, Virginia Governor George Allen successfully advocated a welfare reform plan that would require increased child care spending for at least two years.

Child care is also linked to educational improvement. The nation's governors as well as Presidents Bush and Clinton and Congress have formally declared that all children should start school ready to learn by the year 2000. That goal will be very difficult to achieve unless more children have access to high-quality child care. As the Carnegie Corporation reported, approximately half of all young children today confront one or more major risk factors: inadequate prenatal care, isolated parents, substandard child care, poverty, or insufficient stimulation.[20] High-quality child care is not a perfect antidote to all of these problems, but it can help to correct for some of them.

In some ways child care is also relevant to children's health. Recent studies show that in most states fewer than 60 percent of all two-year-olds are immunized.[21] Other studies show that preventive medicine is much cheaper than emergency care. For example, vaccination against measles, mumps, and rubella saves $14 for every $1 invested.[22] Although independent health care initiatives are needed to address these problems, child care presents an excellent opportunity to monitor and encourage progress toward national immunization goals. Most states require child immunizations, and regulators monitor this when they visit child care facilities. Child care facilities that are exempt from regulations cannot be scrutinized for this purpose.

## Doubts and Reservations

To those unfamiliar with the nuances of these disputes, it may seem clear that the government should intervene aggressively to enhance the well-being of children, especially poor children. Yet that is not obvious, nor is it obvious how the government should proceed when it does intervene.

In the first place, some programs already in existence do not work particularly well, while others work in the short run but not the long run. Still others work in the short run and the long run but only if they are properly designed. Studies of Head Start and other early intervention programs make it clear that government child care programs aimed at disadvantaged children can succeed if they are well funded and properly designed. Even then, there is no guarantee of long-term success.[23]

Some regulations work as intended, but others generate unexpected and undesired side effects. Child care regulations can enhance cognitive and social development, promote health and safety, undermine availability, aggravate affordability, or some combination of the above. The precise consequences may depend not only on the regulations themselves but also on their target populations.[24] Thus it is important to choose regulatory policies and processes with care.

Government has the capacity to shape the child care industry profoundly if it wishes to do so. It can encourage or discourage group day care centers, family day care homes, for-profit centers, church-based centers, care by relatives, neighbors, or friends. It can compete directly with private providers through government centers. It can compete indirectly through programs in public schools. It can pick winners and losers or maintain strict neutrality. Yet experts disagree on which of these strategies makes the most sense.[25]

When exactly are children ready for child care outside the home? And which children benefit the most from it? How good must child care be before societal benefits exceed the costs? How poor must children be before societal benefits exceed the costs? Some of these questions have answers but none that are absolutely precise.[26] Also, each of these questions touches on sentiments that are both varied and deeply felt. As a result, program design must be based on both values and empirical research. A consensus on values has proven elusive in this controversial area.

Finally, subsidies, regulations, programs, services, and other policy initiatives cost money, which governments are reluctant to spend in the current political climate. Federal policymakers are much more cognizant of deficit politics than they used to be and much more skeptical of social programs. State governments face constitutional requirements to balance their budgets, competing interests and interest groups, and vigilant taxpayers. Local governments face shrinking tax bases, mandates from other governments, and burgeoning social problems of their own. Opportunity costs are real for all levels of government. Even if governments do decide to confront social problems, why should child care be high on their list?

## Child Care in Industrialized Nations

The United States is not the only nation to confront child care dilemmas in the late twentieth century. Other nations have coped with the issue to varying degrees and with different strategies. Before considering the U.S. context in detail, it is instructive to examine how other industrialized nations have responded to these challenges.

Esping-Andersen groups industrialized nations into three categories: (1) social democratic welfare states, such as the Scandinavian countries; (2) corporatist welfare states, such as France, Germany, and Italy; and (3) liberal market states, such as Australia, Canada, the United Kingdom, New Zealand, and the United States.[27] Some nations, such as Japan, do not fall unequivocally into one category.[28] Each nation is, of course, unique, but the framework allows for some general observations.

According to Esping-Andersen, the social democratic welfare states are committed to both the right to work (despite young children) and the right not to work (because of young children). The liberal market states, in contrast, recognize no such rights, and the corporatist welfare states fall somewhere between. These differences should result in different child care policies and, more broadly, different social policies towards families with young children.

### Social Democratic Welfare States

By and large, the social democratic welfare states have made the strongest commitment to child care policies that enable parents to combine cheap, reliable child care with gainful employment outside the home. In these countries, child care is heavily subsidized by the central government and is available to all at a nominal fee. In Sweden, for example, parents pay only 10 percent of the costs of a day care center.[29]

The overwhelming majority of centers are run by local governments; a substantial minority are run by nonprofit organizations; for-profit firms are largely irrelevant. Family day care homes also help parents with child care needs, especially those with toddlers (twelve to thirty-six months of age). Local governments play a significant role in both delivering the services and monitoring the facilities. Regulations are relatively strict, and the quality of care is generally high. For example, child-staff ratios are quite low in Sweden and in Finland.[30] Experts have concluded that the quality of child care in Scandinavia is outstanding.[31]

In general, the social democratic welfare states have decided that one year of age (or thereabouts) is a key turning point in a child's life. A combination of maternity benefits and paid parental leave makes it possible for parents (usually mothers) to stay home with their infants for about a year (or more, in Sweden) at substantial rates of pay.[32] Moreover, when they return to work outside the home, they return to a job that has been kept open for them. At that point, state-sponsored child care services become available at very low rates. Not surprisingly, enrollments of toddlers in child care are relatively high in the Scandinavian countries.[33]

## Corporatist Welfare States

The corporatist welfare states have also invested heavily in child care facilities and services. In these countries, child care is relatively cheap and heavily subsidized. Indeed, in Italy and France, child care for three- to five-year-olds is virtually free. Parents are expected to pay for child care for younger children, but these contributions seldom exceed one-fourth or one-third of operating costs.[34] In Germany, child care is not free, but it is very reasonably priced, and parents on social assistance often pay less than other parents.[35]

Child care is often provided by family day care homes and by centers run by local governments or nonprofit organizations.[36] Center sponsorship varies somewhat across countries. In France, 85 percent of the preschools (écoles maternelles) are public;[37] in Italy, 65 percent of the preschools (scuole materne) have public funding;[38] in Germany, 35 percent of the preschools (Kindergärten) are public.[39] In these countries, as in the social democratic welfare states, for-profit centers are virtually nonexistent. Responsibility for regulation varies across countries. In federal systems, such as Germany, regulations are promulgated and implemented by state governments (or *Länder*); elsewhere, regulations are promulgated by the national government and implemented by regional or local governments. An impressive feature of day care centers in Germany and France is that the staff members are well educated, well trained, and well paid.[40] In Germany, however, most of the centers are part-day, which does not meet the needs of mothers who work full time.

In contrast to the social welfare states, the corporatist welfare states seem to have decided that the age of three is a critical turning point in a child's life. When that milestone is reached, child care spaces become available to the general population at substantially reduced rates. Until that point, child care is more expensive, though not prohibitively so. Thus the premise is that mothers should stay at home until their child reaches the age of three. To facilitate this, the corporatist welfare states have typically guaranteed parental leaves with job protection until the child is three. Relatively modest stipends help to compensate for forgone income, though they are often rooted in the premise that a husband has a well-paying job. For single mothers, the choice is usually between work and public assistance.[41]

## Liberal Market States

If differences between corporatist-statist welfare states and social democratic welfare states are fairly subtle, differences between liberal market states and other industrialized nations are striking. In liberal market states, child care subsidies are available to both poor and middle-class parents, but both groups are disappointed and frustrated. The poor are, in principle, eligible for full subsidies in many jurisdictions, but shortages of funding and child care slots often result in long waiting lists. Middle-class parents who purchase child care are eligible for tax breaks, but their child care expenditures remain high because of limited subsidies to child care providers. Finding and paying for good child care is a struggle.

In liberal market countries, day care centers are sponsored by a variety of institutions. The precise role of the for-profit sector varies both across countries and within countries. In the United States, the for-profit sector accounts for more than one-third of all centers and is particularly strong in the southern states, where regulatory standards are relatively low. In Canada, for-profit centers are relatively rare in some provinces (especially Manitoba and Saskatchewan), plentiful in others (such as Alberta and

Newfoundland).[42] Different provincial policies on eligibility for subsidies help to explain these differences.[43] Among the federal systems (the United States, Canada, Australia), regulations are promulgated and enforced by state governments.[44] Such regulations vary considerably across provinces or states.[45] In Canada, for example, Saskatchewan requires all staff members to have some early childhood training or experience, while Alberta requires only one of every six staff members to have early childhood training.[46]

Whereas the social democratic welfare states facilitate a parent's work outside the home when a child reaches the age of one and the corporatist states do so when a child reaches the age of three, the liberal market states do not draw such sharp distinctions. Nor do they actively encourage parents of young children either to work or to stay at home. To many parents, such neutrality seems like indifference. Without paid parental leaves, parents of limited means find it difficult to care for an infant (or toddler) at home. Without heavily subsidized child care facilities, parents find it difficult to place a preschool child at a desirable facility. In the absence of ample government support, many parents must choose cheap child care of dubious quality, while they struggle to make ends meet. Other parents opt for the dole, where child care may not be an issue because parents remain at home.

As a liberal market state, the United States exhibits many of the characteristics described above. The U.S. context, however, is also one in which complacency is particularly difficult to justify. Female employment in the United States is relatively high and more likely to be full time.[47] Thus demand for child care is probably greater, and the consequences of child care quality for children's growth are likely to be greater as well, because children spend more time in such settings. Child poverty is also unusually high in the United States, as is the percentage of families with children headed by single mothers.[48] Due to both factors, affordability problems are worse.

In other respects, the United States also faces unusual problems. For-profit child care constitutes a large and growing percentage of the U.S. day care market, which is troublesome because of persistent doubts about the quality of for-profit care—a subject discussed in depth in chapter 4. Also, the United States has a huge unregulated family day care market. Although a black market or gray market for family day care exists in other industrialized nations as well, the unregulated market here is particularly large (82 to 90 percent of all family day care homes). By way of comparison, an estimated 20 percent of family day care in the United Kingdom is unregulated.[49] For all these reasons, child care in the United States warrants special attention.

## Research Strategy

The approach I take in this book can be characterized as public policy analysis. I combine normative analysis and empirical research to help identify the consequences of public policy choices. Like most policy analysts, I devote considerable attention to problem definitions, policy options, and evidence of public policy impacts. However, I also depart from the norms of public policy analysis in three important ways.

First, I take institutions seriously and I define them broadly. By institutions I mean both formal institutions (such as organizations) and informal institutions (such as norms). Instead of treating institutions as exogenous variables or constraints, I treat them as manipulable variables and attempt to understand their contributions to problems and potential solutions. Elsewhere, I have characterized this approach as "institutional policy analysis."[50] A hallmark of institutional policy analysis is that it considers both the substantive and procedural consequences of alternative institutional arrangements.

Second, I am not content to identify instances of market failure, important though they are. Rather, I discuss market failures, government failures, and societal failures simultaneously and with the same fundamental questions in mind. This should temper any premature expectations that a single institution or institutional type can solve all child care problems. At the same time, it provides a broader repertoire of potential policy solutions to draw upon when devising strategies for reform. In short, I seek a more holistic view of the policymaking process.

Third, I employ a bottom-up methodology rooted in the conviction that federalism offers distinctive opportunities for both policy innovation and policy research. I regard federalism as both a policy constraint and a research opportunity. With that in mind, I have conducted a good deal of research in the hinterlands. Although I have utilized national databases, I have not allowed them to define the boundaries of my research. When databases have not been available to answer a particular question, I have sought to create them from scratch. I have also sought to learn from the people who, in some respects, know child care the best—namely, the state government officials who actually monitor child care facilities on a daily basis.

In this book, I address some difficult social policy questions. Does every parent have a right to stay at home with a child without experiencing substantial financial harm? If so, for how long? With what compensation? At whose expense? Does every child have a right to high-quality child care? If so, should this be contingent upon a parent's ability to pay, willingness to work, attitudes toward child care outside the home? How can the competing claims of employers and employees, mothers who wish to work and mothers who wish to stay at home, mothers and fathers, mothers and children be reconciled? I cannot answer these questions to everyone's satisfaction, but I at least try to make my values clear.

I also seek to answer some equally important institutional questions. Which child care settings are best for children and why? What can government do to improve mediocre facilities or to encourage parents to select better arrangements? Which government agencies are best equipped to monitor child care facilities? How should they go about their tasks? And what are the appropriate roles of schools, churches, private firms, and resource and referral agencies? How can markets, governments, and social institutions collaborate to improve conditions for children, for parents, and for child care providers?

In the next two chapters, I establish some normative benchmarks for making substantive and procedural choices. In chapter 2, I discuss child care as a social problem. I consider two widely used analytic frameworks for thinking about child care problems but find both wanting. I then suggest a broader normative framework suitable for making substantive choices. The framework emphasizes efficiency, justice, and choice.

In chapter 3, I discuss child care as an institutional problem, distinguishing between the formal infrastructure (established organizations) and the informal infrastructure (norms of behavior). I develop a normative framework for making procedural choices involving both infrastructures. That framework emphasizes coordination, discretion, and responsiveness.

The next three chapters present empirical findings on the performance of markets, governments, and society at large. In chapter 4, I focus on two weaknesses of the child care market: a substantial for-profit sector that undermines the quality of group day care centers, and a sprawling family day care sector that is largely untouched by government regulators. I introduce evidence on both and discuss alternative remedies for dealing with them.

In chapter 5, I discuss governmental responses to child care problems, including efforts to strengthen regulatory standards, target regulatory resources, enhance state discretion through block grants, and improve parental choice through vouchers. A close analysis of these and other initiatives suggests that they sometimes work and sometimes backfire.

In chapter 6, I turn to the wider society. Without strong support from schools, businesses, and families, neither free enterprise nor governmental intervention will suffice. Whereas many schools and businesses have ignored child care altogether, others have made token concessions without fundamentally altering their organizational cultures. Resource and referral agencies have sprung up to assist parents as consumers, but their potential has been stunted by a misreading of legal obligations and overly narrow role definitions.

Finally, in chapter 7, I consider alternative models for systemic reform. I argue in favor of institutionalizing the better features of a Mediating Structures Model, an Informed Consumer Model, a Regulatory Bargaining Model, and a Safety Net Model. Different levels of government and different societal institutions must work together if the goals of all four models are to be achieved. Combining certain features of these models will result in sound public policies in the child care domain.

# 2 | Child Care as a Social Problem

I<small>T IS EASY ENOUGH</small> to recognize child care as a serious social problem. It is more difficult to characterize that problem. One can think of child care as a maternal problem, a parental problem, a corporate problem, or a societal problem. Alternatively, one might think of it as a children's problem, in which case one must still decide whether to adopt the vantage point of poor children, at-risk children, or all children. Each of these starting points leads down different paths.

In this chapter, after briefly describing recent changes in the child care market, I consider child care from several vantage points: (1) a work/family perspective, which highlights the conflicts that arise when mothers of young children work outside the home; (2) a parental perspective, which emphasizes such goals as availability, affordability, and quality; and (3) a societal perspective, which attempts to reconcile the often competing interests of children, mothers, fathers, employers, and other members of society. The societal perspective includes consideration of community values. Each of these perspectives has something to offer and will contribute to the analysis that follows. Only the third perspective, however, is comprehensive enough to encompass the most difficult trade-offs that confront policymakers in this field.

15

TABLE 2-1. Primary Child Care Arrangements for Children under Age Five
(Percent)

| Primary child care arrangement | Employed mother | Nonemployed mother | Total |
|---|---|---|---|
| Center | 26.5 | 14.7 | 20.5 |
| Parent | 29.9 | 65.2 | 46.3 |
| Relative in child's home | 6.3 | 5.2 | 5.9 |
| Relative in other home | 11.3 | 5.5 | 8.7 |
| In-home provider | 3.7 | 2.2 | 3.0 |
| Family day care | 18.6 | 2.6 | 10.7 |
| Self-care | 0.0 | 0.1 | 0.1 |
| Lesson | 1.2 | 2.9 | 2.0 |
| Other | 2.3 | 1.7 | 2.8 |
| Total | 100.0 | 100.0 | 100.0 |

SOURCE: Sandra Hofferth and others, National Child Care Survey, 1990 (Washington: Urban Institute Press, 1991), p. 33.

## The New Market for Child Care

Demand for child care has grown dramatically in recent years. Many parents place their children in group day care centers, which care for relatively large numbers of children in a nonresidential setting. Other parents rely upon family day care providers, who care for one or more children in the provider's home, which is adapted for day care use. Still other parents turn to relatives, neighbors, or friends. And a relatively small number hire a nanny or an au pair.

In discussions of child care, it is customary to focus on children under the age of five or six, including infants (up to twelve months), toddlers (twelve to thirty-six months), and preschoolers (thirty-six to seventy-two months).[1] As of 1990, only 46.3 percent of all children under the age of five were primarily cared for by a parent at home (see table 2-1). Not surprisingly, infants are more likely to be cared for by a parent at home than are preschoolers or school-age children. Even mothers of infants, however, are more likely to work than not. Since 1987 a majority of women with children under the age of one have worked outside the home.[2] In 1992, 54 percent of women with infants were members of the labor force.[3]

The single most important reason for the growth of child care in the United States is the sharp increase in female employment. As table 2-2 indicates, labor force participation among women with children under six

TABLE 2-2. Labor Force Participation Rates of Women with
Children under Age Six, 1975–94

| Year | Percent of women employed[a] |
|------|------------------------------|
| 1975 | 39.0 |
| 1976 | 40.1 |
| 1977 | 41.2 |
| 1978 | 44.0 |
| 1979 | 45.7 |
| 1980 | 46.8 |
| 1981 | 48.9 |
| 1982 | 49.9 |
| 1983 | 50.5 |
| 1984 | 52.1 |
| 1985 | 53.5 |
| 1986 | 54.4 |
| 1987 | 56.7 |
| 1988 | 56.1 |
| 1989 | 56.7 |
| 1990 | 58.2 |
| 1991 | 58.4 |
| 1992 | 58.0 |
| 1993 | 57.9 |
| 1994 | 60.3 |

SOURCES: Bureau of Labor Statistics, *Handbook of Labor Statistics* (Government Printing Office, 1989), table 56; Bureau of Labor Statistics, unpublished tables, derived from Current Population Survey, Bulletin 2340 (Washington: Division of Labor Force Statistics, Bureau of Labor Statistics, January 1995).

a. Civilians 16 and older.

years old has climbed from 39.0 percent in 1975 to 60.3 percent in 1994. After reaching a plateau in the early 1990s, the number of working women with young children increased sharply in 1994. Clearly, we have experienced a profound restructuring of social roles.

What accounts for the growth of female employment? Certainly, women's liberation has contributed to this phenomenon. As our life spans have increased, and as women have opted for smaller families, raising children has become less and less the center of women's lives. As Coontz points out, "Both marriage and childrearing occupy a smaller proportion of adults' lives than they did at any time in American history."[4] In addition, women have gone to college and graduate school in record numbers and have acquired marketable skills. Feminist appeals for women to achieve their full potential have coincided with plentiful opportunities for female careers outside the home.

A high divorce rate has also contributed to female employment, with important implications for child care.[5] Although never-married women with children are actually less likely to work than married women with children, divorced, separated, or widowed women with children are more likely to work than married women.[6] Other studies show that single women work longer hours than married women, and they are more reliant on child care outside the home.[7]

Economic difficulties have also encouraged women to work. Most notably, the decline of well-paying manufacturing jobs and the rise of poorly paying service jobs made it difficult for married couples to get by on one income alone, especially if there were other mouths to feed. Between 1970 and 1987 the proportion of mothers in two-parent families who worked outside the home increased from 39 percent to 61 percent.[8] Despite this trend, median family income has remained relatively constant, after controlling for inflation. This suggests that female employment may have become a necessity for many families, including two-parent families that might otherwise have fit the "Ozzie and Harriet" mold.[9]

Although female employment has fueled the growing demand for child care, it has not been the only relevant factor. Many parents of preschoolers have chosen child care in order to give their child an early educational experience or early exposure to other children. Other parents of preschoolers have opted for child care in order to care for sick relatives, to run errands, or simply to take a much-needed break from the rigors of parenting.

Clearly, the traditional family—the father as breadwinner, the mother as housewife, the children at home (or in school and then home)—has become less common. Due to divorce and a sharp increase in the number of illegitimate births, the number of households headed by single women has increased sharply. Due to industrial layoffs and pay cuts, weak economic productivity, and rising expectations among women, the number of dual-income households has also increased sharply. Two-parent families in which only the father works for wages now constitute only 25 percent of all families with children.[10]

These startling social trends have created new opportunities and new problems. On the positive side, they have enabled millions of women to combine a family and a career, which many women prefer. They have also enabled the private sector to fill job vacancies with highly motivated and highly skilled employees. On the negative side, they have created some vexing dilemmas for parents, and especially mothers, who still bear the brunt of child-rearing responsibilities.[11] They have also posed difficult challenges to governments, schools, churches, and corporations that are attempting to cope with the new realities of child care outside the home.

## Work/Family Dilemmas

Guilt. Anxiety. Frustration. Depression. Distraction. Concern. Anger. These are feelings common to many parents, especially mothers, who work while their young children are cared for by someone else. Even on good days, they miss their children and wonder if they have failed them by "abandoning" them to go to work. On bad days, the situation is much worse. A sick child wreaks havoc on a working parent, usually the mother. Many states prohibit centers from accepting very sick children, and few centers are equipped to care for such children. When a child is ill, the working mother must leave work and cope with her sick child or scramble to contrive some other arrangement, on short notice. When a child is seriously ill, the mother winds up staying home 70 percent of the time.[12] Similar crises arise when a child care provider gets sick or quits.[13]

More regularly, working mothers—and some working fathers—must choose between extra time at the office and time with the children, between a tempting business trip and the usual routines at home, between a fast-track career and a less challenging, less remunerative job. These are difficult, wrenching choices, on which much depends—financial earnings, self-esteem, the respect of one's peers, the confidence of one's boss, the love of one's spouse or relevant other, and, of course, the comfort of one's children.

Some parental decisions result in absenteeism, low morale, low productivity, and high turnover. According to a national survey, 15 percent of employed mothers lost some time at work during the previous month because of failures in child care arrangements.[14] The percentage of employed mothers losing time during the previous year is, presumably, even higher.

High turnover is another critical problem, both for mothers and their employers. Women are more likely than men to leave their job when they get married or when they have a child.[15] For example, Schwartz reports that at one multinational corporation, turnover among outstanding women managers exceeded that of their male counterparts by two-and-one-half to one.[16] Turnover is clearly related to the absence of family-friendly policies. For example, a Census Bureau study of turnover between 1981 and 1985 found that 71.2 percent of women with maternity benefits returned to work within six months, while only 42.8 percent of women without such benefits did so.[17]

Unfortunately, work-family problems do not stop when the work day ends. For many employed women, the end of the official work day simply marks the beginning of a second shift at home.[18] Despite growing efforts by fathers to shoulder more responsibilities at home, mothers continue to handle a disproportionate share of household and child care burdens.[19] Thus home life often just substitutes one pressure point for another, making it difficult for parents to spend quality time with their children and one another.

These problems are not unique to the United States, but they are far more prevalent here than in other industrialized countries. As noted earlier, social welfare states and corporatist welfare states provide for paid maternal leave for mothers of very young children and for heavily subsidized child care for mothers of preschoolers. Some liberal market states also provide family allowances, maternity benefits, and paid parental leave.

In Sweden, mothers may remain at home until their child reaches the age of eighteen months. During that period, the mother receives 80 percent of her regular pay (for twelve months), followed by a minimum sickness benefit (for three months), followed by an unpaid leave (for three months).[20] For older children, day care is available at a nominal fee, with parents paying approximately 12 percent of the total cost.[21] And parents may take as many as sixty days per year to care for a seriously ill child.[22]

In Germany, women are entitled to six weeks off at full pay before childbirth and eight weeks off at full pay after. All mothers are eligible for an *Erziehungsurlaub* (job-protected leave) for three years, and approximately 80 percent of all mothers are eligible for *Erziehungsgeld* (cash assistance for child-raising) for two years.[23] Thereafter, parents can choose from a number of child care arrangements, at affordable rates, thanks to substantial state government subsidies. In addition, German parents are entitled to as many as ten paid days off per year to care for a sick child.[24]

Such arrangements do not exist in the United States. Until that changes, working mothers will continue to be at the mercy of their employers. Many employers are well aware of the problems caused by a shaky child care infrastructure. Although approximately 5,600 employers have taken sigificant steps to do something about it, most have done little or nothing.[25] Of the nation's 44,000 employers with more than 100 employees, only 13 percent provide any child care benefits.[26] The track record of very large companies is a good deal better than average, but even they typically provide relatively inexpensive benefits, with predictably modest results.

In principle, reducing parental stress improves productivity at work. For example, studies show that mothers who work part time experience less fatigue and less stress than mothers who work full time.[27] Unfortunately, however, part-time work is relatively uncommon among women in the United States[28] And it usually involves the termination of fringe benefits, such as health care, sick days, and vacation days. In contrast, Sweden guarantees mothers of preschool children the right to reduce their hours without forfeiting their job or their fringe benefits. Mothers enjoy that right until their child reaches the age of eight.[29] Given such incentives, most Swedish mothers of preschoolers have chosen to work part time.[30]

A different solution, recommended by Schwartz, is the so-called mommy-track.[31] As Schwartz sees it, employed women in management positions should designate themselves as "career-primary" or "career-and-family" employees. The former would be treated precisely like men when it comes to assignments or promotions; the latter would receive fewer rewards but would be eligible for flexible work arrangements to facilitate child care, broadly defined. This proposal, though well-intentioned, would institutionalize discrimination against women and absolve fathers of their own legitimate child care responsibilities. Not surprisingly, it triggered an avalanche of criticism.[32]

This work-family perspective highlights the excruciating dilemmas that arise when a mother with young children chooses to work outside the home. It draws attention to the gap between corporate cultures and the contemporary labor market, to the extraordinary mental, physical, and emotional demands that working mothers face, and to the failure of many fathers to offer more than token support.

The work-family perspective, however, suffers from several limitations. It does not consider mothers who have chosen not to work but who do use child care for at least part of the day.[33] It ignores the fact that many child care choices are made—and paid for—by husband-wife teams, not just by the child's mother.[34] It emphasizes the characteristics of the labor market rather than the characteristics of the child care market. And it focuses more on the well-being and comfort level of the employed mother than on the best interests of the child. Useful though it is, the work-family perspective should be augmented by a broader framework.

## Parental Perspectives

One of the more remarkable features of the contemporary child care debate is the extent to which experts agree on the most important child care goals that parents pursue. These include (1) availability, defined as child care for both young and older children that is readily accessible; (2) affordability, which is child care priced or subsidized so that persons of modest means can purchase it; and (3) quality, meaning care that promotes the cognitive, social, and emotional development of the children who receive it.

There is, of course, greater agreement on what the three goals are than on how to measure them or how to achieve them. Nevertheless, most scholarly and popular commentary on child care focuses primarily or exclusively on these three goals.[35] Consequently, we know a great deal about each of them and why each has been so elusive.

### *Availability*

Availability is a concern for many parents. Although the number of child care facilities has increased steadily in recent years, space is not always available at the type of facility parents need or want. For example, a growing number of parents prefer group day care centers to family day care homes. According to a national study conducted in 1990, nearly half of all parents dissatisfied with current child care arrangements would like to switch to a group day care center.[36] Yet centers are often filled to capacity or close to it. Indeed, two-thirds to three-fourths (depending on the type of center) of all centers reported having no vacancies at the moment, when asked in 1990.[37]

Child care for infants and toddlers is especially difficult to find since many group day care centers refuse to care for infants and toddlers. To do so requires more staff members per child, according to state rules and regulations. Infant and toddler care also requires specially designed and specially equipped rooms, to facilitate napping and diaper-changing. Forty-five percent of all group day care centers do not accept children who are not toilet-trained, which means, in effect, infants and toddlers (see table 2-3).[38] Although family day care providers are much more willing to care for infants and toddlers, they too find it easier to care for preschoolers. The result is a shortage of spaces for infants and toddlers.

At the other end of the age spectrum, school-age child care can also be difficult to find. As with infants and toddlers, many group day care

TABLE 2-3.  Admission Policies of Child Care Facilities
Percent

| Children | Group day care centers | Regulated family day care homes |
|---|---|---|
| Non–toilet trained | 55 | 96 |
| Handicapped | 74 | 39 |
| Non-English-speaking | 86 | 31 |

SOURCE: Ellen Kisker and others, *A Profile of Child Care Settings: Early Education and Care in 1990*, vol. 1 (Princeton, N.J.: Mathematica Policy Research Inc., 1991), pp. 54–57.

centers refuse to care for school-age children, in part because it is less lucrative than preschool care. Family day care providers are more willing to care for school-age children.[39] Nevertheless, many school-age boys and girls are "latchkey children" who basically care for themselves. According to one recent study, 5 percent of five- to seven-year-olds and 25 percent of eleven- to thirteen-year-olds take care of themselves.[40]

The availability of school-age child care varies sharply from state to state. According to the U.S. Department of Education, only 5.5 percent of public school children in North Dakota and only 6.9 percent of public school children in West Virginia have access to after-school care at their school.[41] In contrast, 40.9 percent of public school children in North Carolina and 69.3 percent of public school children in Hawaii have access to after-school care at their school.

Within a given community, the availability of school-age child care also varies sharply. In the District of Columbia, for example, school-age child care is available at 63.6 percent of public elementary schools in two relatively affluent wards (Wards 2 and 3), as opposed to 14.6 percent of public elementary schools in two relatively poor wards (Wards 7 and 8).[42] The same pattern can be found in nearby Arlington County, Virginia.

Children with disabilities face special difficulties when it comes to child care. Approximately 26 percent of all group day care centers and 61 percent of regulated family day care homes do not accept such children (see table 2-3). And some of the remaining facilities make decisions on a case-by-case basis. The situation may have improved since passage of the Americans with Disabilities Act in 1990, but admission can still be denied.[43] Children who do not speak English also may experience discrimination. Approximately 14 percent of group day care centers and 69 percent of regulated family day care homes do not accept non-English-speaking children. As Zigler and Lang note, "For families whose children have special needs . . . the struggle to obtain appropriate child care is a constant dilemma."[44]

Other critical availability problems include evening care and sick-child care. For parents who must work evening shifts, regularly or occasionally, conventional child care hours are insufficient. But evening child care is extremely hard to find. In Allegheny County, Pennsylvania, for example, none of 320 group day care centers offers overnight care, and only a few provide evening care.[45] Sick-child care is also quite rare. In Virginia, only two such facilities can be found in the entire state and none in northern Virginia.[46] Yet, as noted earlier, most states prohibit regular child care facilities from caring for really sick children throughout the day. Under such circumstances, parents (usually mothers) have few choices but to leave work when a child becomes ill.

Also hard to find is child care at work. Corporations with on-site child care facilities have received considerable favorable publicity, but only 1,400 corporations actually provide on-site or near-site child care.[47] For most working parents, the dream of being able to check up on or share a meal with a preschool child during the day remains precisely that—a dream.

## Affordability

Affordability is a second serious problem. If parents are able to find the child care that they need, they still may be unable to pay for it. According to recent estimates, full-time child care cost approximately $3,300 per child in 1991, which makes child care the fourth largest household expense beyond shelter, food, and taxes.[48] And some child care is a good deal more expensive than that.

Infant and toddler care is particularly expensive. That is because very young children require more personal attention than older children, which means lower child/staff ratios, which in turn means higher labor costs. In 1993 the average undiscounted fee for full-time infant care at a group day care center was $5,412 per year.[49] In many parts of the country, however, infant care can cost as much as $200 per week or approximately $10,000 per year.[50]

The cost of child care also varies from city to city. In the summer of 1988, researchers systematically compared the costs of full-time infant care in five metropolitan areas.[51] They found sharp variations in cost, ranging from $62.01 per week in Atlanta to $150.96 per week in Boston. Seattle, Phoenix, and Detroit fell somewhere between. By now those rates are undoubtedly higher.

TABLE 2-4. Child Care Spending as a Proportion of Family Income, Employed Mothers with Youngest Child under Age Five

| Family income (dollars) | Mean percent of family income spent on child care |
|---|---|
| < 15,000 | 23 |
| 15,000 – 24,999 | 12 |
| 25,000 – 34,999 | 8 |
| 35,000 – 49,999 | 7 |
| 50,000 + | 6 |

SOURCE: Barbara Willer and others, *The Demand and Supply of Child Care in 1990* (Washington: National Association for the Education of Young Children, 1991), p. 32.

Obviously the affordability of child care depends not just on the rates charged but also on the parents' financial circumstances. As table 2-4 suggests, the impact of child care on the family budget of low-income parents can be quite severe. Thus in 1990, child care constituted 23 percent of family income for those earning less than $15,000 per year.[52]

Because of the relatively high cost of child care and their relative inability to pay, many poor children are effectively shut out of the child care market, despite such well-publicized programs as Head Start and some new federal child care programs established in 1990. For example, the U.S. General Accounting Office found that approximately 35 percent of poor children between the ages of three and five participated in preschool, compared with 45 percent of the nonpoor population.[53] The GAO also found that near-poor children were no more likely than poor children to participate in preschool.[54]

In fact, many middle-class families report that they have difficulty affording child care. One Nebraska mother, testifying at public hearings on the Child Care and Development Block Grant, put it this way: "When I work, everything that I make goes to my child care provider rather than going into my pocket because, to find good quality child care, I have to spend."[55] By the time child care expenses, transportation expenses, and taxes are factored in, many middle-class mothers conclude that they are better off staying home.

## Quality

Whatever else may be said about the quality of child care in the United States, we do know how to measure it. Numerous studies by child psychologists have established that several key factors, described below, contribute to the cognitive, social, and economic development of young children in child care settings.

*Low Child/Staff Ratios.* Lower ratios mean more personal attention to the individual child, which facilitates the child's intellectual and personal growth. That, at any rate, is true for infants and toddlers.[56] The evidence for preschoolers is more mixed.[57]

*Small Groups.* Regardless of ratios, small groups are better. Thus a group of eight children with one provider fares better than a group of twenty-four children with three providers, even though the ratios are identical. Numerous studies have shown that children need to identify with a particular caregiver and with a relatively small group of other children.[58]

*Well-Trained Providers.* The ability to stimulate children, to devise age-appropriate activities, and to provide emergency care if needed depends on provider training. Well-trained providers are better providers, in both group day care and family day care settings.[59] According to some observers, training is the single most important predictor of quality child care, especially in family day care settings.[60]

*Well-Educated Providers.* A college-educated provider is good for children, regardless of which courses the person took in school. Despite some early evidence that formal education does not matter, a substantial number of recent studies indicate a positive relationship between formal education and age-appropriate caregiving.[61]

*Low Provider Turnover.* Children develop personal attachments to child care providers and are puzzled and disappointed when a provider leaves. Studies show that children in centers with higher staff turnover rates have less developed language skills and social skills.[62] More broadly stated, children need an enduring relationship with particular caregivers if they are to feel secure.[63]

This is by no means a comprehensive list. Good record-keeping, good hygiene, nutritious food, reliable transportation, and plenty of age-appropriate toys and books are important. The physical plant also matters, both indoors and outdoors. A well-designed center or home reduces the likelihood of accidents. Smoke detectors, fire exits, secure medicine cabinets, and resilient surfaces in play areas all contribute to a safe environment.

Despite the importance of many quality indicators, focusing on the key factors stated above allows considerable insight into the quality of child care in the United States. Table 2-5, derived from a national survey of group day care centers, offers reason for both comfort and concern. The average child/staff ratio for three-year-olds at group day care centers is 9.9:1, which is about what experts recommend as the maximum.[64] The average group size for three-year-olds is seventeen, which is somewhat lower than the maximum recommended by experts.[65] This means, in effect, that ratios and group sizes for three-year-olds at some centers are higher than experts recommend but that the averages are reasonably good.[66] Indeed, U.S. ratios are considerably lower (that is, better) than those found in Germany, France, or Japan.[67]

The evidence on teacher education and teacher training is also mixed. Although most center teachers have had some education beyond high school, only 47 percent have a college degree (see table 2-5). The percentage of teachers' aides with a college degree is undoubtedly lower still. Although the overwhelming majority of center teachers have had some special training in child care or early education, only 60 percent have taken child-care courses or workshops and only 42 percent have taken child development or psychology courses (see table 2-6).

Compared with workers who receive similar wages, child care providers are unusually well-trained and well-educated. They do not, however, compare favorably with their counterparts in other industrialized countries. In Germany, for example, child care teachers in most states must complete two years of college and a two-year practicum before being certified as child care teachers.[68] In Japan, 85 percent of all preschool teachers have a junior college diploma, have majored in preschool and early education, and have passed a state certification exam.[69] U.S. figures cited refer to center teachers only. Assistant teachers, who constitute a large proportion of the center workforce, typically have less impressive credentials.[70]

One of the most troublesome of quality indicators is the high turnover to be found among child care providers. Table 2-5 reports an average annual turnover among center teachers of 25 percent. Other studies, however, which considered all center personnel, including assistant teachers and teachers' aides, have found turnover rates of approximately 40

TABLE 2-5. Selected Quality Indicators, by Type of Facility

| | | | Nonprofit | | | For-profit | | |
|---|---|---|---|---|---|---|---|---|
| Indicator | Head Start | Public school | Religious sponsor | Other sponsor | Independent | Chain | Independent | Combined |
| Average number of 3-year-olds per staffer | 8.4 | 7.4 | 8.7 | 8.8 | 8.4 | 11.0 | 9.0 | 9.9 |
| Average group size for 3-year-olds | 19 | 16 | 16 | 20 | 16 | 18 | 15 | 17 |
| Teachers with college degree (average)[a] | 45 | 88 | 50 | 52 | 49 | 31 | 35 | 47 |
| Annual teacher turnover rate (average)[a] | 20 | 14 | 23 | 25 | 25 | 39 | 27 | 25 |

SOURCES: Kisker and others, A Profile of Child Care Settings, pp. 234–37; Willer and others, The Demand and Supply of Child Care in 1990, pp. 18–19.
a. Percent.

percent per year.[71] By comparison, the average annual turnover for all occupational categories has been less than 10 percent in recent years.[72] As Phillips notes, "Children are faced with revolving door staff."[73] As a poignant example, Phillips cites a visit to an Atlanta day care center, where investigators were occasionally approached by children and asked if they were their teacher for the day.

Although it is useful to talk about averages, the range of quality is also important. Quality of care varies dramatically from center to center and system to system. As table 2-5 indicates, the quality of care is relatively good at Head Start centers and centers based in public schools. In contrast, quality is significantly worse at centers run by for-profit chains. These generalizations apply less to teacher training than to other indicators (see table 2-6). Teacher training figures are less reliable, because they refer to a single randomly selected teacher at each center rather than to all teachers.[74]

Child care quality also varies significantly across family day care homes. Indeed, Edward Zigler has referred to family day care as a "cosmic crap shoot" because it includes some of the very best and some of the very worst of child care settings.[75] In general, the quality of care is better in regulated than in unregulated family day care homes. For example, a Canadian study found that children in unlicensed homes watched television more and engaged in more solitary play than children in licensed homes, who benefited from more proactive and interactive providers.[76] Similarly, a U.S. study found that unregulated family day care providers were somewhat less "child-focused" than their regulated counterparts.[77] Another study found that unregulated providers had less training and knowledge of child care than regulated providers.[78] On the other hand, unregulated family day care providers do typically care for fewer children.[79] Thus in appraising these different forms of care, one must decide which of several quality indicators is most important.

It is difficult to say whether quality is generally better or worse at centers or family day care homes.[80] Turnover appears to be higher at family day care homes—between 37 percent and 59 percent per year, according to various estimates.[81] Family day care providers are considerably less likely than teachers at group day care centers to have a college degree.[82] Also, few family day care homes boast a written curriculum or a well-equipped playground, as many centers do. On the other hand, family day care homes usually offer very low child/staff ratios, which permits greater attention to the needs of individual children.[83] In addi-

TABLE 2-6. Teacher Training, Type of Facility by Auspices
Percent

| | Nonprofit | | | | | For-profit | | |
| --- | --- | --- | --- | --- | --- | --- | --- | --- |
| Type of facility | Head Start | Public school | Religious sponsor | Other sponsor | Independent | Chain | Independent | Combined |
| Training of randomly selected teachers | | | | | | | | |
| Child care workshops or courses | 65.5 | 51.7 | 66.2 | 61.5 | 61.4 | 54.0 | 58.2 | 60.1 |
| Child development or psychology courses | 49.6 | 39.8 | 42.3 | 47.3 | 41.0 | 36.8 | 38.8 | 42.1 |
| N | 226 | 269 | 222 | 275 | 363 | 87 | 418 | 1,676 |

SOURCE: Calculated by the author from A Profile of Child Care Settings: Center-Based Programs, prepared by Ellen Kisker and Valarie Piper of Mathematica Policy Research Inc. and distributed as a data set by Sociometrics Corp., Los Altos, Calif., February 1992.

tion, family day care homes offer a more relaxed, informal setting. As Modigliani puts it, "A soft, homey atmosphere may be just the thing for a school-ager after a long day in school, as well as for young children who are not ready for more complex, structured institutions."[84]

In child care, the root of much evil is not the love of money but the absence of it. For example, turnover is extremely high because child care providers do not receive pay commensurate with their education, training, or experience. The average day care center worker earned an annual salary of less than $10,000 in 1988, with teachers earning more than assistant teachers.[85] Family day care providers earn even less, particularly when one considers that overhead comes out of their earnings.[86] In fact, child care workers are the second lowest paid workers in the United States, after controlling for education and experience.[87] Only the clergy earn less, and they typically receive other emoluments, such as free lodging.

It is easy to understand the appeal of the availability/affordability/quality framework. By outlining three key goals, it facilitates a succinct summary of the state of child care in the United States. It also lends itself to systematic comparisons of different types of child care facilities, different social classes, and different types of children.

Despite these virtues, however, the iron triangle, as Phillips has called it, falls short of being a comprehensive normative framework. First of all, it fails to indicate how to proceed when availability and quality or affordability and quality tug us in different directions. Should the three goals be lexically ordered, with one taking precedence over the others? What happens when the goals conflict? Are there solutions that reduce or eliminate the need for trade-offs?

The availability/affordability/quality framework, though applicable to many child care policy choices, is incomplete. For example, it presupposes that parents are choosing child care arrangements that permit them to work. But what about parents who prefer to care for their children at home? Should parental choice encompass not just a range of paid child care settings but a more fundamental choice between child care outside the home and parental supervision at home?

Another problem is that substantive goals, such as availability, affordability, and quality, are not directly relevant to systemic or institutional failures. Which is better, a more public or more private service delivery system, greater centralization or greater decentralization? What should the relative roles of federal, state, and local governments be? And what roles should be assigned to churches, schools, and corporations? To answer these questions adequately, we need to consider not just the allocation of resources but the allocation of responsibilities. In short, we need a more comprehensive framework.

## A Societal Perspective

Child care is especially vexing and perplexing, to both analysts and parents, because it is multidimensional. Child care is a labor problem, a social problem, a regulatory problem, an intergovernmental problem, an administrative problem, a community problem, and, of course, a familial problem. To make sense of these multiple problems, we need guideposts. As we move beyond an understanding of difficult child care dilemmas to actual policy choices, we must frame the issues more precisely and more pointedly, with trade-offs clearly in view. We need to be more explicitly normative and to take a wider range of values into account. We also need to decide whose problem child care is, so that particular institutions can be held accountable for particular failures, and so that successful institutions can be rewarded for their accomplishments.

It is not necessary to reinvent the wheel when thinking about child care problems and how to resolve them. For example, child care has a lot in common with regulatory policies, especially those requiring workplace inspections (occupational safety and health, environmental protection). In both instances, "social regulation" seeks to ensure that industry practices are safe, healthy, and in the public interest. Entry requirements, licensing requirements, and standards of conduct also characterize both fields.

On the other hand, child care has sweeping social implications that do not normally figure in regulatory policy disputes. In fact, child care is a regulatory, redistributive, and distributive issue. For example, child care subsidies and eligibility criteria may enhance or inhibit social equality. Increasingly, child care involves considerable income transfers across social classes and substantial industry subsidies. Thus purely regulatory analogies capture a vital component of child care, but only a component.

In some respects, child care problems strongly resemble health care problems. The availability, affordability, and quality issues are as germane to health care as to child care. In both arenas, policymakers must deal with shortages of certain forms of care (such as infant and toddler care); in both arenas, policymakers must cope with affordability problems (around 37 million Americans lack health insurance; millions of Americans are unable to pay for child care); in both arenas, policymakers seek to maintain minimum quality standards (through occupational licensing, inspections, self-regulation, and other techniques).

Yet child care and health care also differ in certain crucial respects. For one thing, child care is a less salient issue, partly because it affects a smaller number of people at any given point in time and partly because young children cannot speak out on their own behalf to advocate improvements. As Peterson has noted, if children had the right to vote, we could expect to see "fundamental political and public policy changes."[88] Lacking the right to vote and the capacity to speak articulately, young children are handicapped politically. A direct result is that child care issues are only intermittently salient, usually when a crisis or scandal erupts. Child care is also perceived to be a less complex issue than health care. Since most adults over the age of thirty have cared for children at some point in their lives, they do not need an interpreter to explain child care issues to them. Also, the issues themselves are usually presented by the mass media in such a way that laypersons can easily grasp them, whether they have had children or not.

Child care and health care also differ significantly in the degree of prestige and autonomy that their professionals enjoy. Medicine, until recently, epitomized the successful self-regulating profession.[89] And doctors continue to enjoy tremendous financial rewards and widespread societal esteem. Even nurses have enjoyed significant wage increases in recent years. Child care workers, in contrast, have only just begun to think of themselves as professionals and have not made much headway in persuading others that they should be thought of in such terms.[90] In terms of pay and prestige, child care is anything but a privileged profession.

Perhaps a better analogy is to education. Like child care, education is characterized by excludability (individual children can be denied services). Like child care, it is also characterized by congestibility.[91] That is, after a certain point is reached, the quality of the service to the individual child is diluted. That is the rationale for classroom size limitations (in teachers' union contracts) and child/staff ratio limitations (in state child care regulations). According to Weimer and Vining, congestibility is troublesome because it usually results in inefficient pricing.[92]

Education and child care are also alike in that they are neither purely private goods nor authentic collective goods. We used to think of education as a private good, but that changed many years ago in elementary and secondary education, and more recently in higher education, as we came to appreciate education's positive side effects for society as a whole.[93] The same shift of perspective could occur in child care, if public attitudes were to change.

Yet that is precisely what has not happened. Although the parallels between education and child care are striking, one important difference remains. Whereas education is widely regarded in positive terms, child care arouses much more ambivalent reactions. The question of whether children between the ages of six and eighteen should be educated outside the home has been largely resolved.[94] The question of whether children under the age of six should be cared for outside the home continues to arouse fierce debate.[95]

On balance, the evidence suggests that child care outside the home does not adversely affect the cognitive or social development of children over the age of one.[96] There is some reason to be concerned about full-time child care for infants, however. A number of studies show that infants in full-time day care are less securely attached to their mothers than other infants.[97] The meaning of this has been hotly debated and more research is clearly needed.[98] A low-risk policy would be for government to facilitate decisions by mothers to care full time for an infant at home or to work part-time until a child reaches the age of one. Such a policy would bring the United States into alignment with most other industrialized nations.

There is also some reason to be concerned about child care of low quality, irrespective of the child's age.[99] Even child care that poses no direct threat to children's health and safety can adversely affect their development, with important implications for the future. Here also, a low-risk policy would be for government to insist upon minimum quality standards, apply them to all child care settings outside the home, and enforce them vigorously.

In developing a normative framework for making collective child care choices, we need to take into account the lack of agreement on the appropriateness of child care for young children. Availability, affordability, and quality are vitally important, but so too is avoidability. As we design new child care policies, we must ask whether parental ambivalence is justified and, if so, what weight to grant that ambivalence.

At the same time, we should consider the possibility that child care is a "merit good." A merit good is one widely regarded as socially meritorious, either because consumers benefit more than they realize or because society as a whole benefits from widespread consumption.[100] If child care is a merit good, or if child care for a certain class of children (for example, poor children) is a merit good, then policies favoring consumption may be justifiable, despite parental ambivalence.

In thinking about child care issues, I have concluded that three core values are a useful starting point: justice, efficiency, and choice. These same values figure prominently in education policy and health policy debates, less so in regulatory policy debates. In adapting and applying them to child care, however, it is important to define them so that they are pertinent to a wide variety of child care dilemmas. It is also desirable to fine-tune them so that they are as compatible with one another as possible.

## *Justice*

According to Rawls, justice is the first virtue of social institutions.[101] Rawls defines justice as a set of rules to govern society that would be adopted by persons unaware of their own place in the social schema. However one chooses to rank it or define it, justice is a central value in many contemporary political theories.[102] Moreover, it is directly relevant to child care debates:

—Should poor children be guaranteed access to child care?

—Should poor children receive free child care?

—Are work-family policies fair to women?

—Are work-family policies fair to children?

—Is it just for child care workers to be paid far less than workers with comparable education and experience?

—Is it just that some for-profit centers make a profit at the expense of children?

These are but a few of the questions that arise. To address them, I suggest the following proposition:

*Child care policies should be characterized by justice across generations, across genders, across social classes, and across occupations.*

This deceptively simple thesis has important implications for the allocation of resources to children, work/family policies, the targeting of children's subsidies, and policies towards the child care industry. It implies, among other things, that child poverty rates far higher than adult poverty rates are unacceptable; that workplace discrimination against women who choose to have children is unacceptable; that the neediest children should be the first priority of government children's programs; and that industry subsidies may be justified in order to correct for market inequities. Yet justice, important though it is, cannot stand alone.

## Efficiency

Efficiency is central to utilitarian thinking and is a key consideration in most contemporary policy analysis.[103] A proposal that would make some people better off without making anyone else worse off is *Pareto optimal* and superior to its alternatives. Beyond that, it is customary to ask whether a proposal could make everyone better off if compensation payments were made by those whom the proposal directly benefits to those whom the proposal directly harms.[104] If so, the proposal is more efficient than the status quo, because the aggregate benefits exceed the aggregate costs. Always important, efficiency is particularly significant in an era of scarce resources. Like justice, it is also directly relevant to child care:

—Is it efficient for parents in general to care for infants at home?

—Is it efficient for poor parents in particular to participate in education and training programs, while the government pays for their child care costs?

—Is it efficient for multiple governments or multiple agencies to regulate child care?

—Is it efficient for child care to be supported through multiple funding streams with different eligibility criteria, ground rules, and reimbursement rates?

—Is it efficient for government inspectors to devote relatively equal amounts of time to good and bad child care facilities?

—Is it efficient for government regulators to enforce standards with high regulatory costs while ignoring standards with low regulatory costs?

These are some of the questions that arise. To address them, I offer a second proposition:

*Child care policies should be pursued that minimize costs to governments, parents, and providers, while maximizing benefits to children and society as a whole.*

This suggests, among other things, the following: that social service delivery systems should be redesigned to eliminate unnecessary duplication and confusion; that regulatory systems should be overhauled to target and correct wrongdoing with greater precision; that scarce resources should be allocated to programs with relatively high benefit-cost ratios; and that both positive and negative externalities should be taken into account. Yet the efficiency criterion also leaves a framework that is incomplete.

## Choice

Choice is central to many social policy debates (abortion, education, health care, for example), and it is of enormous importance to child care as well. Consider the following questions:

—Should parents be free to choose among child care arrangements?

—Should parents be free to purchase care from a provider who is unlicensed and unregulated?

—Is choice meaningful if parents lack information to choose wisely?

—Is choice meaningful if parents lack the money to choose the setting they prefer?

—Should parents be free to choose between staying at home with their children and working outside the home?

—How far should the government go to facilitate such choices?

To address these issues, I suggest a third proposition:

*Parents should be granted considerable discretion in making choices for their children and themselves.*

This proposition has important implications for both government subsidies and government regulations. It suggests, for example, that the flow of information between producers (providers) and consumers (parents) should be improved so that parents can distinguish between inferior and superior child care. It also suggests that child care subsidies should be generous enough so that recipients can purchase the child care that they believe is best for their child.

In considering these three propositions, it does not take long to figure out that they often point us down different policy paths. For example, the regulatory standards that are best for children may also impose the highest costs on providers, consumers, and taxpayers. The policies that enhance parental choice the most may also be least likely to ensure the health and safety of children. Policies that seem highly efficient because they focus on problematic providers may strike many providers as being arbitrary and capricious. A stronger connection between price and quality may deprive poor, near-poor, or even middle-class parents of access to high-quality child care.

These dilemmas, unhappily, are all too common in family policy. For example, Fishkin has argued that it is impossible to promote merit, equal opportunity, and family integrity at the same time, because they tug us in different directions.[105] Thus pursuing equal opportunity and family autonomy comes at the expense of the merit principle. Alternatively, a strict application of the merit principle, when combined with family discretion, guarantees unequal life chances in a society that is already highly stratified.

One solution is to rank principles lexically and to insist that one take priority over the others. Thus, one could rank justice ahead of efficiency and efficiency ahead of choice. However, even the most ardent supporter of social justice might balk at a policy that achieves a slight increase in justice through highly inefficient means. Even the most determined champion of economic efficiency might resist a policy that runs roughshod over parental choice in order to save a few pennies for taxpayers. And even the most committed proponent of parental choice might wonder if parents should be free to make choices that are clearly not in the best interests of their children.

A different strategy is to attempt to reduce conflicts among core values and reformulate the propositions. Thus justice might be tempered by a recognition of opportunity costs. Efficiency might be tempered by sympathy for the disadvantaged. Choice might be tempered by an insistence upon parental duties and obligations. The result could be a somewhat different set of propositions.

Child care policies should be characterized by justice across generations, across genders, across social classes, and across occupations, but the costs of alternative strategies should be taken into account. Justice does not require that every child receive high-quality child care at the government's expense.

Child care policies should be pursued that minimize costs to governments, parents, and providers, while maximizing benefits to children, but impacts on disadvantaged groups should receive special consideration. Policies that benefit poor children in particular generally involve greater net benefits to society than policies that are more diffuse.

Parents should be granted considerable discretion in making choices for their children and themselves, but they should be educated so that their choices are well informed and sensible. Governments should prevent parents from making choices that are demonstrably bad for children.

Even with these reformulated propositions, trade-offs will be necessary. Similarly, studies have shown that there are trade-offs between availability and quality and between affordability and quality.[106] What is striking about these trade-offs, however, is that they can often be avoided or mitigated. For example, some regulations adversely affect the supply of child care, but others do not.[107] Some quality improvements ratchet up costs considerably, while others do not.[108] Before wrestling with zero-sum choices, we should seek creative ways to promote cherished values without undermining other precious values.

## Conclusion

Child care debates are not just about interests but about values. In this chapter, I have approached child care from three different normative vantage points, each of which has something to offer. The first of these, as exemplified by numerous articles in the *Wall Street Journal*, *Working Mother* magazine, and other popular periodicals, is the work-family perspective. This perspective views child care as a women's issue and a labor issue. It notes the tensions and strains posed by female employment when a strong social support system is lacking. It raises issues about gender equity and economic productivity. And it emphasizes, explicitly or implicitly, the responsibility of the private sector. Yet the work-family perspective occasionally loses sight of children, who presumably should be front and center in any child care debate. The test of child care is not just what it does to the company's bottom line or the mother's career but what it does to children. The well-being of children ought to be a central consideration.

The second framework, widely used by child care experts, highlights the importance of three key problems—availability, affordability, and quality. This perspective, in effect, treats child care as a consumer issue. By thrusting parents, and not just mothers, into the picture, it recognizes the growing importance of fathers in child-rearing. By including cost, supply, and quality in the same equation, it anticipates the need for trade-offs. By identifying instances of market failure, it hints strongly at much-needed reforms. Yet child care is more than a consumer product, to be plucked off the shelf by discerning parents. Increasingly, people are coming to recognize that child care has many of the qualities of a collective good, more comparable to education and health care than to groceries and automobiles. A collective good need not be provided by government itself. But a collective good is society's concern, and not just the concern of parents.

The third perspective, which combines political theory and public policy analysis, recommends justice, efficiency, and choice as guideposts for policymakers. This model might be characterized as substantive policy analysis. It also bears a striking resemblance to what Anderson calls pragmatic liberalism.[109] In contrast to the other two perspectives, it may seem fairly abstract. The meanings of justice, efficiency, and choice are not self-evident. These values, however, are highly relevant and readily adaptable to contemporary child care debates. One advantage of this framework is that it facilitates comparisons and contrasts to other policy arenas. Another advantage is that it treats the interests of children and parents as separate and distinct. A final advantage is that it regards child care as a public issue, to be debated in public fora, and to be resolved through public action. Again, that does not presuppose that governments should actually deliver child care services. Nor does it presuppose centralization, universal regulation, or even stringent regulation. But it does imply that governments—federal, state, and local—have a responsibility to evaluate the roles of public and private institutions in delivering child care services and monitoring their performance.

There are limits to what normative analysis can accomplish. To agree on which values are important is not necessarily to agree on how they should be ranked or operationalized. I have attempted to operationalize key values to some degree; I have not attempted to rank them. That is because I cannot claim that quality is always more important than affordability or that justice is always more important than efficiency. The art of policy analysis is in part a question of striking a good balance, of recognizing that one value deserves priority in a particular context, another value in another context. A tidy rank-ordering of values would offer false comfort.

Nevertheless, policy analysis is a science as well as an art. The role of values in policy analysis is not simply to tell us what to do but, more subtly, to tell us, through empirical research, which values are worthy of further inquiry. Thus normative frameworks can help to shape our empirical research agenda. By combining values and empirical evidence, we are in a better position to make sound, informed judgments about trade-offs and probabilities in particular contexts.

Before we turn to that empirical research, however, we should explore yet another world where values and policy choices intersect—the world of institutions. In chapter 3, the focus is on procedural values and institutional choices. Who funds, regulates, and coordinates child care in the United States? What are the respective roles of the federal, state, and local governments? What are the respective roles of the public and private sectors? What are the norms that drive key child care actors? What are the strengths and weaknesses of the child care infrastructure? And what principles might help us to repair or reinvent that infrastructure? These are a few of the questions that need to be addressed.

# 3 | Child Care as an Institutional Problem

THE SUCCESS OR FAILURE of child care policy choices depends not just on the wisdom of substantive decisions but also on the institutions that implement those decisions. Sound policies are easily undermined if the institutions that carry them out are rigid, unresponsive, and disconnected. Thus the challenge that confronts policymakers is not simply to design sound policies but also to build strong institutions.

When we speak of child care institutions, we are really speaking of two interrelated phenomena: a variety of organizations and other groups, both public and private, that care for children and perform other critical child care functions; and an assortment of norms and standard operating procedures that guide the behavior of individuals who perform these key functions. In short, we need to distinguish between formal and informal institutions.

In this chapter, I consider both the formal and informal institutions that together comprise our child care infrastructure. The former receive considerable attention, as they are visible and palpable; the latter are widely overlooked, even among experts. I also introduce several procedural criteria that may be used to evaluate our current system and/or to design a new one. These criteria will supplement the substantive criteria introduced in chapter 2.

TABLE 3-1.  The Formal Child Care Infrastructure

| Regulation | Funding | Information |
|---|---|---|
| State governments | Federal government | Resource and referral agencies |
| Local governments | State governments | Caseworkers |
| Federal government | Private corporations | Mass media |
| Auxiliary regulatory systems | | |

| Training | Providers |
|---|---|
| Community colleges | Group day care centers |
| Resource and referral agencies | Family day care homes |
| NAEYC | Relatives |
| State governments | |

## The Formal Infrastructure

In thinking about the formal child care infrastructure, it is useful to focus on certain basic functions, such as regulating, funding, informing, training, and, of course, caring. These functions are performed in all advanced industrial societies, but they are performed in different ways and by different institutions. In western Europe and Scandinavia, direct provision of child care services by governments is fairly common. In some European countries, churches and governments work hand in hand to provide care. In the United States, a very different division of labor reinforces longstanding commitments to capitalism, federalism, individualism, and the separation of church and state (see table 3-1).

### Providers

The people on the front lines are, of course, the providers themselves, who may or may not be affiliated with a particular organization. They include parents and other relatives; directors, teachers, assistant teachers, and volunteers at group day care centers; providers at family day care homes and group day care homes; nannies; and au pairs. Group day care centers care for children in a nonresidential setting; family day care homes care for a relatively small number of children in a private home; group day care homes care for a larger number of children in a private home. Precise definitions vary from state to state.

Each form of care is more common in some parts of the country than others. Center-based care, for example, is more common in the South. One reason for this is that state standards for group day care centers are less stringent there, which reduces the costs of centers and encourages their proliferation.[1] Another reason is that local zoning standards for family day care homes are more stringent in the South. This discourages family day care, especially regulated family day care.[2]

In contrast, family day care homes are more common in the Midwest.[3] Tougher state standards for centers help to explain this phenomenon. In addition, several Midwestern states (Michigan, Minnesota, and Wisconsin) have taken measures to prevent local governments from keeping family day care homes out of residential neighborhoods.

In recent years, there has been a steady increase in demand for center-based care. Between 1965 and 1990, families with employed mothers relied increasingly upon group day care centers. During the same period, reliance upon relatives declined, while demand for family day care homes fluctuated.[4] The infusion of federal funds into child care may have accelerated these trends. Thanks to government subsidies through the IV-A programs and the Child Care and Development Block Grant, center-based care is now more attractive because it is more affordable.

Another trend has been the growth in the number of for-profit centers, especially centers that are part of a chain. KinderCare, the largest of the chains, is illustrative. In 1980 KinderCare was operating about 510 centers serving 53,000 children.[5] By 1993 the company was operating about 1,200 centers serving 141,000 children.[6] KinderCare centers continue to grow, despite some extremely poor business decisions by central headquarters that culminated in a five-month bankruptcy—a "time-out for bad behavior," as one observer put it.[7] KinderCare emerged as bold as ever, announcing plans for school-age child care programs, on-site corporate centers, and facilities abroad.

## Regulation

The regulation of child care providers is a shared responsibility. State governments and local governments regulate child care providers directly, while the federal government regulates them indirectly, by imposing certain conditions for financial support. Nonprofit organizations and for-profit consultants play auxiliary regulatory roles in certain states.

By far the most important child care regulators are state governments, which establish and enforce standards for group day care centers, group day care homes, and family day care homes.[8] As required by federal law, states also promulgate minimal standards for providers receiving federal funds under the Child Care and Development Block Grant.

State standards vary sharply throughout the United States. In Wisconsin, family day care providers who care for four or more children must complete at least forty hours of training within six months after opening for business and fifteen hours annually thereafter. In Virginia, family day care providers who care for fewer than nine children (the overwhelming majority) need not obtain any training whatever; indeed, family day care homes are currently not licensed by the state.[9] In New York, group day care centers must employ one staff member for every seven preschoolers. In Florida, a center-based staff member may care for as many as fifteen preschoolers at a time.

Enforcement practices also vary considerably from state to state. In eleven states, regulators may post a conspicuous public notice of center violations; in nineteen states, regulators may levy a monetary fine on centers. In some states, neither practice is permitted.[10] Sanctions available for family day care homes vary from state to state as well.

Local governments also regulate child care establishments, though the rules they apply were seldom developed with child care in mind. In most cities, group day care centers must obtain permits from local zoning boards, local fire departments, and local health departments. They must also pass a variety of local inspections. Even family day care homes are subject to considerable local regulation, despite their relatively small size. A survey of 326 cities, conducted in 1990, showed that family day care homes are subject to many local regulatory requirements. For example, family day care homes that care for six children must obtain a business license in 31.4 percent of the cities, an occupancy permit in 36.0 percent, and a zoning permit in 24.9 percent.[11] In some communities, restrictive covenants place additional burdens on family day care homes.

The federal government's regulatory role is quite limited. Although the federal government developed national standards for federally supported child care programs in the 1970s, those standards, known as the Federal Interagency Day Care Requirements (FIDCR), were abandoned by the Reagan administration in 1981, just before they were scheduled to take effect.[12] In 1990 Congress and President George Bush rejected national standards, which had been part of the original ABC child care bill introduced by Senator Christopher Dodd (D.-Conn.). Instead, they approved a very limited regulatory role for the federal government. Under the final bill, states must require providers receiving Child Care and

Development Block Grant (CCDBG) funds to meet certain minimal standards concerning children's health, building safety, and provider training. The states are free to set those standards, and the Department of Health and Human Services has determined that extremely weak standards are acceptable.[13] Also, relatives are effectively exempt from meaningful regulation. To receive CCDBG funds, they must simply "register" with their state, supplying a name, address, and social security number.

In several states, the private sector plays a role in regulating child care facilities, usually under contract with state or county governments. In Wisconsin, nonprofit organizations in the state's two most populous counties "register" or "certify" family day care homes that care for one to three children.[14] In New Jersey, nonprofit organizations "approve" family day care homes that care for one or two children and "register" family day care homes that care for three to five children. In both Wisconsin and New Jersey, registration is voluntary. Seeking approval in New Jersey is also voluntary. Family day care providers in both states must be registered if they wish to receive funds under the Child and Adult Care Food Program.

Although auxiliary regulatory systems are typically aimed at family day care homes, they are sometimes used for group day care centers as well. In Michigan, group day care centers establish their compliance with state fire safety standards by hiring a private consultant to inspect their premises. The consultant must be listed by the state as a qualified fire inspector. The phenomenon of auxiliary regulatory systems seems to be particularly common in the Midwest. In Indiana and Ohio, for example, private individuals also conduct child care inspections from time to time under contract to state or local governments.

## Funding

The federal government has long been involved in providing financial support to child care facilities and to parents who need child care. Indeed, the federal government helped to fund, build, or operate more than 3,000 child care centers for the children of defense industry employees during World War II.[15] Although this practice ended more or less in 1945, the federal government launched an even more ambitious effort when it enacted the Head Start program in 1965.

Under Head Start, one of the most popular social programs in the United States, disadvantaged preschoolers receive educationally enriched child care, in an effort to prepare them for the challenges of formal schooling. The program is administered by local agencies but is funded largely by the federal government and is subject to federal rules and regulations. Although the emphasis of Head Start is on enhanced cognitive and social development in the preschool classroom, ancillary services, such as home visits and health care, contribute to the program's success.

If Head Start is the most visible of the federal government's child care initiatives, it is not the only important federal child care program. Through the Child and Adult Care Food Program (CACFP), created in 1968, the U.S. Department of Agriculture assists eligible group day care centers and family day care homes by defraying the costs of nutritious meals and snacks. The CACFP also funds well-trained "sponsors" who visit participating family day care homes three times a year and offer valuable assistance.[16] Through the Title XX program, created in 1974 and subsequently transformed into the Social Services Block Grant (SSBG), the federal government provides funds to states, which may be used for child care, among other services. According to one estimate, 16 percent of SSBG funds go to child care.[17]

In addition to these direct expenditures, the federal government assists parents of young children through tax expenditures. Under the Child and Dependent Care Tax Credit, parents with taxable earnings may deduct a portion of their child care expenses for children under the age of thirteen. Alternatively, parents who work for participating employers may take advantage of Employer-Based Dependent Care Assistance Plans, whereby anticipated child care expenses of up to $5,000 per year are excluded from the employee's gross taxable income.

The Earned Income Tax Credit, established in 1975 and expanded significantly in 1990 and 1993, might also be viewed as a form of child care support. Under this program, low-income working parents with children receive a tax credit, which declines gradually as earnings increase. Although the money need not go to pay for child care outside the home, it does in many instances do precisely that. In other instances, it helps families to care for their children at home.

Since 1988 federal spending on child care has increased substantially. The Family Support Act of 1988 created a program guaranteeing child care support for parents who receive job training or take courses through the federal Job Opportunities and Basic Skills (JOBS) program. In addition, the Family Support Act provided for transitional child care assistance for parents who have just left AFDC in search of gainful employment. These programs, which require matching funds from the states, were grafted onto Title IV-A of the Social Security Act.

In 1990 Congress created two additional child care programs: the Child Care and Development Block Grant and the IV-A At Risk program. The former provides, among other things, for direct subsidies to parents whose income is less than 75 percent of the median family income in their state; it also provides assistance for early childhood development programs, school-age child care programs, and a variety of quality initiatives determined by each state. The latter provides for direct subsidies to working parents who are at risk of backsliding into poverty and AFDC.

The result of these programs is that the federal government's financial support for child care has grown considerably. According to Hofferth, the federal government was spending $11.7 billion on child care support programs in fiscal year 1994, above and beyond the $11.9 billion in tax expenditures through the Earned Income Tax Credit.[18]

The precise amount spent by state governments on child care is unknown. It is clear, however, that state spending is considerably lower than federal spending. According to one estimate, state spending is no more than one-fifth of federal spending.[19] In per capita terms, that is not a lot of money. Adams and Sandfort found that half of all states spent less than $25 per child on the care and education of young children in fiscal year 1990; a third spent less than $17 per child.[20] Since these studies were conducted, the absolute level of state spending has probably increased, while the relative level of state spending has probably declined.

Still less is known about local government spending for child care, but local governments probably allocate fewer resources to child care than state governments. A survey of 278 larger cities found that only 25 percent are involved in preschool child care in a "major" way.[21] Local government support for early childhood education and family day care homes is even lower, according to the same survey.

The business community's support for child care varies sharply, with bigger businesses being more supportive. Many business initiatives to support child care involve little or no money—flexible hours, job-sharing, or unpaid parental leave. Others involve financial benefits for parents but negligible financial outlays for businesses, such as dependent care spending accounts which allow employees to exclude child care expenses up to $5,000 per year from their gross taxable income. Corporate funding for child care initiatives is currently a very small part of the total picture.

## Information

If parents are to make intelligent child care choices that benefit their children, they need good, timely information on the implications of different forms of care and on the characteristics of particular providers. Beginning in the 1960s, resource and referral agencies were created to play that role. In recent years, resource and referral agencies have enjoyed spectacular growth. Between 1988 and 1993 the membership of the National Association of Child Care Resource and Referral Agencies increased sharply—from 60 to 496. Most parents now have access to a resource and referral agency that serves their community.

Resource and referral agencies differ in their auspices. Most are private nonprofit organizations, but approximately 10 percent are sponsored by local governments. They also differ in the sophistication of their data-bases and in the ancillary services they provide. For example, many resource and referral agencies provide what they call "enhanced refer-rals" to corporate clients who in return provide a lump-sum subsidy. Some work in tandem with county welfare departments or JOBS pro-grams to help educate or inform disadvantaged clients receiving subsi-dized child care. And a growing number of resource and referral agencies manage vendor-voucher programs under contract to the state.

The precise information furnished to parents also varies. The better resource and referral agencies can tell parents whether a particular family day care home participates in the Child and Adult Care Food Program, owns pets, has a fenced backyard, and so forth. Similarly, they can tell parents whether a particular group day care center cares for infants and toddlers, is equipped to handle special needs children, employs a teacher who speaks Spanish, and so forth. More generally, resource and referral agencies can tell parents what to look for in a child care program.

As federal subsidies to poor parents have grown, "street-level bureau-crats" have become increasingly important as potential sources of infor-mation on child care. When AFDC or JOBS caseworkers sit down with clients to determine their eligibility for supportive services, they are in a position to dispense useful information and advice on child care choices. Whether they do so can have a considerable impact on a client's efforts to secure valuable job skills and educational experiences. If child care arrangements crash, a skeptical client's tenuous commitment to self-improvement may crash as well.

The mass media also play a critical role in informing parents, employers, and policymakers about child care problems and opportunities. Much media coverage is reactive; it ebbs and flows with legislative initiatives, scandals, press conferences, and public protests. Some news outlets, however, such as *The Wall Street Journal,* have demonstrated a more sustained interest in child care issues. More specialized magazines, such as *Working Mother* and *Young Children,* also cover these issues on a regular basis.

## Training

Child care training takes many different forms: college courses and degree programs, workshops, seminars, conferences, orientation sessions, and, of course, on-the-job training experiences. To simplify this, it is useful to distinguish between preservice training and in-service training. Preservice training applies primarily, though not exclusively, to center directors and teachers.[22] In-service training usually applies to the same persons and to center assistant teachers and family day care providers as well. But all of this is changing. By the year 2000, preservice training requirements may apply to a broader range of providers, and in-service training requirements may become more intensive.

Community colleges play the lead role in preservice training for center directors and teachers. They also educate a growing number of family day care providers. In addition to offering individual courses in child development and early childhood education, many community colleges offer one-year programs leading to a certificate and two-year programs leading to an associate's degree. Some community colleges have also forged imaginative linkages with four-year colleges and universities. In the state of Washington, for example, Yakima Valley Community College has developed a cooperative program with Central Washington University and Heritage College leading to a baccalaureate degree in early childhood education.[23]

In other jurisdictions, four-year colleges and universities offer their own degree programs. These programs are usually more abstract and always more expensive than community college programs. As a result, they are typically more attractive to persons who envision themselves as teachers of other teachers or as center directors rather than as teachers of children.

Resource and referral agencies are also heavily involved in child care training. Between 1988 and 1993 the number of resource and referral agencies increased by more than 700 percent.[24] According to a 1991 survey by the National Association of Child Care Resource and Referral Agencies, 95 percent of resource and referral agencies offer training for family day care providers; 79 percent offer training for center personnel; and 58 percent offer training for personnel in school-age programs. State governments also play a role in training child care providers in some jurisdictions. For example, they may conduct an orientation session for new providers or offer a course in CPR or first aid.

Another strategy related to training is accreditation. The leading child care accreditation program is run by the Council of Early Childhood Professional Recognition, which was created by the National Association for the Education of Young Children (NAEYC). Based in Washington, D.C., the Council awards a Child Development Associate (CDA) certificate to providers who complete 120 clock hours of approved coursework and who successfully pass an examination or "assessment." The assessment, which includes monitoring of the provider interacting with children, is conducted by a child development expert in the provider's region who has been designated by the council to perform that task. A local advisory team chosen by the provider also participates in the process.

The CDA program has been closely linked to Head Start, because Head Start pays for its teachers to complete the accreditation process, from start to finish, and because federal law requires that every Head Start classroom with twenty children must have at least one teacher with a CDA or an associate's degree in early childhood education.[25] As a result, approximately 80 percent of all persons with a CDA certificate work with Head Start.[26]

Outside of Head Start, the CDA certificate has been slow to catch on, in part because the assessment alone costs $325. Many providers cannot afford the coursework or the assessment without a subsidy. The problem is particularly acute for family day care. As of 1992, only 521 family day care providers nationwide had received the CDA certificate.[27] More broadly, the training of family day care providers poses a special challenge, because it is difficult for family day care providers to get away during the day and because it is difficult to replicate the monitoring process that can take place at a group day care center, with seasoned professionals overseeing the work of their junior colleagues. To remedy this, some family day care training programs incorporate regular home visits into the training process.[28] Others schedule training sessions at relatively convenient times, on weekday nights or during weekends.

## An Appraisal

The formal infrastructure I have described will strike many readers as rational, orderly, logical, and sensible. Without a blueprint or master plan, many enterprises and individuals have combined their energies and talents in the common pursuit of excellence, or at least respectability, in child care. Our system is characterized by a considerable degree of specialization, which permits different sectors, governments, and organizations to pursue their comparative advantage. At the same time, there is considerable diversity, which, in principle, should foster competition; that, in turn, should promote quality at affordable prices.

In one respect, our system is superior to those of Europe and the Far East. Instead of putting all of our eggs in one or two baskets, such as government-run centers or church-based centers, we have institutionalized highly pluralistic arrangements. More than the Chinese, we have allowed 100 flowers to bloom. More than the French, we have adhered to the motto *chacun à son gout* (each to his own taste). There are, however, three key problems with our formal child care infrastructure: decentralization, complexity, and unevenness.

*Decentralization.* For better and for worse, there are no national child care standards in the United States, and there are limited barriers to entry. Decisions are made by public and private entities, with little communication, consultation, or coordination. Funding agencies assume that regulatory agencies are inspecting facilities as required by law; regulatory agencies assume that resource and referral agencies are informing parents of their options; resource and referral agencies assume that community colleges are equipping providers with requisite skills; community colleges assume that providers are applying those skills as they interact with children. If these assumptions are incorrect, we are in deep trouble. No one is checking to see if people are performing their appointed roles, much less coordinating to reduce inconsistencies.

*Complexity.* With so many players involved, so many regulations, and so many different funding streams, it is hard for parents—or providers—to know where things stand. It is difficult to master funding eligibility rules, regulatory requirements, and organizational charts. It is also difficult to know whom to blame when things go wrong. If parents cannot pay the fees at the center they prefer, should they blame the center director for mismanagement? or their employer for Scrooge-like indifference? or their elected officials for failing to appropriate more funds for child care? If providers cannot meet regulatory requirements, should they blame their local government for "going by the book"? or their state government for failing to inform them of local requirements? or the federal government for failing to provide financial support? Complexity breeds confusion, which undermines accountability.

*Unevenness.* Child care in the United States is strikingly uneven. Some child care facilities are heavily regulated, while others are regulated by no one. This is especially true of family day care, where we have managed to combine underregulation and overregulation with perverse consequences.[29] Even for centers, which are usually regulated, standards vary dramatically. In the Northeast and the upper Midwest, ratios are low and training requirements are high; in the Southeast, ratios are high and training requirements are low. Funding levels also vary. Head Start programs receive 95 percent of their funding from government sources (mainly the federal government), while for-profit chains receive 3 percent of their funding from government sources.[30] In fiscal year 1990, Massachusetts spent $152 per child on direct child care and early childhood services, while Idaho spent 24 cents.[31]

In short, we have created a "loosely coupled" system that makes it difficult to achieve such substantive goals as justice and quality. A loosely coupled system is one characterized by tenuous connections between subunits and weak hierarchical controls. It is distinguishable from a tightly coupled system, such as a Weberian bureaucracy, in which a clear chain of command guarantees a substantial degree of cohesiveness, consistency, and control.[32] Although loose coupling and tight coupling are ideal types, many real-world systems approximate them. The public school is a frequently cited example of a loosely coupled system.[33] Child care is, in some respects, an even better example.[34]

A loosely coupled system resembles organized anarchy, especially when compared to a tightly coupled system. Individual subsystems often march to the beat of different drummers, to the detriment of system goals (if indeed there are any system goals). Also, as a general rule, loosely coupled systems are less able to capture economies of scale, to provide comprehensive services, and to ensure social equity.[35] These are real drawbacks that cannot be lightly dismissed.

On the other hand, loosely coupled systems do possess certain virtues that should not be overlooked. As a general rule, they are more innovative, because discretion breeds creativity. They are more responsive to changing conditions, because they are more outward-looking and because new directions do not require numerous approvals. Furthermore, they are less likely to break down if a particular course of action proves foolhardy, because independent or quasi-independent subunits seldom opt for identical strategies. In short, they are more resilient. From diversity and discretion many real benefits flow.

Family day care, among the loosest elements of our loosely coupled system, illustrates some of these virtues. To parents who yearn for the relaxed, casual rhythms of a home environment, family day care offers a middle course between placing their child in a center and staying home themselves. When the demand for infant and toddler care increased dramatically, family day care providers met that need, while other segments of the child care market did not. Also, family day care providers are less insistent on punctual pickups, more willing to care for sick children, and more tolerant of late payments. If the family day care sector were tightly coupled, it might be less versatile, less adaptable, and less understanding.

Yet loose coupling has its drawbacks. When state and local governments impose conflicting requirements on family day care providers, that is a loose-coupling problem. When diverse funding streams make it difficult for clients to retain the same child care provider as they shift from one program to another, that is a loose-coupling problem. When information networks and child care counselors operate independently of one another, that is a loose-coupling problem. The absence of meaningful performance review is also a loose-coupling problem. These are not trivial challenges.

In the final analysis, loose coupling can be a major irritant but it need not be a fatal flaw. That is because informal norms, if well-crafted and well-diffused, can substitute for formal structural controls. Professionalism is one such norm. Collegiality is another. Thus in thinking about our child care system, we need to consider not just the formal infrastructure but the informal infrastructure as well—the norms that are not written down anywhere but that determine the ebb and flow of organizational and personal behavior.

## The Informal Infrastructure

Most studies of child care—and most reform efforts—have focused on the formal infrastructure—the skeletal framework of institutions

TABLE 3-2. The Informal Child Care Infrastructure

| Regulation | Funding | Information |
|---|---|---|
| Speak loudly and carry a little stick | You go first! | Public information that never reaches the public |
| Equal treatment of unequals | Entitled but capped | Honest brokers |
| Going by the book | Zero-sum conflicts | Look it up in the Yellow Pages! |

| Training | Providers |
|---|---|
| Training is its own reward | Babysitters for hire |
| Experience is the best teacher | Reluctant businesspersons |
| Invisible gems | Don't tread on me! |

that perform critical child care tasks. Neglected are the tasks themselves and the ground rules that undergird them. The norms that govern what formal child care institutions do may be thought of as the informal infrastructure. These norms have developed without much introspection or public debate. Like prairie weeds, they have grown, willy-nilly, in unexpected and sometimes unfortunate ways (see table 3-2).

## Regulatory Rituals

Child care inspectors in all fifty states have the option of recommending license revocation or denial of renewal if they do not like what they see at a particular center. But license revocations and renewal denials almost never occur. During a recent three-year period, for example, Virginia revoked or refused to renew only 11 center licenses.[36] Why? Because no one wants to see a child care facility shut down at a time when parents are scrambling for child care. And because inspectors are loath to initiate the cumbersome process required to terminate a license. The informal norm, widely understood, is that a center must be truly horrible before it will have its license revoked.

If inspectors have difficulty punishing bad providers, they also have difficulty rewarding good providers. Unlike dentists, who hand out free toothbrushes to patients every six months, child care inspectors do not have free samples to dispense. They can and do offer words of encouragement. But they are urged by their superiors to praise both good and bad providers, on the assumption that positive reinforcement helps both types. At times, this is difficult. While visiting a particularly dreadful facility, one inspector looked for something nice to say and finally settled on the director's blouse: "I love that shade of pink!"

If every regulatory visit includes its obligatory compliment, the rest of the regulatory process is also highly standardized. Because of time constraints, inspectors must focus on obvious rule violations rather than less obvious opportunities for improvement. Thus they dutifully record odors in the bathroom and missing ipecac bottles in the first-aid kit. These observations require less thought and less time than observations on staff-child interactions, which take more time to notice and record. The tendency in child care, as in other policy domains, is to "go by the book."[37] As a result, problems displace opportunities and tangible rule infractions displace intangible signs of dysfunctional behavior.

The cumulative effect of all these norms is that good and bad providers become virtually indistinguishable, judging from the regulatory agency's output. Inspectors know who's been naughty and who's been nice, but that remains their little secret. Constrained by time, by tradition, and by legal expectations, inspectors treat providers with radically different performance records fundamentally the same.

## Funding Flaws

In an era of scarce resources, the simplest rule of thumb is to wait until somebody else takes the initiative. Consequently, businesses hope that governments will come to the rescue, local governments look to the statehouse for financial support, and state governments urge the federal government to intervene—with funding, that is, not regulation. Under such circumstances, funding levels tend to be inadequate. And special problems, such as sick-child care and evening care, remain largely unaddressed.

Despite a built-in bias towards stinginess, agencies of various sorts do provide significant funding, thanks to demographic changes, new cultural values, interest group advocacy, and policy entrepreneurship. Full funding, however, is rare. Thus authorizations exceed appropriations, and the number of persons eligible for funding exceeds the number who actually receive it. Along the way, a strange phrase has crept into the political vocabulary—the "capped entitlement." In practice, the capped entitlement is not an entitlement at all but rather a fixed appropriation for a worthy cause that in a more expansive era might have warranted a real entitlement. The IV-A At-Risk program, with a budget fixed at $300 million per year and a bulging potential clientele, illustrates this phenomenon.

Because of funding limitations, spending programs are usually targeted to the neediest of the needy. In this case, child care programs are superior to older social programs, which often favored middle-class constituents at the expense of the hard-core disadvantaged—the Comprehensive Employment and Training Act (CETA), for example.[38] However, middle-class parents have serious child care problems too, problems that are only partially addressed by the Child and Dependent Care Tax Credit, which primarily benefits the middle class. Indeed, child care quality at centers that primarily serve middle-class children is actually lower than the quality at centers that primarily serve low-income children (upper-income children enjoy the best care).[39]

Given multiple problems and scarce resources, a division of labor makes sense. For example, the federal government might concentrate on the special needs of the poor, while other governments and the private sector focus on the needs of middle-class children. In practice, however, the federal government has been asked for child care support for both the poor and the middle-class. Those constituencies are now locked in zero-sum conflicts.

## Information Islands

The regulatory process generates large quantities of data on the attributes of group day care centers, group day care homes, and family day care homes. Most of that information never reaches the consuming public. Regulators see themselves as serving consumers through dyadic relationships with providers, not as part of a multilateral network that includes civil servants, resource and referral specialists, providers, and consumers. While they respond politely to polite inquiries, state officials do not make heroic efforts to disseminate inspection results to a wider audience.

Resource and referral agencies also possess large quantities of data on the attributes of providers, which they readily share with consumers, usually in return for a nominal fee. Most of this information comes directly from providers; contacts between resource and referral agencies and regulatory officials are few and far between. In their dealings with consumers, resource and referral specialists offer general advice and specific information but seldom specific advice. Thus they urge parents to look for certain things in a day care facility, and they supply basic information on facilities of interest. But they avoid making connections between general rules of thumb and specific center characteristics. To do so, they fear, would jeopardize their status as "honest brokers."

The other relevant brokers are caseworkers, who dispense information on job training and educational opportunities to clients receiving government funds. Increasingly, they dispense information on child care as well. Like resource and referral specialists, caseworkers are loath to offer specific advice. Unlike resource and referral specialists, who may have to bite their tongues to avoid divulging what they know, caseworkers usually know very little about child care opportunities and pitfalls. They are also pressed for time, due to bulging caseloads. If asked for advice on child care, they may produce a brochure or perhaps even a videotape. Or they may echo James Earl Jones on TV: Look it up in the Yellow Pages!

Role specialization makes perfect bureaucratic and political sense but it works to the detriment of consumers. State inspectors, local caseworkers, and resource and referral specialists have defined their roles so narrowly that no one gets into hot water, except for consumers who need help they are not getting. By eliminating strong advice to consumers from their repertoire, information brokers save time in the short run and escape political controversy, but they fail to help many consumers who desperately need guidance.

## Training Troubles

It is possible to be a child care provider without having much training—indeed, without having any training at all in some states. The marketplace, the polity, and the society send similar signals to potential providers. The dominant message is that child care is a personal service of relatively modest value best handled through informal transactions between consenting adults. Low wages, low entry requirements, and low prestige strongly reinforce that message.

Child care differs from nursing, social work, teaching, and other human services, which have developed strong professional associations, powerful credentialing bodies, and supportive public policies. At best, child care is a semi-profession. In keeping with that perception, training requirements are rather limited. Comparisons with other countries are instructive. We measure our training requirements in terms of hours; they measure theirs in terms of years. In Germany, for example, at least two years of college are required to teach in *Kindergärten*. In France, the equivalent of a master's degree is required.[40]

In practice, many providers do obtain training, either because they are required to or because they want to. But training carries with it meager financial rewards. As Walker has noted in a study of family day care homes, the rates charged by well-trained and poorly trained providers are virtually identical.[41] Under such circumstances, training must be its own reward.

Critics of higher training requirements muster all sorts of arguments to bolster their position: Will additional training requirements make it more difficult for parents to find child care slots? Will additional training requirements make it difficult for minorities to find jobs as child care providers? What is the point of training if providers go out of business in one or two years?

These arguments can be rebutted, but their pervasiveness illustrates the problem. Of all the regulatory requirements in the government's arsenal, none contributes more to the personal growth and professional development of child care providers than training requirements. Yet many regulators attach little value to professional training, and parents seem to value it even less. Even resource and referral agencies, which supposedly have a strong commitment to quality, are frequently unable to disclose which day care centers in their community employ teachers with outstanding training or CDA credentials. Until this changes, child care will not be a full-fledged profession.

## Provider Problems

Despite abundant training opportunities, active professional associations, and a deeply rooted service ethic, child care remains a semi-profession. As Spodek has noted, the child care field lacks accepted standards for admission and practice, protracted periods of preparation, and high levels of public trust.[42] Moreover, many parents continue to think of providers as "babysitters" despite vigorous efforts to purge that word from the child care vocabulary. Indeed, a substantial minority of providers still see themselves as babysitters. This is especially true of family day care providers, whose commitment to a child care career is more tenuous than that of center-based teachers.[43]

A related problem is that many providers have trouble thinking of themselves as small businesspersons. Lacking business savvy and skill, they are often overwhelmed by paperwork requirements imposed by government agencies. When that occurs, they may fail to take advantage of valuable programs, such as the Child and Adult Care Food Program. Here again, family day care providers are usually less sophisticated and more easily frustrated than their center-based counterparts. The latter have the advantage of being able to pay someone—the director—to handle health insurance, liability insurance, record-keeping, and regulatory requirements. Family day care providers do not enjoy that luxury.

Despite a growing awareness that governments have legitimate roles to play in regulating and funding child care, many providers view government regulation with skepticism, fear, or outright hostility. Family day care providers are often exasperated by the number of hurdles they must overcome just to get started. They are also troubled by the hidden costs of licensing, which can be substantial.[44] Directors of group day care centers are more likely to take government regulation in stride. Even they get upset, though, when government regulators huff and puff over technicalities.

No master plan undergirds the diverse norms that guide politicians, civil servants, information brokers, educators, and child care providers. These norms do not add up to a coherent system. Many of the norms make it extremely difficult to achieve justice, efficiency, and choice. Many of the norms also interfere with more modest procedural goals.

## Procedural Criteria

Throughout this chapter I have hinted at procedural criteria that may help to evaluate our child care infrastructure, formal and informal. The most important of these criteria are coordination, discretion, and responsiveness. These words have mantra-like qualities—they are so soothing that it is easy to miss their significance. Before embracing them and moving on, it is important to ask what they mean, how they differ from related concepts, and how they fit into a broader scheme of values.

### Coordination

Serious efforts to link agencies, programs, and policies entail coordination. A fitting goal for most policy systems, coordination helps to ensure that organizations with somewhat dissimilar purposes move in somewhat similar directions. Coordination is not as powerful as collaboration, which implies the actual sharing of power, resources, and authority.[45] However, it may be better suited to loosely coupled systems than collaboration, because it demands somewhat less of the participants. Thus if we accept the basic outlines of our formal child care infrastructure, coordination seems very appealing.

What exactly might coordination look like in a child care context? In practice, it might suggest some of the following propositions:

—Funding streams should be well integrated so that shifts from one stream to another are as smooth as possible for clients;

—Regulations imposed by different levels of government should be consistent;

—Disadvantaged clients should be able to obtain all the information they need on employment, training, and child care options at one site;

—Child care grants should be administered by the same agency or by agencies successfully linked through interagency agreements, interagency task forces, or similar arrangements;

—Public and private agencies should share information with one another to the maximum extent possible; and

—Child care services, educational services, and health care services should be integrated as much as possible (for example, by situating child care programs in hospitals and schools).

## Discretion

Discretion implies that regulators, producers, and consumers should be free to choose courses of action that seem most appropriate in a particular case. At its best, discretion promotes creativity and a sense of responsibility. Closely related to flexibility, it is clearly compatible with a loosely coupled system. It does not, however, imply total freedom. Nor does it imply the absence of accountability. Choices can be evaluated, by political superiors and by voters, and consequences may flow from those evaluations. Discretion is particularly important in human services programs. Unless street-level bureaucrats are free to improvise, contacts with clients quickly become impersonal and dehumanizing.[46]

What are the implications of discretion for child care? Here are a few possibilities:

—State governments should be free to promote quality through higher provider reimbursement rates, even if this means that fewer children are served;

—State governments should be free to promote affordability through higher child/staff ratios for preschool children, even if this means that quality suffers somewhat;

—Child care inspectors should be free to punish bad performers and reward good performers;

—Child care providers should be allowed to meet the spirit of regulatory requirements, if the costs of literal compliance are unusually and unnecessarily high;

—Caseworkers should be free to refer clients who need child care assistance to a resource and referral agency; and

—Businesses should choose child care support strategies that maximize the autonomy of their employees.

## *Responsiveness*

Responsiveness means listening to customers and taking into account what they say. Despite its association with Total Quality Management (TQM), responsiveness is not a new-age concept. Our political system, with its emphasis on federalism and checks and balances, was designed to promote responsiveness, among other values. And capitalism promotes responsiveness to customers through the invisible hand of the marketplace.

Responsiveness and accountability are closely related but not identical concepts. Accountability suggests the ominous inevitability of a judgment day, when transgressions and mistakes will be noted and punished. Responsiveness, in contrast, implies more of an ongoing relationship. Accountability also implies more of a top-down hierarchical structure, as in a tightly coupled system. In contrast, responsiveness suggests greater influence from below. So long as our child care infrastructure remains loosely coupled, responsiveness seems the more appropriate concept.

What might responsiveness look like in a child care context? Among other possibilities:

—Providers should be required to grant parents access to their premises and some voice in decisionmaking processes at the home or center;

—States should be required to hold public hearings on how to spend federal child care funds;

—Notices of violation of child care rules should be posted so that parents can read them and act on them;

—Voucher arrangements should supplant contractual arrangements wherever possible;

—Employers should consider the preferences of their employees before embarking on new child care initiatives; and

—State and federal agencies should be subject to vigorous legislative oversight as they administer child care programs.

## Discussion

Coordination, discretion, and responsiveness in various forms are certainly legitimate goals to pursue. Each of these concepts, however, covers an enormous amount of territory. When we favor coordination, do we mean coordination across governments, across programs, across agencies, or across bureaus? When we endorse discretion, do we mean state discretion, inspector discretion, provider discretion, or parental discretion? When we advocate responsiveness, do we mean responsiveness to employees, interest groups, parents, or children?

Coordination, discretion, and responsiveness also tug us in different directions. Weak coordination poses no threat to administrative discretion, but strong coordination may, and collaboration surely does. As coordination grows stronger, discretion may weaken. Responsiveness also poses a threat to administrative discretion, particularly if it requires administrators to respond favorably to constituencies with an obvious axe to grind. Do we want a child care system in which inspectors cannot stand up to disreputable providers? Do we want a child care system in which state agencies do precisely what parents want, regardless of the implications for quality?

Those who favor coordination and responsiveness may be willing to sacrifice discretion, just as those who favor efficiency and justice may be willing to sacrifice choice. Or they may attach little weight to particular forms of discretion, such as provider discretion or inspector discretion. These forms of discretion appear less dispensable and more precious when linked to other values, such as professionalism. Without considerable discretion, the pursuit of professional norms and standards becomes impossible. Thus if we wish to nurture professionalism, within the provider community and elsewhere, we must sustain a considerable degree of discretion within a loosely coupled system.

In fact, professional status offers unusual opportunities to solve a number of value trade-offs. If provider professionalism were stronger, providers—especially those with exemplary records—could be given greater slack. If inspector professionalism were stronger, inspectors could escape dysfunctional bureaucratic controls. Professionalism is no magic bullet, but it does encourage quality and consistency without resorting to bureaucratization or political interference. As Sykes explains, "The classic bargain struck by the elite professions substitutes regulation of the worker for regulation of the work itself."[47] If we struck a similar bargain in child care, street-level bureaucrats and service providers could enjoy greater freedom, while children experienced fewer risks.

Our child care system is a failure not because our formal infrastructure is irretrievably flawed but because our informal norms fail to compensate for the looseness of our formal infrastructure. In case after case, those informal norms reflect the absence of strong professional standards. State inspectors and AFDC caseworkers are guided by bureaucratic rules and conventions, corporate executives and politicians are guided by profit-seeking and blame avoidance, and child care providers are guided by habits of the heart, pocketbook reflexes, and cultural expectations. The result is a system of incentives that favors standardization, mediocrity, and indifference.

Is professionalism attainable or even desirable in a policy arena where every parent claims to possess relevant expertise? Does not professionalism pose its own dangers, such as insulation, impenetrability, and elite dominance? Might professionalism result in excessive attention to some substantive values, such as quality, at the expense of others, such as affordability? Professionalism has not solved our health care dilemmas, and it has proven only partially successful in education. Yet it stands out as a solution that is fully compatible with the loosely coupled infrastructure that defines child care. Ever since the Progressive Era, it has offered a safe haven for those who favor both technical expertise and political democracy. And it does reduce the costs of monitoring and supervision.

There are, of course, alternative paths. The most conspicuous would be to pursue a tightly coupled system, in which centralization is strong, accountability is high, and control is tight. In pursuit of such a system, we would need to overhaul our formal infrastructure. We would shift responsibility from the state to the national level, we would tighten regulatory enforcement, we would impose new mandates on business, and we would strengthen barriers to entry. Such a system might resemble child care in Sweden or perhaps France. Both quality and cost could be high. To replicate the highly regarded French system, for example, could require a tripling of current government spending for child care in the United States.[48]

A more complex alternative would be to create a different kind of loosely coupled system, in which the principal adhesive is not professionalism but collegiality. Within the provider community, the emphasis would be on support groups. Within the regulatory community, the emphasis would be on retreats or quality circles.[49] Within the legislative community, the emphasis would be on party caucuses. In each instance, norms would evolve through a series of ad hoc discussions rather than through the adoption and transmission of professional standards. Instead of "purposive" incentives, we would rely upon "solidary" incentives to keep people marching in the same direction.[50]

In succeeding chapters, I will consider these and other alternatives. Some require a new formal infrastructure; others require a new informal infrastructure. Substantive or procedural criteria may be used to evaluate these alternatives. In either case, the stakes are unusually high. A strong, robust, resilient child care system is essential not just to child care policy but to education policy, employment policy, and welfare policy as well. Beyond that, it signifies a civilized society that cares about its future and that cares for its most vulnerable citizens.

## Conclusion

Two child care infrastructures exist in the United States, one largely visible, the other largely invisible. Our formal infrastructure is a classic loosely coupled system—untidy but fully functional when combined with appropriate norms. If our formal infrastructure does not look very European, that is hardly surprising. Neither our health care system nor our educational system looks European either. Perhaps that is bad. On the other hand, looseness has its advantages. Innovation, experimentation, and adaptability are not trivial virtues. As for decentralization and complexity, they present problems, but not insoluble ones.

If our formal infrastructure has redeeming features, our informal infrastructure does not. The norms embedded in our child care system are dysfunctional and perverse. They impel well-meaning individuals to play counterproductive roles. Instead of complementing our formal infrastructure, our informal infrastructure reinforces some of its worst features. Standardization, caution, fear, inertia, and suspicion have become commonplace. Centrifugal forces have grown out of control. Time horizons have shrunk. Unintentionally, we have created a system that encourages mediocrity.

Several procedural criteria help to pinpoint problems with our two infrastructures. Coordination, discretion, and responsiveness are vital if a loosely coupled system is to succeed. To varying degrees, each is lacking. Connections between information gatherers and information sharers are weak. Street-level bureaucrats are hobbled by standard operating procedures that discourage distinctions between good and bad providers. Parents are casual observers rather than full-fledged participants in decisionmaking processes. Seamless services, regulatory reasonableness, and responsive governance seem elusive goals.

Even more distressing is that substantive goals are not being met. Without coordination and discretion, how does one achieve efficiency? Without coordination and responsiveness, how does one promote informed choice? Without discretion and responsiveness, how does one guarantee social justice? The elusiveness of important procedural goals hints strongly at the difficulty of achieving important substantive goals.

It is possible to imagine several paths out of this morass. One strategy would be to redesign the formal infrastructure, with a tightly coupled system in mind. Several precedents exist, even in the United States, for such an approach. A different strategy would be to introduce a strong dose of professionalism as a much-needed tonic for our loosely coupled system. Instead of striving for greater control, we would institutionalize greater self-control. This approach, increasingly popular in education policy, may have merit in child care policy as well.

Hierarchy and professionalism are not the only techniques for achieving greater cohesion. In the chapters that follow, we consider a variety of reforms aimed at improving service delivery, government intervention, and social support. Clearly, problems are multifaceted. As such, they require remedies that transcend particular institutions. Industry, government, and society must all be part of the solution.

# 4 | Markets and Black Markets

THE CHILD CARE INDUSTRY in the United States is characterized by considerable diversity or unevenness, which is partly a reflection of a highly decentralized, pluralist, federal political system. But it also reflects a weak constituency for young children, ambivalence toward both government regulation and child care, nervousness about new entitlement programs, and a reluctance to defer to experts.

A Pennsylvania child care inspector likens the situation to an old Clint Eastwood movie—*The Good, the Bad, and the Ugly.* That characterization is probably too harsh. No one doubts that there are good and bad facilities. The debate is over how to characterize the rest. Depending on one's perspective, they are adequate, undistinguished, or mediocre.

For example, most group day care centers and most regulated family day care homes comply with key state regulations, but many fail to meet higher standards offered by the National Association for the Education of Young Children and other child care experts.[1] Thus it is important to distinguish between those facilities that are unacceptably bad and those whose improvement is desirable but not urgent.

For analytic purposes, it is possible to be fairly precise about where the biggest problems lie. Although there is considerable diversity within the child care industry, the fault lines that separate the good from the bad facilities are clear.

In this chapter, I focus primarily on the quality of care in two settings— for-profit group day care centers and unregulated family day care homes. A substantial minority of centers are for-profit and the vast majority of family day care homes are unregulated. The quality of care in both settings leaves much to be desired. By focusing on these two areas, I hope to illustrate the potential for targeted reforms in the child care industry. I discuss one such reform (provider education and training) and a broader reform strategy (total quality management) later in this chapter.

## The For-Profit Sector

The single most unusual feature of the child care industry in the United States is the relatively prominent role played by for-profit group day care centers. A national study, conducted in 1990, found that 35 percent of all group day care centers are for-profit ones.[2] Another national study, conducted in 1991, found that 34 percent of all school-age child care programs are for-profit.[3] The for-profit sector is growing somewhat in other countries, but they still constitute an extremely small percentage of all group day care centers in western Europe and Scandinavia.[4]

For-profit chains are another unusual feature of the U.S. child care landscape. More than one-sixth of all for-profit centers are owned by chains, leading some critics to charge that the child care industry is becoming more and more like the fast-food industry, with its emphasis on low cost and its lack of emphasis on quality. KinderCare, the largest of the chains, is sometimes referred to as "Kentucky Fried Children," which conveys precisely the critics' concerns.

Is it wrong for companies to make money caring for small children? Is it wrong for chains to secure a firm niche in the child care market? My answer to these questions is no. After all, is it wrong for companies, including chains, to make money feeding people or sheltering people? If it were, we would want to nationalize McDonald's, Howard Johnson, and Holiday Inn.

Nevertheless, it is appropriate to raise questions about the for-profit sector of the child care industry because of persistent allegations of inferior care. Using public policy levers, we can encourage or discourage the provision of child care by for-profit firms. In Canada, for example, some provinces allocate discretionary grants to for-profits, while others do not. Industry norms or incentives can be greatly affected by regulatory actions. Before choosing a course of action, however, it is necessary to examine the evidence.

## Findings

For-profit centers are cheaper than nonprofit centers and for-profit chains are cheaper than "mom and pop" for-profits. In 1990 for-profit chains charged an average of $1.47 per hour and for-profit independents charged an average of $1.53 per hour. In contrast, nonprofit religious centers charged an average of $1.65 per hour, and nonprofit independents charged an average of $1.73 per hour.[5] One explanation for these price differentials might be that for-profit centers are more efficient than nonprofit centers, because market discipline induces them to make sound business decisions. The evidence suggests, however, that for-profit centers are no more efficient than nonprofits.[6]

A more troubling explanation, which receives some empirical support, is that for-profits sacrifice quality to achieve cost reductions. Across a wide range of indicators, for-profit centers are worse than other centers.[7] They pay their personnel less, which encourages staff turnover, which is harmful to children. They hire fewer teachers per child, which reduces opportunities for positive interactions between children and adults. They also hire fewer teachers with college degrees. Similar findings apply to school-age child care programs, with one notable exception.[8]

Within the for-profit sector, chains look worse than independents.[9] In 1990 the average hourly wage of center teachers was $5.43 at for-profit chains, $6.30 at for-profit independents. As a result, the average annual turnover at for-profit chains was much higher. Whereas for-profit independents maintained an average child/staff ratio of 9:1 for three-year olds, for-profit chains allowed an average ratio of 11:1. For-profit independents boasted a somewhat higher percentage of teachers with a college or graduate degree.

Of course, these are descriptive statistics. Do the findings hold up when one controls for other relevant variables? Does public school sponsorship or church sponsorship make a difference? And how important is for-profit status relative to other policy-relevant variables, such as subsidies, regulations, and parental involvement?

To answer these questions, I have estimated the effects of institutional status and several other variables on teacher education, staff size, and teacher turnover. Research shows that children's cognitive and social development is enhanced by high levels of teacher education, low child/staff ratios, and low turnover.[10] To assess the effects of institutional auspices on these three variables, I have utilized either ordinary least squares regression analysis or two-stage least squares.[11] Each model includes institutional auspices variables, public policy variables, and other appropriate control variables. The unit of analysis is the group day care center.

The primary source of data for this analysis is the *Profile of Child Care Settings Data Base,* which includes detailed information on the characteristics and practices of 2,089 center-based early education and care programs in 1990.[12] Because Head Start programs are not directly regulated by state governments, I have excluded them from the analysis. In theory, this leaves a total of 1,876 centers for further analysis. In practice, because of missing data for particular variables, the samples range from approximately 700 to approximately 1,200 centers. Most—but not all—of the variables used in the different models have been obtained from the *Profile of Child Care Settings* data set.[13]

Table 4-1 confirms that for-profit status affects teacher education, even after controlling for other variables. For-profit centers are less likely than other centers to hire teachers with a college degree. Neither the number of inspections, nor the size of state subsidies, nor the degree of parental involvement has a statistically significant impact on teacher education. A state requirement that teachers have a high school diploma and further course work or experience does, however, encourage the employment of college-educated teachers.

For-profits are also associated with lower quality because they use fewer staff members than other day care centers (see table 4-2). The effects of other institutional sponsors are not statistically significant. As expected, state regulatory ceilings for child/staff ratios have an impact on staff size, after controlling for the number of children and the mean age of children. Here, too, the number of inspections, the size of state subsidies, and the degree of parental involvement do not have statistically significant effects.

It is particularly interesting to note that the number of inspections has little or no impact on staff size. Presumably, one of the purposes of inspections is to ensure that child care facilities are adequately staffed. Yet the data do not assure us that increasing the number of inspections will increase the number of staff members. To investigate this further, I considered the possibility that staff size helps to determine the number of

TABLE 4-1. Determinants of Teacher Education:
Multiple Regression Results

| Variable | Unstandardized $B^a$ |
|---|---|
| For-profit sponsorship | −.267* |
| | (.134) |
| Church sponsorship | .291 |
| | (.179) |
| Public school sponsorship | .489 |
| | (.261) |
| Number of teachers | .196*** |
| | (.012) |
| High school diploma and coursework or experience required | .914*** |
| | (.131) |
| Percent of children, parents on AFDC | −.008** |
| | (.003) |
| Number of inspections | −.019 |
| | (.016) |
| State subsidies | −6.459E-04 |
| | (.002) |
| Parental involvement | .283 |
| | (.149) |
| $R^2 = .25$ | |
| $N = 1,054$ | |

a. Standard errors are in parentheses.
*Significant at the .05 level.
**Significant at the .01 level.
***Significant at the .0001 level.

inspections and not just vice versa.[14] Through two stage least squares, it is possible to purge the effects of one endogenous variable on another and then reestimate the effects of the latter on the former by using a newly created instrument derived from a reduced form equation that includes all exogenous variables in the system of equations as predictors.[15] The results of these procedures, however, are not encouraging (see tables A-1 and A-2 in the appendix). I found that when two-way causality is taken into account, the effects of inspections on staff size are even weaker and definitely not statistically significant.

The effects of for-profit status are also apparent when one considers teacher turnover. Here also, for-profit status makes a difference (see table 4-3). Specifically, for-profit sponsorship leads to higher turnover. Neither the number of inspections nor the level of state subsidies nor parental involvement has statistically significant effects. There is, how-ever, a statistically significant negative relationship between the percent-

TABLE 4-2. Determinants of Staff Size: Multiple Regression Results

| Variable | Unstandardized $B^a$ |
|---|---|
| For-profit sponsorship | −1.773* |
| | (.441) |
| Church sponsorship | −.725 |
| | (.630) |
| Public school sponsorship | −1.107 |
| | (1.365) |
| Number of children | .129** |
| | (.004) |
| Mean age of children | −2.782** |
| | (.358) |
| Allowed ratio, 3-year-olds | −.294* |
| | (.081) |
| Percent of children, parents on AFDC | .006 |
| | (.009) |
| Number of inspections | .081 |
| | (.051) |
| State subsidies | .004 |
| | (.008) |
| Parental involvement | .512 |
| | (.500) |
| $R^2$ = .62 | |
| $N$ = 702 | |

a. Standard errors are in parentheses.
*Significant at the .001 level.
**Significant at the .0001 level.

age of the center's budget spent on salaries and fringe benefits and teacher turnover. Centers that allocate more money to teacher pay are better able to retain teachers. By extension, this suggests that state initiatives targeted at boosting teacher salaries could reduce turnover. Since 1990 states have been free to use a portion of their Child Care and Development Block Grant (CCDBG) money to boost salaries. Whether such efforts have borne fruit is not yet clear.

Overall, this analysis of national survey data confirms the negative impact of for-profit status on quality. The effects of for-profit status on three key dependent variables remain statistically significant, after controlling for other variables. For-profit status has a stronger impact on center quality than church sponsorship or public school sponsorship. It also has a stronger impact on center quality than the number of inspections, the level of state subsidies, or the degree of parental involvement in center affairs. Among policy-relevant variables measured here, only state

TABLE 4-3. Determinants of Teacher Turnover:
Multiple Regression Results

| Variable | Unstandardized $B^a$ |
|---|---|
| For-profit sponsorship | .343* |
| | (.169) |
| Church sponsorship | −.193 |
| | (.211) |
| Public school sponsorship | −.010 |
| | (.348) |
| Number of teachers | .218*** |
| | (.014) |
| Allowed ratio, 3-year-olds | −.010 |
| | (.029) |
| Percent of budget spent on salaries, fringes | −.011** |
| | (.004) |
| Percent of children, parents on AFDC | .001 |
| | (.003) |
| Number of inspections | .025 |
| | (.018) |
| State subsidies | −.002 |
| | (.002) |
| Parental involvement | −.197 |
| | (.173) |
| $R^2 = .26$ | |
| $N = 861$ | |

a. Standard errors are in parentheses.
*Significant at the .05 level.
**Significant at the .01 level.
***Significant at the .0001 level.

regulatory standards (teacher education requirements and child/staff ratios) rival for-profit status in importance.

As mentioned earlier, the quality of care at for-profit chains appears to
be considerably lower than the quality of care at independent for-profit
centers. Thus the question naturally arises: Would for-profit centers still
be worse than nonprofit centers if we could wave a magic wand and
banish the chains? Although this sounds like a thought experiment, an
in-depth empirical analysis of child care in Vermont actually permits a
tentative answer to that question, because none of the national chains has
chosen to settle in Vermont.[16] Indeed, it is difficult to find examples even
of local chains in Vermont.[17]

To assess the effects of institutional sponsorship on child care quality
in Vermont, I have examined state inspection reports for all group day

TABLE 4-4.    Number of Problems Detected by Inspectors in
Vermont, For-profits versus Nonprofits, 1989–1993[a]

| Year | For-profits | Nonprofits |
|------|-------------|------------|
| 1989 | 3.63 | 2.75 |
| 1990 | 4.77 | 4.78 |
| 1991 | 2.99 | 3.71 |
| 1992 | 5.06* | 3.09 |
| 1993 | 6.74 | 4.70 |

a. Entries refer to the number of problems (such as code violations) per group day care center detected by Vermont inspectors during license renewal visits.
*Significant at the .05 level.

care centers relicensed in 1991 in Vermont.[18] For that group of 167 centers, I conducted a content analysis of inspection reports for the period from 1989 through 1993. I coded the number of problems identified by inspectors during relicensing visits; I also coded the number of substantiated complaints against each facility. To determine the institutional status of the facility (for-profit versus nonprofit), I conferred with the inspector responsible for that facility. When the inspector wasn't sure, I contacted the Chief of the Children's Day Care Unit, the local resource and referral agency, or the facility itself to clarify institutional status.

As table 4-4 reveals, for-profit status is associated with more problems in three years and fewer problems in one year, but the positive relationship between for-profit status and problems identified by state inspectors is statistically significant at an acceptable level in only one of the years. The effects of for-profit status on quality appear somewhat stronger when one focuses on the number of substantiated complaints (see table 4-5). In all five years, there is a positive relationship between for-profit status and the number of substantiated complaints.[19] In two of the years, that relationship is statistically significant at an acceptable level.

What are we to make of all this? The negative relationship between for-profit status and child care quality persists, even when chains are eliminated from the picture. That relationship is stronger, however, for substantiated complaints than for problems detected in routine relicensing inspections. When for-profits sin, that is, they sin more grievously and more conspicuously than nonprofits. Problems noted by inspectors in their official reports may or may not be code violations.[20] In contrast, substantiated complaints are, by definition, code violations.

A content analysis of substantiated complaints reveals that a disproportionate share of for-profit code violations are money-related. Of 187

TABLE 4-5. Number of Substantiated Complaints in
Vermont, For-Profits versus Nonprofits, 1989–93[a]

| Year | For-profits | Nonprofits |
|------|-------------|------------|
| 1989 | .139 | .086 |
| 1990 | .241 | .118 |
| 1991 | .177 | .118 |
| 1992 | .380 | .075* |
| 1993 | .304 | .086* |

a. Entries refer to the number of complaints per group day care center substantiated by Vermont inspectors during on-site visits. Some centers received more than one substantiated complaint.
*Significant at the .01 level.

substantiated complaints lodged against for-profit centers, 35.8 percent included a confirmed ratio violation or a confirmed numbers violation. Of sixty-eight substantiated complaints filed against nonprofit centers, only 8.8 percent included a confirmed ratio violation or a confirmed numbers violation.[21] Centers can make more money by allowing ratios to fall below required levels or by allowing enrollments to climb above allowed levels. Evidently, for-profits are more likely than nonprofits to deviate from state regulations when large expenditures or revenues are at stake.

Even in Vermont, where chains do not dot the child care landscape, for-profit centers violate state rules more often, especially when substantial amounts of money are at stake. The quality gap between for-profits and nonprofits narrows, but does not vanish, in a state without chains.

## Explaining the Quality Gap

It is customary to explain the quality gap between for-profits and nonprofits by focusing on the profit motive, or the proverbial "bottom line." The owner of a for-profit facility (or group of facilities) expects a return on his or her investment. In contrast, the income earned by a nonprofit facility must be plowed back into program improvements, physical plant improvements, or higher staff salaries. Also, nonprofit executives may be more "public-spirited" than their for-profit counterparts.[22] The manifest result is higher quality at nonprofit facilities.

Yet this is not the only explanation for the quality gap. Nonprofits have greater access to government resources, including both direct expenditures and tax expenditures. For example, for-profit centers pay federal, state, and local taxes, while nonprofits are exempt from some or all of them. This places for-profits at an obvious disadvantage. In addition, for-profits are not always on an equal footing with nonprofits in competing for government funds. For example, for-profit centers are not automatically eligible to participate in the Child and Adult Care Food Program (CACFP). Under federal law, for-profit centers may participate only if 25 percent of their children are receiving funds under the Social Services Block Grant, formerly known as Title XX.[23] In contrast, nonprofit centers may participate even if they care for no disadvantaged children.

The quality gap between for-profit chains and other for-profits is more of a puzzle. In theory, chains should be better equipped to capture "economies of scale." For example, they are able to purchase insurance and equipment at a discount.[24] They are also able to pool resources for training programs, architectural design, and curriculum development. The result should be greater efficiency, with opportunities for higher quality, lower prices, or both.

Chains, however, have greater capital requirements than mom-and-pop providers, especially if they are expanding, which most of them are. Larger companies seem to believe that "growth is essential to survival."[25] This encourages them to use retained earnings from one region to expand in another. Like other large companies, chains are also more likely to be publicly held. This requires them to divert substantial portions of their earnings to dividends, even during nonexpansionary periods. Thus, KinderCare, as a publicly held corporation, must offer reasonably attractive rates of return on investment if it wishes to attract investors.[26]

Another factor at work could be the rough equivalent of the absentee landlord syndrome. Lacking community roots, chains may care less deeply and less personally about a particular community and its citizens. A local entrepreneur may see a day care center not only as a money-making venture but also as a community service. Local day care center owners, like local newspaper owners, may be more willing to boost their community and its prospects, even at the expense of the bottom line.

Evidence on the relative profitability of for-profit chains and for-profit independents is mixed. In 1990, a national study found that 60 percent of for-profit chains said they made a profit the previous year, as opposed to 48 percent of for-profit independents.[27] A more recent study of day care centers in four states found no statistically significant differences in actual profits between for-profit chains and for-profit independents.[28]

Perhaps chains are somewhat more likely to make some money but somewhat less likely to make substantial amounts of money per child.

TABLE 4-6.  Financial Data of For-Profit Chains
Percent

| Institution | Return on equity[a] | Return on assets | Return on sales |
|---|---|---|---|
| KinderCare | 9.7 | 3.8 | 3.6 |
| La Petite Academy | Loss | −1.3 | −0.1 |
| Children's Discovery Centers | 8.1 | 4.7 | 2.9 |

SOURCES: KinderCare Learning Centers, Inc. (Montgomery, Ala.), Form 10-K, for fiscal year ended June 3, 1994, submitted to U.S. Securities and Exchange Commission, p. 23; La Petite Holdings Corp. (Overland Park, Kan.), Condensed Form 10-K filed with U.S. Securities and Exchange Commission for the year ended August 27, 1994, p. 7; Children's Discovery Centers (San Rafael, Calif.), Form 10-K, for fiscal year ended December 31, 1993, submitted to U.S. Securities and Exchange Commission, pp. F2, F3.

a. A return on equity is not considered meaningful when either the net income or the shareholders' equity is negative. Consequently, I have not computed this figure for La Petite Academy.

Whatever the precise explanation, for-profit chains do not appear to be unduly profitable. Consider, for example, the fortunes of three of the largest child care chains in the United States: KinderCare (with centers in thirty-eight states in 1994), La Petite Academy (with centers in thirty-four states and the District of Columbia in 1994), and Children's Discovery Centers (with centers in eighteen states and the District of Columbia in 1994). As table 4-6 suggests, the return on equity, return on assets, and return on sales for all three firms were generally unimpressive during the latest year available (fiscal year 1994 or calendar year 1993).[29]

It may be that 1993 and 1994 were bleaker than average years for child care firms, but this does not appear to have been the case. Kinder-Care, recovering from bankruptcy, had lost money for several years in a row.[30] Children's Discovery Centers lost money during the two preceding years. And La Petite Academy, which did earn a 3.7 percent profit in 1992, was even then performing below average for businesses as a whole. Whatever their other virtues and vices, it would appear that for-profit chains are not reaping unusually high profits at the expense of consumers.

## Solutions

How might for-profit centers improve? One step would be to make them automatically eligible for the Child and Adult Care Food Program (CACFP), as nonprofits already are. Among centers currently participating in the program, the average value of participation is approximately $17,000.[31] The actual value of participation to a for-profit center could be considerably less, because reimbursement rates are pegged to the income levels of enrolled families, and for-profits are less likely to care for disadvantaged children.[32] Still, this step might help to narrow the performance gap between for-profits and other centers.

A similar strategy would be to change various state laws, administrative rules, and informal practices to ensure that for-profits and nonprofits compete on an equal footing for various state grants. In some states, child care improvement grants are earmarked for nonprofit organizations. In Oklahoma, for example, for-profit centers are ineligible for certain Child Care and Development Block Grant program grants. As of 1990, for-profit centers received only 3 to 6 percent of their revenues from government sources.[33] If for-profits became eligible for additional government grants, the percentage could increase somewhat.[34]

Both of these strategies would benefit the for-profit sector. Neither strategy, however, would necessarily benefit children enrolled in for-profit centers, because there is no guarantee that increased revenues would be used to enhance program quality. As it stands, additional program revenues generated by the CACFP or other government subsidies could be used to boost profits, rather than to hire more or better staff. Thus the principal beneficiaries would be owners and investors, not parents or children.

Another problem with these strategies is that they may not improve the quality of for-profit chains in comparison to other for-profit centers. As we have seen, the chains warrant special concern and attention. Stronger self-regulation might be a partial solution. It has worked to some degree in occupational licensing and occupational safety in the United States.[35] It has also worked in the child care industry in Germany, where self-regulation by the churches and other associations augments state regulation.[36] German churches, however, are financially secure, thanks to a well-established system of church taxes collected by the government. And they are philosophically committed to human service, as opposed to profit-making. Also, even Germany uses self-regulation as an auxiliary regulatory system.

A more promising variation on this theme, still largely at the proposal stage, is "enforced self-regulation." Ayres and Braithwaite explain how this might work.[37] Instead of or in addition to industry-wide standards, the government enters into contractual arrangements with particular firms. The contract specifies certain standards, drafted by the firm and ratified by the government. The firm establishes a compliance group and a compliance director. If management fails to comply with group directives, the director must report this to the government; failure to do so subjects the director to criminal penalties.

In child care, such an arrangement could result in regulatory standards for a chain both higher and lower than those applicable to other child care firms in the same state. For example, the chain might secure permission for higher child/staff ratios in return for tougher training requirements, tougher safety standards, and on-site health services. If the chain failed to keep its promises, the contract could be terminated immediately and the usual rules would apply.

Enforced self-regulation would give chains powerful reasons to comply with regulations that they themselves developed. Creative experiments could result, and chains might compete with other firms by enhancing quality in some program areas, while cutting costs (and perhaps lowering quality) in others. On the other hand, enforced self-regulation would involve considerable paperwork for all concerned and would be difficult to justify except for relatively large chains operating in relatively populous states.

Regulators might also target chains for special programs and initiatives. For example, the Massachusetts Office for Children, which licenses child care facilities throughout the state, has occasionally held special training sessions for center directors from particular child care chains. From the state's point of view, this enables regulators to get their message across clearly, quickly, and emphatically; from the chain's point of view, it enables them to combine regularly scheduled meetings with state training sessions. It also ensures that center directors hear and comprehend the same message.

I would characterize this as a catalytic control strategy because it relies upon outside catalysts (in this case, state officials) to offer advice aimed at self-improvement. A tougher, more hortatory control strategy would be to use negative publicity—or the threat of negative publicity—to embarrass a chain into upgrading its quality. More than other for-profit firms, chains seem to be extremely sensitive to negative coverage by the mass media. Consider, for example, the $3 discount that used to accompany any Domino's pizza not delivered within 30 minutes. Following numerous accidents, lawsuits, and unfavorable publicity, Domino's abandoned the policy late in 1993. How would KinderCare or La Petite Academy react if its code violations were publicized with equal vigor by the mass media? A chain's good name is ultimately as valuable as its physical plant. If state regulators were more aggressive in disclosing problems with particular chains, and if the mass media were more aggressive in reporting such problems, the chains would have powerful incentives to improve their performance.

A more draconian solution would be to try to squeeze chains out of existence or to prevent their growth. This could be done by ratcheting up regulatory standards, especially child/staff ratio standards, which chains regard with special fear and loathing. Or it might be done through more aggressive enforcement of the Robinson-Patman Act, which prohibits buyer discounts that substantially lessen competition.

Hardball solutions may be tempting, given the poor quality at many for-profit chains. Such strategies, however, fail to pass the Aunt Polly test. Aunt Polly spent a considerable portion of every day upbraiding Tom Sawyer for his mischievous behavior. But upon learning—erroneously—of Tom's death, Polly wept bitter tears, as did the rest of Tom's critics. If KinderCare and La Petite Academy were suddenly to vanish from the child care scene, they would leave a conspicuous hole that the nonprofit sector might or might not rush to fill.[38] People would probably grieve over their passing and call upon government officials to approve more child care subsidies to help cope with this disaster. With child care chains, as with Tom Sawyer, improving their character may be more sensible.

## Unregulated Family Day Care Homes

The United States is not unique in relying heavily on family day care homes. In other countries, family day care homes also play an important role, especially in caring for infants and toddlers. For the most part, however, family day care homes in other countries are regulated. In contrast, between 82 and 90 percent of family day care homes in the United States are unregulated.[39]

Unregulated family day care homes fall into two categories: family day care providers who are exempt from state regulations because they care for a relatively small number of children; and family day care providers who are operating illegally. According to a recent Families and Work Institute study of three metropolitan areas, 81 percent of the unregulated family day care providers in their sample were operating illegally.[40] If this is true nationwide, it suggests that approximately two-thirds of all family day care providers may have illegally exempted themselves from regulatory review.

## Findings

Several studies show that regulated family day care providers offer superior care. For example, a study conducted in British Columbia during the 1980s found that unlicensed family day care providers had less formal training than licensed providers and were considerably less committed to child care as a profession.[41] The same study found that licensed family day care homes scored higher on space and furnishings, basic care, language development, learning, and social development. In addition, children in the licensed homes were more likely to engage in group and pair play. This study is particularly revealing because children in licensed and unlicensed care came from similar demographic backgrounds, which is not always the case.[42]

A larger, more recent study of family day care homes in the Dallas-Fort Worth, Charlotte, and San Fernando-Los Angeles areas reached similar conclusions. Regulated providers were more sensitive and more responsive than their unregulated counterparts.[43] They were also more likely to plan things for children, more likely to have participated in training exercises, and more likely to view family day care as their chosen occupation. Overall, being regulated was a very good predictor of child care quality.

Regulated and unregulated family day care providers may differ at the outset to some degree, in which case performance differences would be partly a function of self-selection. For example, researchers found that regulated family day care providers were better educated than unregulated providers.[44] If education is a purely exogenous variable, in this context, then regulation's primary contribution could be to screen providers rather than to modify their behavior.

Nevertheless, there is reason to believe that regulation does have a positive impact on family day care providers and the children they serve. Regulation enables the state to reduce health and safety risks to children and encourages receptive providers to take positive steps to nurture children. In forty-one states, regulation involves inspections of some, or even all, regulated facilities on a regular basis.[45] This brings providers into contact with experts who can help them with particular problems. In sixteen states, regulations require pre-service training; in twenty-eight states, they require in-service training.[46] And training helps providers to cope with a wide variety of challenges. This is especially important in family day care, where, typically, only one adult is present for most of the day.

Regulation also may encourage providers to think of themselves as professionals, not babysitters. Professionalism sometimes boils down to common sense in multisyllabic form. But a healthy dose of common sense is desperately needed in child care, where emergencies often require quick responses that have been proven effective in comparable situations. Norms of good practice often seem more obvious in restrospect than they do when problems arise. Regulatory handbooks, orientation sessions, and conversations with inspectors help providers to inoculate themselves against horrible tragedies. Increasingly, they also help providers to inject planning, purpose, and perspective into their daily activities.

On balance, the evidence suggests not only that regulation matters but also that it matters more than the number of children in care. As noted in previous chapters, several studies have concluded that lower child/staff ratios are associated with child care quality. Yet regulated family day care providers care for more children, on the whole, than unregulated family day care providers.[47] Thus their ratios are higher. Despite that fact, regulated family day care providers perform better, and their children fare better on a wide range of indicators.

This has important implications, not only because of the prevalence of unregulated family day care but also because reliance upon unregulated care varies across social strata. Specifically, lower-income families are much less likely than upper-income families to use regulated family day care as opposed to unregulated family day care.[48] Lower-income families are also less likely than middle-income families to use regulated family day care, though the difference is less dramatic.[49] Thus the persistence of unregulated family day care homes may undermine social justice by reinforcing differences attributable to circumstances of birth.

## Life Underground

Despite the benefits of regulation to children, the overwhelming majority of family day care providers have chosen to remain unregulated. Are they rebellious scofflaws who resent and despise government regulators? Naive provincials who do not understand the connection between regulation and quality? Caring persons who believe that flexible, informal arrangements are best for all concerned? Struggling small businesspersons whose earnings are so meager that they cannot afford to run the regulatory gauntlet?

Evidence suggests that they are all of the above. Although most unregulated family day care providers are aware that state governments regulate family day care homes, a substantial percentage mistakenly believe that they are exempt from these requirements.[50] Most states exempt some family day care homes from regulatory requirements. The precise cutoff points change over time, and state and local governments do not always utilize the same cutoffs. In Arlington County, Virginia, for example, family day care providers who care for fewer than eight children are exempt from state licensing requirements, those who care for fewer than four children are exempt from local licensing requirements, but no family day care providers are exempt from local certificate of occupancy requirements. There is considerable confusion as to who is regulated and by whom.

Unregulated family day care providers are also less likely than regulated providers to view child care as their chosen occupation.[51] Their commitment to child care as a profession is tenuous at best. If they expected to stay in business for long, perhaps licensing (or its equivalents) would be worth the effort. But why get licensed when they intend to be doing something else in two or three years? They can make more money as waitresses, sales clerks, or airline reservationists. Licensing implies a long-term commitment that they do not feel or share.

Licensing is not only a hassle, it is costly. The nominal cost, as measured by the state's licensing fee, is the tip of the iceberg.[52] State regulations require, in many instances, that providers purchase fire extinguishers and smoke detectors, erect a fence around their backyard, and fix faulty equipment used by children. Local regulations may trigger a variety of other expenses, such as electrical repairs, plumbing repairs, window repairs, stair repairs, and furnace repairs.

The sheer volume of inspections required may be daunting in itself, regardless of what the inspectors detect and require. In De Kalb County, Georgia, family day care providers must pass at least three separate local inspections before securing a license. To many providers, this is regulatory overkill, and they want no part of it. Separate inspections also invite the possibility of contradictory instructions from inspectors who are upholding different laws. This infuriates providers, and horror stories spread quickly, reducing the urge to cooperate.[53]

Perhaps the most fundamental reason why unregulated providers eschew regulation is that the personal benefits are too subtle. Although the literature attests to the benefits of regulation for children, providers are likely to ask what is in it for them if they choose to get regulated. The answers are real enough—self-esteem, security, visibility. Also, regulated providers are eligible for certain government programs, such as the Child and Adult Care Food Program. Yet these benefits, though far from trivial, seem distant or abstract when compared to the immediate effects of regulation on their pocketbooks. To many providers, regulation just doesn't seem to be worth it.

## Solutions

A partial solution to some of the problems described above would be to extend the scope of regulatory coverage, so that all or most family day care providers were covered. As of late 1993, some family day care homes were exempt from state regulation in thirty-nine states.[54] If the definition of what constitutes a family day care home requiring state regulation were broadened, the availability of regulated facilities would improve. Some providers might go out of business, and others might remain underground, but the number of regulated family day care homes would undoubtedly increase.[55] Also, if everyone were covered under the law, confusion about exemptions would diminish or vanish.

It is not obvious how far policies should extend. Is Wisconsin wrong to exempt providers who care for fewer than four children from state licensing requirements? Is California wrong to exempt providers who care for children from only one family? Is Minnesota wrong to exempt providers who care for only one child? These exemptions are rooted in both philosophical and practical judgments about the desirability of regulation and the state's ability to regulate large numbers of family day care providers in a meaningful way. Regulation can become a sham if everyone is regulated in theory but the state is unable or unwilling to monitor the quality of the regulated parties. Thus if more providers are to be regulated, the challenge is to ensure that regulation, already weak in many states, is not further diluted as regulatory coverage is extended to more providers.

As noted earlier, many family day care providers are illegally unregulated. To cope with this problem, state governments might move more vigorously to detect, expose, and punish illegal operators. At the moment, most states intervene when they receive a complaint about illegally operated child care but do not otherwise attempt to ferret out illegals. A more aggressive effort to identify such facilities might bear fruit; automatic fines could increase the costs of evasion. On the other hand, such an approach converts state inspectors into enforcers rather than helpers at a time when many states are trying to move in the opposite direction. The question arises: Can substantial increases in the number of regulated family day care homes be achieved through positive rather than negative incentives?

In fact, the government might entice family day care providers by offering tangible benefits in return for regulation. As Nelson has pointed out, family day care providers might like to have access to a pool of substitute providers, who would pinch hit for them when they were sick, when they needed to be out of town, or simply when they needed a break.[56] A van service (for field trips), a toy lending library, and an advice line might also be available. Such services could be provided by a family day care system or network funded in part by the government. If such a system existed, and were available to all regulated family day care providers, regulation might look much more appealing.

Such an initiative would cost money, but it could be funded in whole or in part by the federal Child Care and Development Block Grant, which reserves 6.25 percent of total funds for quality initiatives. Support might also be obtained from private foundations that have already demonstrated a willingness to assist and improve family day care homes.[57] Beyond the benefits accruing to individual providers and their children, a robust family day care network could help to develop a stronger sense of community among family day care providers, many of whom are disconnected from other providers (indeed, other adults) for most of the day. It could also signal to them that they are providing a community service for which the community is properly grateful.

At the moment, that is not the signal many family day care providers receive. On the contrary, many sense that they are unwelcome in their community. Restrictive covenants in certain neighborhoods flatly prohibit family day care homes. In other communities, zoning requirements make it difficult for family day care providers to operate.[58] Unlike other regulatory hurdles, these requirements are not even remotely related to the health and safety of children. They are designed not to protect children but to protect grouchy neighbors from children.

## Industrywide Problems

It would be a mistake to conclude that the quality of care provided by certain child care facilities is the only serious problem that afflicts the child care industry. It would also be a mistake to conclude that for-profit centers and unregulated family day care homes are the only problematic sectors of the industry. Many nonprofit centers and regulated family day care homes fail to meet quality standards established by state regulatory agencies, much less those recommended by such groups as the National Association for the Education of Young Children (NAEYC). And even if quality were to improve suddenly and dramatically, availability and affordability problems would remain. Indeed, they might well worsen as a result of quality improvements.

The problems faced by the child care industry as a whole are sobering: low wages, high turnover, poorly trained providers, insufficient staff members, inadequate supervision of children, limited programs, limited equipment for children to develop gross motor skills and small motor skills, safety hazards, poor hygiene, and poor record-keeping. Of course, there are exemplary programs, terrible programs, and many in between. Is a systematic strategy available for addressing these problems all at once? Can these deficiencies be remedied without massive government intervention? Can the industry heal itself, with a little help from its friends? Are there lessons to be learned from other fields?

## A TQM Approach to Child Care

One approach that has captured the imagination of industry leaders from Motorola to Federal Express is total quality management (TQM). Originally developed by the late management guru W. Edwards Deming, TQM was initially applied, with great success, to large manufacturing industries in Japan.[59] It has recently been rediscovered in the United States and has led to the revitalization of several major companies. It has also been integrated into Vice President Al Gore's reinventing government initiatives.

Total quality management is a multifaceted management strategy that stresses teamwork, customer satisfaction, and collaborative problem-solving. It rejects hierarchy, elaborate worker controls, and a preoccupation with short-term profits. Does TQM have anything to offer to the child care industry? Its most conspicuous triumphs have been in industries radically different from child care—heavy manufacturing industries, not human services industries. Nevertheless, some elements of the TQM approach would appear to be directly applicable to child care.

One of the hallmarks of TQM is a customer focus. According to Deming, companies need to keep their customers in mind at all times. They should listen to customers' complaints and respond imaginatively. They should look at proposed product designs from the customer's perspective. They should ask not whether a particular strategy will make money but whether it will increase customer satisfaction; the presumption is that if customers are satisfied, profits will take care of themselves.[60]

If the child care industry were to take customers seriously, efforts to involve and empower parents would be far stronger than they are today. Parents would help to design programs and policies. They would participate in the selection of staff. They would serve as volunteers. They would donate money and muscle to special projects. They would work with providers to secure funding from public and private sources.

Within the child care industry, one can find examples of significant parental involvement. In Harrisburg, Pennsylvania, for example, several state-sponsored day care centers are governed primarily by parents. At each center, a contract is issued to a private firm for a fixed time period. When the contract expires, competitive bids are invited, and parents collectively choose the winning bidder. In practice, parents have not hesitated to press the eject button.[61]

Child care in the military has developed another technique for involving parents. Within all four services, and on every military base, center inspection teams must include at least one parent. The parent not only participates in the inspection process but also is in a position to inform other parents of the center's strengths and weaknesses. In principle, this empowers at least one parent per center to serve as an informer, an educator, and a surrogate for other parents. In addition, the military requires a parent advisory board for every center and requires that parents be interviewed during major command and installation commander inspections.

Does parental involvement make a difference? Earlier in this chapter, we saw that parental involvement had no discernible impact on teacher education, staff size, or teacher turnover at group day care centers. This suggests that there are limits to parental involvement. But it is important to stress that two of these three quality indicators (low child/staff ratios and low turnover) can be achieved only through substantial spending.

TABLE 4-7.  Determinants of Physical Exam Provision:
Logistic Regression Results

| Variable | Regression coefficient[a] |
|---|---|
| For-profit sponsorship | −.857* |
| | (.372) |
| Church sponsorship | −1.603* |
| | (.756) |
| Public school sponsorship | 1.447*** |
| | (.339) |
| High school diploma and coursework or | .183 |
| experience required | (.328) |
| Percent of children, parents on AFDC | .020**** |
| | (.004) |
| Number of inspections | .067 |
| | (.031) |
| State subsidies | −.001 |
| | (.005) |
| Parental involvement | −.880** |
| | (.300) |
| Model chi square = 109.33**** | |
| N = 1,060 | |

a. Standard errors are in parentheses.
*Significant at the .05 level.
**Significant at the .01 level.
***Significant at the .001 level.
****Significant at the .0001 level.

And all three of them are customarily thought of as personnel matters usually handled by center directors.

Under what circumstances might parents have an impact on child care quality? Several hypotheses can be stated. First, parents should be able to influence center practices when recommended reforms are relatively cheap. Second, parents should be able to influence center practices when services to children are clearly at stake. Third, parents should be able to influence center practices when there is a relatively high consensus as to what is appropriate.

Tables 4-7 through 4-9 show the effects of parental involvement on three variables that would appear to meet all three criteria.[62] These dependent variables indicate whether physical, dental, or cognitive exams for children are available through the center. Because the dependent variables are dichotomous, I have used logistic regression analysis as the estimating technique.[63]

TABLE 4-8.  Determinants of Dental Exam Provision:
Logistic Regression Results

| Variable | Regression coefficient[a] |
|---|---|
| For–profit sponsorship | –.977* |
| | (.330) |
| Church sponsorship | –.798 |
| | (.463) |
| Public school sponsorship | 1.744*** |
| | (.335) |
| High school diploma and coursework or experience required | –.248 |
| | (.283) |
| Percent of children, parents on AFDC | .015** |
| | (.004) |
| Number of inspections | .048 |
| | (.029) |
| State subsidies | –.000 |
| | (.004) |
| Parental involvement | .873* |
| | (.267) |
| Model chi square = 121.735*** | |
| N = 1,060 | |

a. Standard errors are in parentheses.
*Significant at the .01 level.
**Significant at the .001 level.
***Significant at the .0001 level.

In each instance, parental involvement has a statistically significant, positive impact on the availability of an exam. In contrast, the number of inspections and the size of state subsidies are once again irrelevant, as they were in tables 4-1 through 4-3. For-profit centers are less likely to provide the various tests, while public schools are more likely to provide them. Church-sponsored centers are less likely to provide physical exams.

Basic education and training requirements do not affect the provision of physical or dental exams but do affect (positively) the provision of cognitive tests. Perhaps this suggests something about the nature of coursework and training modules in the child care field.[64] On balance, cognitive development may receive greater emphasis than health or hygiene. Under such circumstances, education and training may be more effective in promoting sensitivity to general learning than to preventive medicine.

The findings reported here are consistent with the arguments made earlier. Administering physical, dental, and cognitive tests at group day care centers is not particularly costly.[65] It is certainly less costly than

TABLE 4-9. Determinants of Cognitive Testing Provision:
Logistic Regression Results

| Variable | Regression coefficient[a] |
|---|---|
| For-profit sponsorship | -.292 |
| | (.153) |
| Church sponsorship | -.128 |
| | (.203) |
| Public school sponsorship | 1.403*** |
| | (.321) |
| High school diploma and coursework or experience required | .609** |
| | (.153) |
| Percent of children, parents on AFDC | .008* |
| | (.003) |
| Number of inspections | .001 |
| | (.019) |
| State subsidies | .001 |
| | (.002) |
| Parental involvement | .366* |
| | (.167) |
| Model chi square = 87.532** | |
| N = 1,060 | |

a. Standard errors are in parentheses.
*Significant at the .05 level.
**Significant at the .001 level.
***Significant at the .0001 level.

hiring additional personnel. Moreover, testing provides tangible benefits
to children and does not necessarily intrude upon managerial preroga-
tives, as personnel decisions might. And parents certainly have a common
interest in healthy children and in early detection of potential cognitive
problems.

If this reasoning is correct, one should expect parental involvement to
make a difference in other areas as well. Parents might be expected to
mobilize in support of better playgrounds, better toys, and more books—
all services to children and all relatively cheap. Parents might also be
expected to mobilize in support of longer operating hours, for their own
convenience.

In contrast, parents may be reluctant to champion smaller group
sizes—a technical issue and a managerial issue as well. Parents may also
rely upon the center director to decide how much training is necessary or
desirable. Parents may also be inactive or ineffectual on policies concerning sick children, because they—and their children—will have different

interests in this regard. A contagious child is a potential threat to other children, but a child who must be sent home is a potential burden to the parent(s).

These propositions should not be construed as an argument to impose permanent boundaries on what parental involvement can accomplish. It is possible to convince parents to carve out a broader role for themselves. As parents become more aware of the factors that contribute to quality, they may be willing to focus more on personnel issues, despite the perception that these are largely managerial concerns. In the short run, however, parents will probably feel more comfortable working on other kinds of issues.

If significant outreach to parents exemplifies a customer focus, as recommended by Deming, it also exemplifies a fairly traditional notion of who the customer is in child care arrangements. A more radical application of Deming's ideas would be for child care providers and center directors to think of children as their customers and to act accordingly. In such a world, providers might place greater emphasis on stimulating and enriching activities, less emphasis on handsome offices and colorful displays. Providers might place greater emphasis on quality, less emphasis on affordability, despite parental concerns. Providers might place greater emphasis on play, less emphasis on education, also despite parental concerns. Some, if not all, of these choices are controversial. But if children are the real customers, should not providers think primarily about their well-being and not about parental expectations?

## Worker Education and Training

Another cornerstone of TQM is a conscious effort to reduce the need for inspections by building quality into the production process. Deming put it succinctly: "Inspection with the aim of finding the bad ones and throwing them out is too late, ineffective, costly."[66] Deming's solution is to get things right the first time. Just as preventive medicine is more cost effective than surgery, building quality into a production process is more cost effective than ensuring quality through frequent monitoring. Error prevention, not error correction, is the key.

Is it possible to achieve a quantum leap in child care quality sufficient to reduce the need for frequent inspections? The most promising approach would seem to be provider training and education. By sensitizing and educating providers up front, when they begin their trade, we could reduce the need for government regulators to scrutinize them. By ensuring that they sharpen their skills regularly through refresher courses, we could further reduce the need for inspections. In addition, the resulting sense of professionalism could improve the field's reputation, making it easier to recruit and retain competent, dedicated personnel.

Several states have launched new initiatives aimed at improving child care quality through major upgrades in staff training and education. One of the most ambitious of these initiatives is North Carolina's TEACH (Teacher Education and Compensation Helps) program, which began officially in February 1993 after some demonstration projects proved successful and after a gubernatorial campaign in which child care was a central issue.[67] Based on ideas developed by the Day Care Services Association of Orange County, TEACH is a multifaceted program that offers financial incentives to child care providers to take courses at local community colleges.

The cornerstone of the TEACH program is a two-course college curriculum known as the North Carolina Child Care Credential (see table 4-8). The courses, offered by fifty-three of the state's fifty-eight community colleges, follow a common outline developed by child care professionals in collaboration with the state's Division of Child Development and the Department of Community Colleges.[68] Persons who work at least twenty hours per week as child care providers, either at centers or in licensed family day care homes, are eligible to participate in the Credential program (provided that they promise to work at least one year as a provider after completing the program).

The big inducement is that the state pays 80 percent of the tuition costs and 80 percent of the book costs for Credential program participants.[69] For center staff members, the center contributes an additional 10 percent of tuition and book costs, while the staff member contributes the remaining 10 percent. Family day care providers are responsible for 20 percent of the total costs. Upon completion of the two-course sequence, participants receive a $100 bonus from the state.

A similar, but more complicated arrangement has been made for providers who wish to work toward a diploma, a certificate, or an associate's degree in early childhood education. Center-based teachers have two options (see table 4-10), one of which is for the state to pay 80 percent of the tuition costs and 90 percent of the book costs. Under this option, centers pay 10 percent of tuition costs and provide three to six hours of release time per week.[70] The release time may be used to prepare for classes or however the provider sees fit. Family day care providers are more constrained—the state will pay 50 percent of their tuition and book costs, but the provider is expected to make up the difference.[71]

To qualify for an associate's degree scholarship, a student must be working at least 30 hours per week as a provider (and must promise to work at least one additional year as a provider after finishing the program). Upon completing the associate's degree, center-based teachers receive a 4 to 5 percent raise or a $550 to $700 bonus, depending on which option they selected. Family day care providers automatically receive a $300 bonus.

The TEACH program has generated considerable interest in early childhood education in North Carolina. Since February 1993, 1,786 providers have enrolled in the Child Care Credential program and 523 providers have enrolled in the associate's degree program. In addition, ninety-four directors have enrolled in a comparable program for directors, and forty-three teachers have agreed to serve as mentors to less experienced teachers. An early childhood bachelor's degree scholarship program began in the fall of 1994.[72]

The TEACH program has several attractive features. It significantly reduces the costs of training and education for child care providers. Each Credential course costs center-based providers only $13.50 in tuition and books; family day care providers pay $27.50 per Credential course. The costs of obtaining an associate's degree are also quite low, especially for center-based providers. For example, at the Asheville-Buncombe Technical Community College, the tuition for the two-year associate's degree is $1,300, while books cost between $1,000 and $1,200. Thanks to the TEACH program, a center-based student pays only $130 for tuition, $100 to $120 for books. The cash bonus more than covers these costs.

A high degree of quality control has been built into the Credential curriculum. The two Credential courses have been designed with considerable care and are to be taught consistently at community colleges throughout the state. To ensure this, no one may teach the Credential course without first completing an eight-hour state-sponsored course. A shared instructor's manual further guarantees that course content will be consistent from one instructor to another.

The two Credential courses automatically count towards an associate's degree in early childhood education at every community college that offers one in North Carolina. Although associate's degree courses do not automatically count towards a bachelor's degree in early childhood edu-

TABLE 4-10. TEACH Program in North Carolina

| Program of study | Credits received | Scholarship support | Required commitment | Compensation awarded |
|---|---|---|---|---|
| Credential courses | 6 credit hours at community college | 80% Tuition<br>80% Books<br>Travel stipend | Additional year in child care | $100 bonus |
| Group day care, associates degree | 12 to 20 credit hours per year at community college | 80% Tuition<br>90% Books<br>Travel stipend<br>Release time<br>OR<br>50% Tuition<br>50% Books<br>Travel stipend<br>Release time | Additional year in center | 4 to 5 percent raise<br>OR<br>$550–$700 bonus |
| Family day care, associates degree | 12 to 20 credit hours per year at community college | 50% Tuition<br>50% Books<br>Travel stipend<br>Reimbursed release time | Additional year as provider | $300 bonus |
| Center director, associates degree | At least 18 credit hours per year at community college | 80% Tuition<br>80% Books<br>Travel stipend | Additional year in center | $300–$600 bonus |
| Model/mentor program | 3-credit-hour course in mentoring | 95% Tuition<br>90% Books<br>3 Hours release time | Additional year in center/home | 3 percent raise |

SOURCE: Day Care Services Association of Orange County, June 1994.

cation, several four-year colleges and universities have developed "articulation agreements" with local community colleges to do precisely that.

Finally, the Credential courses are almost always offered on weekday evenings or weekends so that all providers, in principle, can attend them. At many community colleges throughout the state, courses leading towards the associate's degree are offered at convenient times as well. To address the needs of center-based providers who cannot easily commute from work or home to a community college site, some community college instructors have agreed to offer Credential courses on the premises of a center, provided that a critical mass of a dozen or so students will enroll. For example, Katherine Wilder of the Nash Community College has taught Credential courses at a Nash County Head Start program and at the First Methodist Preschool in Rocky Mount. These extraordinary efforts have helped the TEACH program to reach providers who would otherwise be unable to participate.

The TEACH program is not the only worthwhile education and training program adopted by a state government to improve child care quality, but it illustrates the potential for improving quality without imposing additional regulatory requirements.[73] It also exemplifies a successful partnership between the public and private sectors. And it demonstrates that when child care catches fire as a political issue, creative public policies can result.

## Conclusion

The child care industry is afflicted by many serious problems. Some of them are structural in nature. The absence of economies of scale, for instance, makes it difficult for chains to compete with other centers, except by sacrificing quality to secure a modest price advantage. The ease with which family day care homes can go underground makes it difficult to police the family day care sector and exposes regulated family day care providers to large numbers of hidden competitors. The fact that most provider earnings come directly out of parents' pocketbooks, as opposed to government coffers, dampens wages and thereby reduces the appeal of child care as a vocation. This is not the only cause of low wages, but it is a factor: Parents lack the government's deep pockets, and providers are reluctant to raise fees at the expense of parents whose financial stress is palpable.

Other industry problems relate to culture rather than to economics. Many family day care providers eschew government regulation not because they object to a particular regulation but because they reject the premise that the government has a right to tell them what to do inside their own home. As a Nevada family day care provider put it, "No one's going to go through my closets!"[74] Many family day care providers feel guilty about charging higher rates because they think of themselves as babysitters and because they do not view themselves as businesspersons. Many parents choose child care chains for the same reasons that they choose McDonald's, Days Inn, and K-Mart—familiarity, convenience, and low prices. Other parents choose unregulated family day care homes for similar reasons. These decisions reflect a limited awareness of how quality varies across sectors, a tendency to weigh affordability more heavily than quality, and a different conception of quality than that held by child care experts.

Neither our formal infrastructure nor our informal infrastructure is strong enough for us to rely exclusively on self-regulation and competition to guarantee industry performance. Professionalism is too weak for self-regulation to work as it does in medicine or law or teaching. Information is too limited for competition to work as it does in grocery shopping or the purchase of durable goods. This is not to say that self-regulation and competition have no role to play. Chapter 6, for example, describes how competition has enhanced the availability of school-age child care programs. But self-regulation and competition are not sufficient in an industry as fragile and as disconnected as the child care industry. The market failures are too pronounced.

What, then, might work? Although I have stressed industry problems in this chapter, I have also tried to suggest that solutions are within our grasp. For example, differences between for-profit and nonprofit centers tend to support the proposition that subsidies work as intended. Nonprofits receive more direct and indirect government subsidies (grants and tax expenditures) than their for-profit counterparts; their quality is higher as a result.[75]

Similarly, differences between regulated and unregulated family day care homes tend to support the proposition that regulation works as intended. Regulated family day care homes are superior to unregulated family day care homes in many ways, thanks in part to the greater scrutiny that regulation provides. We have also seen that tougher child/ staff ratio requirements result in lower ratios (more staff members, controlling for the number of children) and that tougher education and training requirements result in the hiring of better-educated providers, who place a stronger emphasis on cognitive tests.

It is tempting to conclude from this that what we need is more government spending and more government regulation. But the findings reported in this chapter suggest that such a conclusion must be qualified and refined. For example, the number of center inspections has no discernible effect on several quality indicators. Also the level of state subsidies has no noticeable effect on these same indicators.

Some of these findings can be attributed to methodological limitations. The number of inspections, for example, refers to the number of inspections recalled by center directors. No distinction is made between state and local inspections, and center directors may not recall the number of inspections with precision. The level of state subsidies is a more valid measure, but state subsidies constitute a relatively small fraction of total government subsidies. Moreover, state child care subsidies have typically sought to make child care more affordable to poor parents rather than to improve child care quality.

Still, it would appear that a closer look at traditional tools of government and their effects on child care quality is merited. It is also important to broaden the inquiry to examine the effects of government intervention on availability as well. And it is important to look beyond traditional tools to other techniques, such as deregulation and privatization. The problems facing the child care industry are too numerous, too important, and, in some instances, too subtle to be solved using traditional approaches alone.

# 5 | Dos, Don'ts, and Dollars

WHEN INDUSTRY FAILURES become acute, there is a tendency to ask government for remedies, such as regulation and subsidies. These are two of many instruments in the government's collective tool kit, instruments that really are multidimensional.[1] Regulation, for example, might refer to more stringent standards, more vigorous enforcement of existing standards, or the extension of existing standards to previously uncovered populations. Subsidies might mean block grants, categorical grants, tax expenditures, or vouchers. Moreover, each of these concepts has its flip side. Dissatisfaction with regulation has led to deregulation and other regulatory reforms; dissatisfaction with subsidies has led to user fees. Dissatisfaction with government itself has led to privatization. So the government's tool kit has become much bulkier and more robust.

When government intervention becomes necessary, it is not always easy to choose the right tool or combination of tools. Yet that is absolutely essential, because the government's tools are no more interchangeable than, say, a hammer and a wrench. As Hood puts it, "Government's tools are not like the magic rings, lamps, or charms we read about in fairy tales. Indeed, there are many circumstances in which 'overload' or misuse can prevent those instruments from operating as government might wish."[2]

In this chapter, I subject government to the same scrutiny that the child care industry received in chapter 4. It is not possible to dissect all of the government initiatives undertaken at the federal, state, and local levels. Therefore, I focus primarily on a more manageable set of tools: regulation (at the state level), regulatory reform (at the state level), categorical grants (at the federal level), and block grants (at the federal level). Because the Child Care and Development Block Grant includes a significant voucher component, I examine that as well.

## Regulation

State regulation is the cornerstone of governmental child care policies in the United States. It allows state governments to intervene to correct such market failures as externalities and information asymmetries. It allows state governments to set rudimentary standards of justice, as they seek to protect innocent children from threats to their health and safety. It reduces the information burdens of parents who must choose from a wide variety of providers, some good and some bad. It also enables, but does not require, state governments to minimize costs to taxpayers, which may or may not promote efficiency. If rules are well-crafted, overall costs can be reduced; if not, rules may carry a high price tag.

Although regulation has considerable potential for improving child care quality, that potential is not always realized. Regulatory standards are relatively weak in many states. Their impact is diluted by numerous exemptions. Their impact is further diluted by compliance and enforcement problems. Compliance levels vary from state to state, and it appears that states with relatively high standards have relatively low compliance levels.[3] States with relatively high standards are also somewhat less likely to possess robust enforcement tools, such as the authority to fine recalcitrant providers.[4]

Why are states so reluctant to upgrade their standards and to enforce them? One reason is that tougher requirements may force providers to raise their fees, which many parents cannot afford. For example, North Carolina recently tightened its child/staff ratio requirements for infants at group day care centers.[5] Almost immediately, state officials noticed an increase in center fees.[6] Family day care homes also raised their fees, even though their ratios were unaffected. Apparently, in an industry marked by extremely low wages, providers must take advantage of every opportunity to raise their rates without triggering a public outcry.

Lower child/staff ratios may be justified, even if fees increase. North Carolina still has ratios higher than those found in most other states. And the case for tougher ratio requirements is strongest in infant care, where the quality impacts of ratios are most pronounced.[7] Thus the point is not that North Carolina made a bad decision, but that changes in ratio requirements almost certainly involve trade-offs. If affordability does not worsen, availability does. In a cross-sectional study of all fifty states, I found a statistically significant negative relationship between tougher ratios for center-based care and the supply of centers in each state.[8] When states tighten child/staff ratios at centers, they can expect higher prices in the short run, fewer centers in the long run.

## Family Day Care: The Exit Option

Tougher ratios do not affect family day care homes that much, largely because family day care providers prefer to care for relatively small numbers of children. There is reason to believe, however, that family day care providers are more sensitive to government regulation than their center-based counterparts. For one thing, government regulation applies not just to their place of employment but to their home. A center-based teacher who is told that her/his center is unsuitable for children can shrug that off more easily than a family day care provider who is told the same thing about her/his home. At home, the sting is sharper, more personal.

Family day care providers may experience more stress, overall, than center-based teachers. They put in longer hours and they cannot shield themselves from messy financial details. Also, they must cope with routine tensions and alarming crises more or less on their own. If they become ill, they cannot easily find a substitute, so they are likely to soldier on. For all these reasons, family day care providers may be tempted to take drastic measures when regulation becomes (or seems) oppressive. And they usually enjoy a wider range of options than their center-based counterparts. Unlike centers, family day care providers can go underground if they become exasperated with government officials. Alternatively, they may alter their regulatory status by reducing the number of children they care for. Depending on the state, that may enable them to avoid regulation altogether or it may subject them to certification requirements rather than more onerous licensing requirements.

FIGURE 5-1. Family Day Care Growth in Missouri, 1988–93

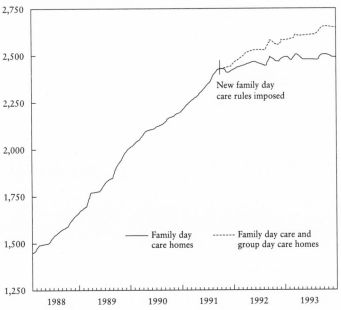

Number of licensed
family day care homes

How do family day care providers actually respond to sudden surges in state regulation? To answer that question, I obtained and examined monthly data on the number of regulated family day care homes from three states. I then used time-series analysis to isolate the effects of the policy intervention on the supply of regulated family day care homes.[9] Time-series analysis requires a substantial number of data points both before and after the policy intervention. Therefore, I selected states where new family day care rules took effect recently (so that pre-intervention figures were still available) but not too recently (so that postintervention figures were also available).

Missouri is a good place to start, because the policy intervention occurred at an ideal time for analytic purposes and because there were fewer complications than in other states. In October 1991, Missouri implemented new family day care rules that imposed new provider training requirements, tightened outdoor safety requirements, clarified policies towards sick children, and added provisions on pets, field trips, transportation, and nutrition. As figure 5-1 indicates, the number of regulated family day care homes in Missouri continued to climb after the

TABLE 5-1.  Effects of Rules Changes on the Supply of Regulated
Family Day Care Homes in Missouri

| Independent variable | Unstandardized $B^a$ | 2-tailed significance |
|---|---|---|
| Rules change | −20.60 | .0000 |
| | (3.26) | |
| Female employment, 4-month lag | 1.50 | .2147 |
| | (1.20) | |
| Births, 2-year lag | −0.01 | .1048 |
| | (0.00) | |
| AR(1) | −0.20 | .1102 |
| | (0.12) | |

Constant = −20.77
$R^2$ = .36
Adjusted $R^2$ = .32
Durbin-Watson statistic = 2.12
F statistic = 8.82
$N$ = 68

a. Standard errors are in parentheses.

rules change but at a lower rate than before. The key question is: Is this decline in the rate of increase due to the new family day care rules?

To answer that question, I analyzed the family day care series (FDCS) and found it to be nonstationary.[10] Through first differencing, I was able to create a stationary series (DFDCS) suitable for further analysis. An analysis of the autocorrelation and partial autocorrelation functions of FDCS and DFDCS suggested a classic AR(1) model.[11] Therefore, I included an AR(1) component in a least squares equation. I also controlled for the monthly percentage of employed women in Missouri, lagged by four months, and for the number of births in Missouri, lagged by two years.[12]

As table 5-1 reveals, the effects of the family day care rules change on the supply of regulated family day care homes are negative and statistically significant at the .0001 level. It is important to note, however, that the family day care rules change coincided with the creation of a new category of facilities in Missouri—the group day care home. Is it possible that the rate of increase in homes (family and group) remained constant while the rate of increase in family day care homes declined? The answer to that question is an unequivocal no. As table 5-2 suggests, the impact of the rules change on the total number of homes is also clearly statistically significant at an acceptable level.[13] In concrete terms, this means that there were fewer regulated child care homes in Missouri as a result of the rules changes than there would have been had the rules changes never taken place.

TABLE 5-2. Effects of Rules Changes on the Supply of Regulated
Child Care Homes in Missouri

| Independent variable | Unstandardized $B^a$ | 2-tailed significance |
|---|---|---|
| Rules change | −14.85 | .0000 |
| | (3.17) | |
| Female employment, 4-month lag | 1.28 | .2767 |
| | (1.16) | |
| Births, 2-year lag | −0.01 | .1002 |
| | (0.00) | |
| AR(1) | −0.22 | .0855 |
| | (0.12) | |

Constant = −8.78
$R^2$ = .26
Adjusted $R^2$ = .22
Durbin-Watson statistic = 2.12
F statistic = 5.61
N = 68

a. Standard errors are in parentheses.

In contrast to Missouri, which implemented a fairly comprehensive rules change in 1991, California adopted what would seem to be a much more modest policy shift in 1992. In an effort to alleviate pressure on a beleaguered general treasury, the California legislature imposed a state licensing fee on child care facilities, including family day care homes, effective September 1992. The fee schedule, which distinguished between small and large family day care homes, included both an initial fee and an annual fee.

To estimate the effects of the new fees on the supply of licensed family day care homes, I transformed a nonstationary series (FDCS) into a stationary series (DFDCS) through first-differencing. Based upon an analysis of the autocorrelation and partial autocorrelation functions, I concluded that an AR(1) term should be included in the model.[14] As in Missouri, I controlled for female employment and the number of births.[15] It was also necessary to include dummy variables to account for several abrupt upward shifts in the series. In California, counties may, at their discretion, license family day care homes themselves or cede that authority to the state. During the time period in question, several counties transferred licensing responsibility to the state, which suddenly increased the number of regulated family day care homes at the state level (see figure 5-2). Dummy variables take these jurisdictional changes into account.

As table 5-3 illustrates, the new family day care fees had a statistically significant negative impact on the number of regulated family day care homes in California. Unlike Missouri, which experienced a decline in the

FIGURE 5-2. Family Day Care Growth in California, 1986–93

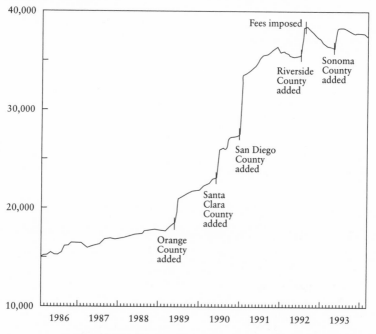

Number of licensed
family day care homes

rate of growth of licensed family day care homes, California experienced a decline in the actual number of licensed family day care homes, disguised only in part by the addition of approximately 1,000 family day care homes from Sonoma County. In California, as in Missouri, new regulatory requirements resulted in fewer regulated family day care homes than would otherwise have existed.

In Texas, where family day care homes are "registered" rather than licensed, two recent policy shifts are worth examining. In July 1990 new family day care rules took effect. They included new training requirements and a requirement that a 20 percent sample of family day care homes be inspected on a regular basis.[16] In January 1992, Texas began to implement another new requirement—that all new family day care registrants be inspected before opening for business.[17] Either intervention might be expected to discourage the provision of family day care.

To estimate the effects of these policy interventions on the supply of registered family day care homes, I focused on the Houston metropolitan

TABLE 5-3. Effects of New Fees on the Supply of
Licensed Family Day Care Homes in California

| Independent variable | Unstandardized $B^a$ | 2-tailed significance |
|---|---|---|
| New fees | −1471.00 | 0.0112 |
|  | (567.43) |  |
| Female employment | 248.75 | 0.0069 |
|  | (89.95) |  |
| Births, 2-year lag | −0.08 | 0.0032 |
|  | (0.02) |  |
| Orange County added | 296.14 | 0.2480 |
|  | (254.61) |  |
| Riverside County added | 1306.45 | 0.0169 |
|  | (536.20) |  |
| Santa Clara County added | 886.30 | 0.0197 |
|  | (373.03) |  |
| San Diego County added | 299.26 | 0.3825 |
|  | (340.98) |  |
| Sonoma County added | 304.50 | 0.3603 |
|  | (331.13) |  |
| AR(1) | −0.09 | 0.4129 |
|  | (0.11) |  |
| Constant = −10253.83 |  |  |
| $R^2$ = .25 |  |  |
| Adjusted $R^2$ = .18 |  |  |
| Durbin-Watson |  |  |
| statistic = 2.01 |  |  |
| F statistic = 3.28 |  |  |
| N = 97 |  |  |

a. Standard errors are in parentheses.

area, where an uninterrupted time-series dating back to September 1986 happened to be available.[18] As in the other cases, I transformed a non-stationary series into a stationary series through first-differencing. I also determined that an AR(1) term should be included in the model.[19] As in the previous cases, I controlled for female employment and the number of births.[20] I also added a dummy variable for the incorporation of Initiatives for Children, a Houston resource and referral agency that launched a major effort to recruit and retain family day care providers in 1988.

As table 5-4 indicates, Initiatives for Children was successful in boosting the number of registered family day care homes (p < .05). Grants from the state Department of Human Services, Mervyn's, and IBM enabled "Initiatives" to recruit new providers and assist established providers through training and support groups. The new family day care rules,

TABLE 5-4.  Effects of Policy Changes on the Supply of Registered
Family Day Care Homes in the Houston Area

| Independent variable | Unstandardized $B^a$ | 2-tailed significance |
|---|---|---|
| Initiatives for Children | 40.65 | 0.0450 |
| incorporated | (19.97) | |
| Family day care rules implemented | –34.80 | 0.0152 |
| | (14.04) | |
| Initial inspections required | 1.62 | 0.9126 |
| | (14.73) | |
| Female employment | 469.23 | 0.4131 |
| | (570.43) | |
| Births, 2-year lag | –0.00 | 0.4320 |
| | (0.00) | |
| AR(1) | 0.12 | 0.2856 |
| | (0.11) | |

Constant = –226.41
$R^2 = .18$
Adjusted $R^2 = .12$
Durbin-Watson statistic = 1.99
F statistic = 2.99
$N = 91$

a. Standard errors are in parentheses.

implemented in 1990, resulted in a temporary decline in the number of registered family day care homes ($p < .05$). The new inspection requirements, however, had no noticeable impact on supply (see figure 5-3).

## Sensitive Providers

The picture that emerges from this analysis of family day care policy changes is one of extremely sensitive providers. In all three states, a tightening of regulatory requirements adversely affected the supply of regulated family day care homes. This is a serious matter, even if, for the sake of argument, the total number of unregulated homes increased. Regulated homes are considerably more visible than unregulated homes, not just to regulators but to parents as well. Thus a diminution in the number of regulated homes makes child care less accessible and available, regardless of what happens to unregulated homes.

At first glance, it would appear that almost any regulatory stimulus negatively affects supply. But perhaps the rules changes described have something in common. Two of the rules changes—in Missouri and Texas—

FIGURE 5-3.  Family Day Care Growth in the Houston Area, 1987–93

Number of registered
family day care homes

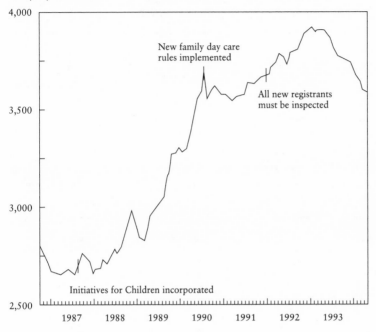

imposed provider training requirements for the first time. In Missouri, providers were required to complete twelve clock-hours of training per year; in Texas, providers were required to complete a state-sponsored orientation session and twenty clock-hours of training per year.

In general, training is an unlikely source of discontent among providers. In interviews with sixty-four potential family day care providers in Milwaukee County, I found that only one objected to state training requirements, perhaps the toughest in the nation.[21] In a cross-sectional analysis of data from all fifty states, I found that training requirements were not associated with a reduced supply of regulated family day care homes.[22] On the other hand, the Texas training requirements may have come as a shock to some providers, long accustomed to a laissez faire climate in a conservative state.

I am reluctant to attribute the Missouri downturn to new training requirements, especially because Missouri took significant steps to ensure that the requisite training was available throughout the state at little or no cost. A more plausible explanation is that some providers objected to a new play area equipment rule that could prove costly. Under the old rules, all equipment was to be kept in good condition and swings and climbers were to be securely anchored.[23] Under the new rules, any equipment from which children can fall can be no more than six feet high; swings must have seats of rubber, plastic, canvas or nylon; equipment with moving parts which might pinch or crush children's fingers must have protective guards or covers; and ropes or loops that might close or tighten upon a child are not permitted.[24] At the very least, the new rules are likely to require new swing seats and new protective covers.[25]

How costly must a rule be for providers to react negatively to it? The California results suggest an answer: not very costly at all. The new fees imposed by California were very modest indeed: $25 upon initial licensing and $25 annually thereafter for small family day care homes (fewer than seven children), which constitute the bulk of all family day care homes. Even the fees for large family day care homes (seven to twelve children)—$50 initially and $50 annually after that—are not particularly high. Of course, providers may fear that a modest fee will become immodest over time. Or providers may object to paying something for nothing. In this respect, training presents an interesting contrast. While it may be inconvenient to obtain training, at least training offers tangible benefits that most providers can readily understand.

Do providers react negatively to new inspection requirements? The Houston evidence does not permit a good answer to that question. When Texas required that 20 percent of all family day care homes be inspected, supply declined, but new training requirements kicked in at the same time. When state officials in Houston began to implement the requirement that all new registrants be inspected, nothing happened to supply.

In an analysis of data from all fifty states, I found that a higher number of state inspections was associated with a lower number of regulated family day care homes.[26] In an analysis of reports from 1,206 mothers from thirty-seven states, researchers found that the number of inspections had no negative effect on availability, defined as mothers' perceptions of proximity to a family day care home.[27] Clearly, more research is needed in this area. The key would seem to be to identify those inspections that are perceived to impose substantial costs on providers. Perhaps there are interaction effects between inspections and other requirements. In a state with relatively weak rules, an inspection may not be much of a threat. In a state with relatively tough rules, an inspection may presage demands to purchase new equipment or to make costly repairs.

The absolute number of regulated family day care homes does not always drop as a result of tougher regulatory requirements. In some instances (such as Missouri), the rate of growth declines, but the absolute number of regulated homes continues to climb. Perhaps a small decline in the growth rate of regulated family day care homes is an acceptable price to pay for quality improvements.

There is, however, another option that state regulators might consider. When upgrading family day care rules, state regulators could simultaneously expand the scope of coverage to previously exempt providers. In this fashion, they would not only boost the quality of care in regulated homes but would also ensure an increase in the number of regulated family day care homes.

Of course, this strategy is possible only in those thirty-five states that currently exempt some family day care homes from regulatory requirements. In the other states, regulators might take the sting out of new regulatory requirements by offering one-time-only subsidies from quality improvement funds to bring family day care providers into compliance with new rules. Some states are already doing precisely that. For example, Oregon has allocated $70,000 from Child Care and Development Block Grant funds to help family day care providers meet health and safety standards.[28] As Houston demonstrates, a major initiative to assist family day care homes can boost supply. That initiative combined the resources of the public, nonprofit, and for-profit sectors.

If money presents opportunities, it also imposes constraints. If states were to upgrade their family day care standards and expand the scope of coverage to previously unregulated homes, parents would have access to a greater number of regulated family day care homes of higher quality. But those homes would probably be somewhat less affordable than unregulated homes of lower quality. Under such circumstances, affordability suffers for the sake of quality and availability. And availability is a rather hollow concept if available care is not also affordable.

The same problem arises in the context of group day care centers. Depending on the regulation, efforts to improve quality may result in center-based care that is less affordable, less available, or both. This is especially true of rules changes providing for lower child/staff ratios. Whatever the merits of such changes in terms of quality, they are clearly associated with a reduced supply of group day care centers.[29] Thus regulators and legislators must decide whether the quality gains that flow from lower ratios can justify the adverse effects on affordability and availability that also follow.

## Regulatory Enforcement

Many state regulatory agencies have revised their child care standards in recent years, through the rulemaking process. This is true of rules for centers, group day care homes, and family day care homes. In most states, these rules have been rewritten—and almost always made more stringent—every few years.

Yet the same states that have upgraded their standards have been reluctant to enforce them. Consider, for example, Pennsylvania, where the rules are relatively strict. In 1993 Pennsylvania revoked or refused to renew the licenses of only six group day care centers and the registrations of only seven family day care homes. This is a state with nearly 3,000 licensed centers and over 6,000 registered family day care homes.

Nor is this an isolated example. In state after state, one finds single-digit entries for license revocations in a given year. One also finds single-digit entries for other punitive sanctions against licensees. This would not be surprising or disturbing if 95 percent of all facilities were good or even adequate. But that is not what some studies show. For example, the Families and Work Institute found that the quality of care provided in 13 percent of all regulated family day care homes was "inadequate."[30] If that is the case, why are so few of them disciplined by state officials?

In fact, there are several reasons for weak enforcement of regulations. First of all, no one is particularly anxious to invoke the ultimate sanction of shutting a facility down. This is especially true in rural communities, where centers are often few and far between. A North Carolina inspector with a rural jurisdiction puts it this way: "Of my centers, 30 percent are superior. Another 10 percent should be closed, but there is no other day care in the area." Under these circumstances, the inspector has concluded that license revocation is simply not a viable option.[31]

Of course, the community may be better off without a particular provider, even if that aggravates supply problems, but shutting down a facility normally requires extensive documentation, frequent site visits, and numerous conversations with nervous attorneys. If state regulators proceed anyway, providers are not powerless. They may appeal a negative action, seek the support of a friendly politician, or both.

An Oklahoma case is illustrative. A for-profit center continually violated important state rules. The facility was understaffed, there was no air conditioning in the summer, it was too cold in the winter, and there were rats, mice, and roaches. The facility was so bad that the inspector visited it twenty-four times in one year. She threatened to close the center if conditions did not improve. The owner responded by calling a state legislator, who complained to state officials about harassment. The state relented and allowed the center to remain open. When conditions failed to improve, the state declined to renew the owner's license, but the owner appealed, which enabled the center to stay open. Eventually, a state attorney prepared an emergency order to close the facility. Informed of this, the owner finally shut down. But the entire process took approximately eighteen months.

In theory, inspectors can punish a recalcitrant provider without putting him or her out of business. But that presupposes a range of sanctions not available in many states. According to a General Accounting Office survey conducted in 1991 and 1992, only nineteen states can impose monetary fines on centers, and only twenty-nine states can place a center on probation.[32] The same survey revealed that only sixteen states can levy a fine on a family day care home, and only twenty-three states can place a family day care home on probation. This means that many inspectors must choose between innocuous and draconian sanctions.

Yet intermediate sanctions could be more constructive than license revocation, more effective than a written warning. As Braithwaite has argued, regulatory agencies are most successful when supported by an "enforcement pyramid" with sanctions that escalate as the offense worsens.[33] As Ayres and Braithwaite explain, "Defection from cooperation is likely to be a less attractive proposition for business when it faces a regulator with an enforcement pyramid than when confronted with a regulator having only one deterrence option."[34] Unfortunately, regulatory agencies often possess a drastic remedy (the top of the pyramid), an inconsequential remedy (the base of the pyramid), and little in between. The missing intermediate sanctions are the key.

Even when intermediate sanctions are available, however, they may not be used. In a number of states, the monetary fine is available in theory but almost never used in practice. In Pennsylvania and Colorado, for example, no monetary fines were imposed on any group day care centers in 1993, even though state statutes permit them.

Some regulators oppose a monetary fine on the grounds that it contributes to an adversarial relationship. These same regulators believe that a fine is too harsh a penalty in an industry marked by extremely low wages. Right or wrong, some regulators also feel that they must document deliberate noncompliance over a period of several days or even weeks before imposing a fine. This belief comes from state attorneys who prefer a limited number of airtight cases to a larger number of reasonably good cases, so that they can cope with substantial caseloads.[35] For these and other reasons, fines are much rarer in child care than they are, for example, in occupational safety regulation, where one of every three inspections results in a monetary fine.[36]

In short, lax enforcement of child care standards has several underlying causes: inspectors have mixed feelings about punitive sanctions; they possess a limited range of tools to deal with code violations; and they are put off by a cumbersome legal process. Another reason why inspectors don't penalize really bad facilities is that they are extremely busy policing all facilities, both good and bad. With high caseloads, numerous rules to enforce, and lots of paperwork to complete, inspectors often conclude that they cannot afford to become preoccupied with any one facility. This state of affairs has led some to propose deregulating good facilities in order to concentrate on the bad ones. Effective regulation, according to some observers, requires careful targeting. Otherwise, inspectors will come to resemble poor Mickey Mouse in "Fantasia"— coping frantically with so many water-toting brooms that only magic can prevent a flood.

## Regulatory Reform

Regulatory reform is a broad concept. It can mean the elimination of regulation altogether (as in the case of the airline industry), the substitution of one form of regulation for another (pollution taxes instead of command-and-control), or a more streamlined regulatory process (through administrative reorganization). It can mean greater reliance on regulatory bargaining, a wider array of enforcement options, or smarter enforcement strategies. Often, regulatory reform seeks to improve the efficiency of government regulation.[37]

In child care, numerous regulatory reforms have been proposed. The most intriguing, however, are those that seek to reallocate regulatory resources where they are needed the most. The basic premise is that "good apples" and "bad apples" do not deserve equal attention from government inspectors. As Bardach and Kagan put it, "Inspectors should be concentrated where they can prevent the greatest harm to the greatest number."[38] This implies that inspectors should distinguish sharply between firms with good and bad track records. The latter would then receive much more scrutiny than the former. Thus some facilities would be "deregulated" while others would be watched more closely.

## Differential Licensing Systems

One way to distinguish between good and bad firms that need government licenses to operate would be to link the firm's license term to performance. In 1991 Vermont implemented a differential licensing system that does precisely that. The impetus for Vermont's reform was a caseload crisis in the Children's Day Care Unit. A downsizing phase in state government resulted in the loss of two full-time inspectors over a two-year period; a prominent supervisory position was also eliminated. At the same time, the number of registered family day care homes was increasing dramatically. With only four full-time child care inspectors, Vermont was unable to visit every center annually and respond to every complaint against licensed centers and registered family day care homes.

Coleman Baker, Chief of the Children's Day Care Unit, concluded that business as usual would no longer work. In 1990 Baker announced his intention to establish an "extended licensing" system to cope with the worsening caseload crisis. In anticipation of such a possibility, the Department of Social and Rehabilitation Services had rewritten its rules to permit the issuance of licenses for up to three years. Under the new system, to be implemented in January 1991, inspectors would be free to award a one-, two-, or three-year license to group day care centers at renewal time. Initial licensees would continue to receive one-year licenses. The hope was that the new system would be more efficient, enabling the Department to "do more with less."

To assess the effects of Vermont's differential licensing system on center quality, I decided to examine state inspection reports covering a five-year period (from 1989 through 1993).[39] To ensure a large number of cases for analysis, and to avoid generalizations based on selected regions or cities, I analyzed all centers in the state. As a first step, I identified centers in existence in 1991, when the differential licensing process first took effect. For each such center, I recorded problems noted in inspection reports based upon 1991 renewal inspections.[40] These were most frequently listed under the heading, "Recommendations for Improvement."[41] I

TABLE 5-5. Change in Center Conditions Following 1991
Relicensure in Vermont
Percent

| Type of change | One-year license | Two-year license |
|---|---|---|
| Number of problems | | |
| Worse | 27.3 | 62.0 |
| Same | 20.5 | 12.7 |
| Better | 52.3 | 25.4 |
| N | 44 | 71 |
| Number of very serious problems | | |
| Worse | 20.5 | 45.1 |
| Same | 34.1 | 29.6 |
| Better | 45.4 | 25.4 |
| N | 44 | 71 |

NOTE: Based on t-test results, using raw data, the difference of means (between one-year and two-year licensees) is statistically significant at the .01 level for the change in the number of problems, at the .05 level for the change in the number of very serious problems. The data have been grouped into three categories for ease of presentation.

also distinguished between very serious and less serious problems, relying heavily upon interviews with the state's inspectors.

For each license renewed in 1991, I determined the length of the license term.[42] I then repeated this process for the two preceding years, where possible, and for the two following years, where possible. This enabled me to calculate each center's performance in 1991, as well as its prior history and its subsequent history. If a center was licensed for the first time in 1991, I excluded it from analysis, because initial licensing differs fundamentally from the relicensing process.[43] If no relicensing activity occurred during 1992 or 1993, I extended my content analysis of inspection documents into early 1994 in an effort to assess the center's performance during its second renewal following the implementation of the new regulatory regime.

How has the differential licensing process actually worked? Table 5-5 reveals the trajectory of centers granted one-year and two-year licenses at renewal time in 1991.[44] Of those granted one-year licenses, the majority improved by their next renewal. Of those granted two-year licenses, the majority deteriorated by their next renewal. A t-test indicates that the difference between the two types of licensees is statistically significant at the .01 level.

Of course, it is theoretically possible that one-year licensees are getting better in trivial ways or that two-year licensees are getting worse in trivial ways. A separate analysis of very serious problems, however, reveals similar results. Of those centers granted one-year licenses in 1991, a plurality improved by their next renewal. Of those granted two-year licenses, a plurality worsened by their next renewal. Here also, the difference between the two groups is statistically significant, this time at the .05 level.

From these figures, we may draw two inferences. First, the one-year licensees, who were essentially awarded a booby prize for poor behavior, seem chastened by the experience. Embarrassed by the dubious distinction of a one-year license, they apparently resolved to do better the next time. And most of them did. Among centers relicensed in 1991 and granted a one-year term, 63.2 percent received a two- or three-year term in 1992.

Second, the two-year licensees, who received a vote of confidence from the regulatory staff, seem to have let their guard down afterwards. Perhaps smugness set in. Or perhaps they missed the welcome assistance that accompanies unwelcome nagging. Whatever the reasons, two-year licensees, as a group, deteriorated over time, though they were still superior in 1993 to centers that received one-year licenses in both 1991 and 1992.[45]

Before regarding this as the last word on the subject, we should consider a potential objection to this analysis: that the behavior of licensees over time simply reflects a statistical artifact known as "regression toward the mean." It is well established that high and low test scores on a given date will gravitate towards medium-range scores over time. If one thinks of 1991 inspections as a sort of test, with inspectors assigning high-scorers and low-scorers to different groups (three-year licensees, two-year licensees, one-year licensees), then regression toward the mean could be a result.

A closer analysis of the data suggests that this is probably not the case. When inspectors decided in 1991 which centers would receive licenses of different lengths, they were guided less by the licensee's 1991 "test" score than by the licensee's cumulative history.[46] As table 5-6 indicates, the relationship between 1991 observations and license length thus is weaker than the relationship between the cumulative history and license length. Moreover, this is true of both very serious problems and problems generally. In assigning centers to different groups, inspectors made an obvious effort to take each center's past track record into account.

116 DOS, DON'TS, AND DOLLARS

TABLE 5-6. License Term Granted at 1991 Relicensure in Vermont: Correlation Coefficients

| Variable | Simple correlation coefficient |
|---|---|
| Number of problems (1991) | −.242** |
| Number of problems (1991, 1990, and 1989 combined) | −.344*** |
| Number of very serious problems (1991) | −.189* |
| Number of very serious problems (1991, 1990, and 1989 combined) | −.310*** |

*Significant at the .05 level.
**Significant at the .01 level.
***Significant at the .001 level.

In conclusion, the Vermont experiment has had two strikingly different effects. By stigmatizing problematic centers with the opprobrium of a one-year license, regulators have sent a strong negative signal that served as a wake-up call to these providers. This is precisely what the regulation intended. By rewarding better centers with longer licenses, however, regulators have unwittingly pressed the snooze button on the alarm clock. Buoyed by the state's vote of confidence, some providers have slackened their efforts to maintain high quality. Positive reinforcement, in this instance, does not seem to have worked.

The Vermont results are particularly interesting because Vermont probably has a smaller percentage of hopelessly bad day care centers than other states. They have no for-profit chains, which in itself should guarantee higher quality. In addition, Vermont has been singled out by experts in the field as one of the best states for child care.[47] If day care centers deteriorate in the absence of frequent monitoring in Vermont, they almost certainly deteriorate in the absence of frequent monitoring elsewhere.

Does this mean that more attention to "bad apples" and less attention to "good apples" is a bad idea? Not necessarily. The problem with the Vermont experiment may be not the concept of differential monitoring but the time interval between inspections. A differential monitoring system with more frequent inspections could accomplish two important goals: It could send a strong warning to poorly performing centers; and it could devote enough attention to better-performing centers that they do not slip into mediocrity. The Vermont results suggest that poorer centers need regular attention and occasional embarrassment, while better centers simply need regular attention.

In Texas, a differential monitoring system was established several years ago with precisely the characteristics described above. Under the Texas system, centers are placed into one of three categories after a renewal inspection: Plan 1 (three inspections per year), Plan 2 (two inspections per year), and Plan 3 (one inspection per year). It is not possible to do a before and after study of the Texas system, because the system was implemented in 1986 or 1987 and inspection records do not go back that far. In principle, however, the Texas approach should yield the best of both worlds: enough attention to better centers to keep them from deteriorating; greater attention to poorer centers to prod them to improve.

Thus it would be a mistake to conclude from the Vermont experiment that inspector discretion and differential treatment of day care facilities are bad. Child care regulatory systems need more flexibility, not less. Child care facilities also need regular attention. Directors change, staff members change, regulatory requirements change, and parental expectations change. An annual renewal visit, with lots of paperwork, may not be necessary. But an annual visit of some sort is probably essential, even at centers with good track records and good intentions.

## Indicator Checklists

The premise behind differential licensing is that good facilities do not need to be visited as often as bad facilities. The premise behind indicator checklists is that visits to good facilities need not be as lengthy as visits to bad facilities. An indicator checklist is a relatively short collection of regulatory requirements culled from a comprehensive set of regulatory requirements.[48] Items chosen for inclusion are based on how well conformity to a particular requirement predicts conformity to the whole range of items. Thus if compliance with training requirements is an excellent predictor of overall compliance, while compliance with field trip requirements is not, then training requirements—and not field trip requirements—should be included on the indicator checklist.

Like differential licensing, the indicator checklist is a regulatory reform aimed at more efficient regulatory enforcement. It was developed in the early 1980s by Rick Fiene, a psychologist and policy analyst who works for Pennsylvania's Office of Children, Youth and Families. Fiene saw the indicator checklist as a mechanism for shifting the emphasis in regulatory enforcement from compliance to quality. Meanwhile, many state governments saw the indicator checklist as a chance to do more with less.

Fiene, the guru of indicator checklists, is a purist on the subject. He believes that a true indicator checklist has two key components: a weighting scheme that gives greater emphasis to items judged by experts to pose a greater threat to the health and safety of children; and a statistical sifting and winnowing process that distinguishes between good and bad predictors of overall compliance and tilts towards the former.[49] Based on these criteria, only a handful of states currently use true indicator checklists.[50] Based on looser criteria, nearly thirty states use some form of indicator checklist.[51] Most commonly, indicator checklists apply only to center-based care.

The big advantage of indicator checklists is that they save time and thus money. A typical indicator checklist reduces a cumbersome list of 200 or so regulations to a more manageable list of about twenty-five or so key regulations. Although recent studies are not available, a West Virginia study conducted in the early 1980s found that the indicator checklist saved approximately $800 per year per center.[52] That money can be returned to taxpayers or invested in more attention to "bad apples." Either way, it contributes to efficient regulatory enforcement.

According to Fiene and others, indicator checklists are very popular with providers. This is understandable, because indicator checklists shorten the time of an inspection considerably. They are not always popular with inspectors, however. In Pennsylvania, for example, nearly half of all inspectors oppose indicator checklists, which are now used only when license renewal backlogs become acute. Some cite the old adage that anything worth doing is worth doing well. Others worry that providers will focus on the indicators and not the full set of rules. An unspoken objection of regulators may be the most telling—that indicator checklists can be used to justify layoffs, higher caseloads, or both.

Perhaps the solution is for inspectors to use indicator checklists selectively. Instead of employing such lists at every renewal, inspectors could use them at centers with good track records and low turnover. A center with a poor track record or a new director would receive the full treatment. North Carolina has used a system with some of these characteristics, and it has won the warm support of its inspectors (see table 5-7). West Virginia has also linked the use of indicator checklists to center performance.[53] Although logistical problems remain, the indicator checklist is a promising technique for enhancing the efficiency of the regulatory process.[54]

TABLE 5-7. Inspectors' Beliefs about Indicator Checklists[a]
Percent

Statement: When inspecting centers at renewal time, inspectors should be free to use an abbreviated set of regulatory requirements, such as an indicator checklist.[b]

| State | Disagree | Not sure | Agree |
|---|---|---|---|
| Colorado | 10.5 | 0.0 | 89.5 |
| (N) | (2) | (0) | (17) |
| North Carolina | 3.6 | 0.0 | 96.4 |
| (N) | (1) | (0) | (27) |
| Oklahoma | 42.3 | 11.5 | 46.2 |
| (N) | (11) | (3) | (12) |
| Pennsylvania | 48.0 | 12.0 | 40.0 |
| (N) | (12) | (3) | (10) |

a. Numbers in parentheses are totals.

b. This statement was one of several read to child care inspectors in four states, as part of a broader study of child care regulatory enforcement. The interviews were conducted during May, June, August, and September 1994.

## Regulatory Reform in Perspective

Regulatory reforms differ from one another in several crucial respects. Some impose tougher rules on regulated firms, while others relax regulatory requirements. Some redefine relationships between regulatory agencies and regulated firms, while others redefine relationships between government agencies. Some increase the costs of compliance, while others increase the costs of noncompliance. The case for a particular approach depends on the problem at hand.

In thinking about regulatory reforms, it is useful to distinguish between broad and narrow reform strategies. Some reforms apply to all licensed centers or all registered family day care homes. For example, Kansas established a self-certification system for family day care providers in 1980. More recently, in 1992, California eliminated license renewals (but not periodic inspections) for all providers. Other reforms, in contrast, enable regulators to take the unique characteristics of individual providers into account. Thus Massachusetts sometimes requires recalcitrant providers to hire a consultant or to undertake appropriate training to remedy a specific problem. Imposing monetary fines illustrates the same broad strategy, though a different tactic.

Selective and uniform approaches to regulation are not mutually exclusive and can in fact be complementary. In rulemaking, there is much to be said for uniformity and consistency. All providers in a certain class or category should be expected to meet identical or similar expectations. In enforcement, however, there is much to be said for flexibility and selectivity. Both monitoring and sanctioning should be tailor-made if possible. Regulators should be encouraged to discriminate between good and bad providers.

I have deliberately used the word discriminate because that is how some providers perceive selective regulation and selective deregulation. It is important to stress, however, that injustice is the unequal treatment of equals, not the unequal treatment of unequals. Efforts to distinguish between good and bad providers at the enforcement stage are in fact fairer than across-the-board approaches that treat saints and sinners alike.

Nor does differential treatment present special legal difficulties. It is a time-honored principle of administrative law that administrative agencies are free to exercise broad discretion so long as they do not behave "arbitrarily and capriciously."[55] Neither differential licensing nor the indicator checklist violates that presumption. On the contrary, they constitute good-faith efforts to allocate resources more efficiently and to introduce greater flexibility into the regulatory process.

It is important to emphasize that selectivity can be built into either regulatory or deregulatory initiatives. The case for one approach rather than another will depend on the scarcity of regulatory resources, the balance that has already been struck between quality and availability, and other factors. Moreover, regulatory and deregulatory approaches are not incompatible. For example, a state might combine tougher rules (uniform regulation) with more relaxed enforcement of exemplary providers (selective deregulation).

Regulators should also consider effective ways to improve child care quality by combining regulatory and nonregulatory approaches. A timely subsidy, for example, can help take the sting out of new regulatory requirements. When providers do not comply with regulatory standards, the problem may be not that they oppose them but that they lack the financial wherewithal to comply. Regulatory tools and nonregulatory tools, when combined, can help to overcome the financial weaknesses of an unusually troubled industry. Thus it is important to ask how subsidies have been structured in the past and how they might be restructured to promote efficiency, justice, and choice more effectively.

## Grants-in-Aid

Government spending on child care in the United States pales in comparison to such spending in other industrialized countries.[56] Nevertheless, government spending on child care is considerable and growing.

The federal government's role is particularly significant. According to recent estimates, the federal government presides over approximately four dozen separate child care programs. Total federal spending on programs related to child care, including tax expenditures, now comes close to $12 billion per year.[57]

Of this amount, I estimate that 74 percent primarily benefits the poor (for example, Head Start, the Child and Adult Care Food Program, the Child Care and Development Block Grant, the Social Services Block Grant, and the various IV-A programs), while 24 percent primarily benefits middle- and upper-income taxpayers (the Child and Dependent Care Tax Credit), and 1 percent benefits all users of child care services through infrastructure support. The principal beneficiaries of the remaining 1 percent could not be determined.[58] Child care spending by the federal government has become considerably more redistributive since 1988, when tax expenditures constituted approximately two-thirds of all federal child care spending.[59] Since that time, federal child care spending has focused much more sharply on the child care needs of AFDC clients and the working poor.

Various studies suggest that government subsidies can help to improve the quality of child care that children receive. Some of these studies are program-specific; others consider the effects of aggregate spending levels on particular quality indicators. One of the more sophisticated studies shows that higher subsidies result in more formalized instructional programs, greater parental participation, and higher salaries.[60] According to the same study, however, higher subsidies do not necessarily result in lower child/staff ratios. This is roughly consistent with the findings reported in chapter 4.

Studies of particular child care programs, such as Head Start, are also encouraging, but not unambiguously so. Clearly, Head Start produces short-term gains in cognitive development for disadvantaged children.[61] In addition, Head Start graduates are less likely to repeat a grade and less likely to be placed in special education classes.[62] Head Start children also benefit from timely immunizations and regular physical examinations.[63] On the other hand, analysts generally agree that Head Start's cognitive gains diminish over time. Also, the most compelling evidence that early education programs can generate substantial long-term benefits to both children and taxpayers comes from a study of an Ypsilanti, Michigan preschool program and not from a Head Start program per se.[64] That preschool program differed significantly from run-of-the-mill Head Start programs.[65] Thus Head Start should not be oversold.

Other child care spending programs have also enriched the lives of children, especially disadvantaged children. The Child and Adult Care Food Program, for example, provides free or reduced-price meals and snacks to approximately one million children every day. Over 500 million meals are served per year. Centers that participate in the Child and Adult Care Food Program are more likely to serve some food and much more likely to provide meals than other centers.[66] Centers that participate are also much more likely to care for disadvantaged children. That is understandable, because food subsidies vary inversely with children's income. Thus the Child and Adult Care Food Program helps to redistribute income by rewarding centers that care for a relatively large number of disadvantaged children. The same cannot be said of family day care homes, however, which are generally free to participate in the Child and Adult Care Food Program, regardless of children's income.[67]

## Categorical Versus Block Grants

Both Head Start and the Child and Adult Care Food Program are categorical grants. Such grants are designed with relatively narrow and specific purposes in mind, leaving little discretion in the hands of those organizations that administer them. Other federal child care programs are also administered through categorical grants. These include: the IV-A JOBS program, which offers child care support to AFDC recipients participating in an approved education or training program; the IV-A Transitional Child Care program, which provides child care to working parents who have just left AFDC; and the IV-A At-Risk program, which assists working parents who are in danger of slipping into AFDC dependency.

The federal government's child care programs also include two block grants. The Social Services Block Grant, formerly known as Title XX, provides relatively unrestricted assistance to state governments that may spend the funds on a wide variety of social services, including child care. The Child Care and Development Block Grant, enacted in 1990, provides approximately $1 billion per year to the states to purchase child care services for disadvantaged children and to promote quality improvement. Children whose families earn less than 75 percent of their state's median family income are eligible for "direct services" grants to the extent that funds are available. The program's principal intent was to assist the working poor.

In principle, block grants are better designed than categorical grants to promote such goals as discretion, flexibility, and responsiveness. As Wright points out, block grants usually allow state governments to spend money as they see fit or where they believe it will do the most good.[68] Monitoring and reporting requirements are reduced so that state governments can concentrate on service delivery. Funds are allocated according to a fixed formula so that states do not dissipate energies in grantsmanship games. Also, matching funds requirements are usually quite low, sometimes nonexistent.

Although these characteristics seem to describe the Social Services Block Grant, they do not accurately describe the Child Care and Development Block Grant, the more important of the two programs to the child care community. Both Congress and the U.S. Department of Health and Human Services have placed significant restrictions on the use of CCDBG funds. Three-fourths of the money must be devoted to direct services, and a voucher system must be in place to facilitate parental choice. All recipients of direct services, including relatives, must "register" with their state government, and all recipients, excluding relatives, must meet basic health and safety requirements. Although these provisions are aimed at promoting quality, other restrictions are not. For example, HHS prohibits states from reimbursing high-quality providers within a broad category (such as family day care homes) at significantly higher rates than other providers within the same category. Overall, the Child Care and Development Block Grant seems to illustrate what the U.S. Advisory Commission on Intergovernmental Relations has called "regulatory federalism."[69] Intergovernmental restrictions make the CCDBG look more like a hybrid than a pure block grant.

The IV-A programs, in contrast, are genuine categorical grants. They have their own set of problems, however. Perhaps the most fundamental problem is insufficient funding. All of these programs require a state match, and many states have had difficulty coming up with the funds. For example, 21 percent of the At-Risk funding available in fiscal year 1992 had not been claimed by the states as the end of the fiscal year approached.[70] Waiting lists for the working poor are commonplace. In many states, parents on AFDC must pay for child care themselves and get reimbursed from the state one or two months later. This arrangement places a real hardship on parents and puts providers in an awkward situation (many providers are unwilling to accept AFDC clients who must pay for care themselves, because they fear that bills will not be paid). The IV-A programs also restrict state efforts to promote quality by limiting provider reimbursement rates to a level no higher than those charged by

124    DOS, DON'TS, AND DOLLARS

the least expensive 75 percent of local providers. The intent behind this provision is to stretch scarce resources. It also means that many funded parents cannot purchase high-quality child care unless they make up the difference, which many are unable to do.

These restrictions have had spillover effects on the Child Care and Development Block Grant. In pursuit of consistency across programs, most states have established identical reimbursement rates for multiple child care programs.[71] Because the 75 percent limit applies to all IV-A programs, this means that it also applies to the CCDBG program in those states that have placed a high value on consistency. Insufficient funding for the IV-A programs also undermines the Child Care and Development Block Grant. As of late 1993, at least sixteen states have used CCDBG funds to help prop up underfunded IV-A programs for AFDC recipients.[72] While this is entirely legal, it undermines the ability of the CCDBG program to meet the needs of the working poor.

What effects are these programs having on state spending priorities and parental choices? Does program structure matter? Are particular programs too restrictive or not restrictive enough? Although the available data could be better, it is possible to reach some tentative conclusions about program impact and implementation.[73] Consider, for example, block grant beneficiaries. According to some political scientists, policymakers should be wary of social programs that delegate substantial discretion to state and local governments in "redistributive" policy domains.[74] That is because state and local governments will be tempted to convert redistributive programs aimed at benefiting the poor into distributive programs aimed at benefiting more affluent clients. Thus one might expect that state governments would use most of their CCDBG money to assist persons with incomes above the poverty level, rather than persons with incomes below the poverty level. Under the 1990 law, states are free to support families with incomes up to 75 percent of the state median family income, which corresponds roughly to 200 percent of the federal poverty level.

In practice, this has not occurred. According to the U.S. Department of Health and Human Services, 67 percent of the children supported under CCDBG during the first year of implementation (fiscal year 1992) were at or below the poverty level.[75] If anything, the states have made a fairly redistributive program even more redistributive, by diverting funds originally intended for the working poor to AFDC clients participating in welfare-to-work programs. Some states have done this because the IV-A

TABLE 5-8. Proportion of Children Receiving CCDBG Funds Who
Are Cared for in a Family Day Care Home:
Multiple Regression Model[a]

| Independent variable | Unstandardized B |
|---|---|
| Group day care centers per child | −3.740 |
| | (11.909) |
| Percent of residents born in state | −0.001 |
| | (.002) |
| Percent of residents who are black | −0.004* |
| | (.002) |
| Family day care homes per child | 3.864* |
| | (1.836) |
| Inspection required of FDCs that would otherwise be exempt | −0.016 |
| from an inspection | (.047) |
| Constant = 0.178 | |
| Adjusted $R^2$ = .19 | |
| N = 47 | |

a. Standard errors are in parentheses; the data on child care arrangements were obtained from ACF-700 forms for fiscal year 1993.
*Significant at the .05 level.

programs require matching funds, whereas CCDBG does not. Thus if states begin with the premise that their first priority is to assist AFDC clients in welfare-to-work programs (such as JOBS), they will sometimes use "free" federal dollars for that purpose when state budgets get tight. Clearly, the implementation of redistributive block grants depends on a complex mix of political, financial, and policy considerations. Delegation to the states does not necessarily undermine redistributive goals.

Another key question is whether federal regulatory requirements have undermined parental choice. One such requirement is the statutory mandate that family day care providers meet basic health and safety standards if they are to be eligible for CCDBG funds. In implementing this requirement, some states have required family day care providers receiving CCDBG funds to be inspected even though other family day care providers need not be, or to receive training that other family day care providers need not receive.[76] One might imagine that this would discourage some family day care providers from accepting CCDBG clients. If so, parents could be less able to find appropriate family day care in such states. Table 5-8 suggests that this has not happened.[77] Certain regulatory requirements may reduce the supply of regulated family day care homes, as discussed earlier, but not enough to prevent parents from pursuing family day care options if that is what they prefer.

## Vouchers

One of the most intriguing features of the Child Care and Development Block Grant law was its requirement that states establish voucher or certificate programs to deliver child care services. Although states may use a combination of vouchers and contracts if they wish, Congress insisted that states facilitate parental choice to the maximum feasible extent.[78] If the use of contracts were to interfere with this principle in a particular state, the U.S. Department of Health and Human Services could require greater reliance on vouchers. In practice, however, states have not balked at the use of vouchers, and many states now rely exclusively upon vouchers to deliver child care services to parents under CCDBG.

Vouchers have long been used in social welfare policy (the Food Stamp program is, in effect, a voucher program), and they have become a staple of housing policy, as clients use vouchers to choose rental properties in the open market in lieu of public housing sites. Vouchers have also been touted by some as a promising tool in education policy. According to Chubb and Moe, an extensive voucher system would inject a healthy dose of competition into our public school system and would ultimately improve the quality of both public and private schools.[79] That thesis has been challenged by others, who doubt that significant quality improvements flow from vouchers.[80]

Vouchers are controversial in education policy because they could further weaken a beleaguered public school system and because they could upset delicate balances between the races and between church and state. Vouchers are somewhat less controversial in child care policy because most of the child care sector is already private, because religious instruction is presumed to play a modest role when directed at preschoolers, and because the racial implications of child care have been largely ignored.[81] Child care vouchers still arouse debate, however, because of the fear that they will encourage the use of low-quality informal care (that is, by relatives) and discourage the use of high-quality formal care (that is, at centers).

Do vouchers have such an effect? One strategy for determining the answer might be to look at the choices made by or for parents receiving federal subsidies through different funding streams, including CCDBG. None of the IV-A programs mandates that vouchers be used; the CCDBG program mandates that vouchers be used to some extent. Thus program

TABLE 5-9. Child Care Choices by and for Parents Receiving
Federal Subsidies
Percent

| Program | Relative | Nonrelative, child's home | Family day care home | Group day care center |
|---|---|---|---|---|
| IV-A (JOBS) | 19.5 | 7.3 | 32.0 | 41.2 |
| IV-A (NON-JOBS) | 13.9 | 4.9 | 28.5 | 52.7 |
| CCDBG | 6.6 | 1.2 | 26.6 | 65.6 |

SOURCE: Administration for Children and Families, U.S. Department of Health and Human Services. The percentages are averages, with the state as the unit of analysis. The JOBS figures are for fiscal year 1992; the NON-JOBS figures are for the first quarter of calendar year 1992; the CCDBG figures are for fiscal year 1992. The CCDBG figures were obtained through a Freedom of Information Act request.

comparisons might offer some clues as to the mix of child care arrangements that results when parents are free to pursue their own preferences. As table 5-9 indicates, CCDBG parents choose centers (formal care) more often than other parents, and IV-A parents choose relatives (informal care) more often than other parents.

These figures, however, cannot really be used to gauge the effects of vouchers. The CCDBG program is not a pure voucher program. Contracts are also used. Also, the IV-A programs often include voucher components. Indeed, many states have gone to great lengths to employ identical service delivery mechanisms for their various child care programs. Finally, child care arrangements under the different programs probably reflect clientele characteristics more than program characteristics. For example, IV-A JOBS clients, many of whom take classes only three days a week, often need only part-time care, and many centers spurn part-timers. Moreover, parents who participate in JOBS part-time may be better able to prevail upon relatives to spend fifteen to twenty hours a week with their children than full-time workers ever could. Thus the child care arrangements selected by or for parents under the different funding streams do not really enable us to pinpoint the impact of vouchers.

A more promising strategy is to look at CCDBG choices exclusively, just before and just after vouchers became mandatory. As of October 1, 1992 (the beginning of fiscal year 1993), states were required to have voucher systems in place. Thus a comparison of enrollment patterns in fiscal year 1992 and fiscal year 1993 gives us some sense of whether the new voucher requirement had an impact on the kinds of child care choices made. To ensure a fair comparison, I have examined only those

TABLE 5-10. CCDBG Spending Patterns Before and After Vouchers
Became Mandatory, Fiscal Years 1992 and 1993
Percent
(N = 38)

| Fiscal year | Relative | Nonrelative, child's home | Family day care home | Group day care center |
|---|---|---|---|---|
| 1992 | 6.9 | 1.3 | 25.0 | 66.8 |
| 1993 | 6.8 | 2.7 | 23.7 | 66.9 |

SOURCE: These figures, which indicate how CCDBG direct services funds were spent, are derived from ACF-700 forms for fiscal year 1992 and fiscal year 1993. The percentages are averages, with the state as the unit of analysis. States were excluded from the analysis if data were available for only one of the two years. The fiscal 1992 data were obtained through a Freedom of Information Act request. The fiscal 1993 data were obtained by contacting the individual states and the District of Columbia.

thirty-eight states for which spending data were available for both fiscal years. As table 5-10 indicates, the percentage of children cared for by nonrelatives in the child's home doubled during this transition period, while the percentage of children cared for by family day care providers declined to accommodate this shift. Of course, it is possible that this is part of a trend away from family day care homes and towards other forms of child care. This should become apparent within two or three years. On the other hand, these figures may also understate the impact of vouchers, because many states were already using vouchers or voucher equivalents in fiscal year 1992.

According to one appraisal of school vouchers, parents are enthusiastic about them, but their effects on children are negligible.[82] There is every reason to believe that parents are also enthusiastic about child care vouchers, which enhance their discretion and which flatter them by assuming that they are capable of making sensible decisions. That assumption, incidentally, is an integral part of recent welfare reforms, which seek to get parents to take charge of their own lives. Yet a lingering question remains: Could vouchers be good for parents but bad for children?

Critics of vouchers might well point to three facts. First, the quality of care provided by relatives is lower than the quality of care provided by regulated or even unregulated family day care homes.[83] And vouchers clearly permit relative care. Even if children are not at risk in these settings, they could do better. Second, center-based care chosen by voucher recipients may not compare favorably with center-based care chosen by other parents. The 75 percent ceiling, widely used for both

IV-A and CCDBG programs, imposes de facto quality constraints on child care purchased with CCDBG funds. And that includes voucher purchases. Third, parental choice does not necessarily mean informed parental choice. If parents receive bad advice or no advice at all, they may select a child care arrangement that matches their untutored preferences but is not best for their child.

While these are not trivial objections, they certainly do not imply that vouchers should be abandoned. The use of relative care is actually quite modest under the CCDBG program. Fears that relative care would be widespread, exposing large numbers of children to care of dubious quality, have not materialized. The use of relative care is more widespread under the IV-A programs, but understandably so. Part-time care, which many IV-A recipients need, is often hard to arrange, and relatives perform a useful service by helping out under such circumstances. Financial constraints apply to vouchers and contracts alike. If federal reimbursement rates are set too low to permit the purchase of high-quality care through vouchers, these same limitations apply to contract purchases. The key would seem to be to allow states greater discretion in their rates, not to abolish vouchers. And parents do indeed suffer from an information gap, and perhaps state officials could do better, through a contract system. But state officials are partly responsible for the information gap, as the next chapter reveals. If certain informal norms were to change, and the child care infrastructure were to improve, the negative features of vouchers would greatly diminish or disappear. The positive features—discretion, flexibility, and competition—would remain.

## Seamlessness

A common problem in social policy is that diverse programs, created at different points in time and administered by different personnel, are difficult to coordinate. Instead of a "seamless" garment, with one fabric gracefully joining another, government tailors often produce an unsightly patchwork, with protruding seams attesting to the awkwardness of the stitching. That, in fact, is an apt characterization of our nation's child care programs. A wide variety of programs, rooted in varied political intentions and perceptions, contain different eligibility rules for parents, different payment expectations for parents, different regulatory requirements for providers, and different reimbursement rates for providers. This confuses parents and limits their options. It also frustrates providers and discourages them from caring for subsidized children.

Rules adopted by the U.S. Department of Health and Human Services in 1992 exacerbated these problems. Its rules for IV-A programs prohibited states from using federal funds to reimburse providers at rates higher than those charged by 75 percent of providers in the local market (even though the CCDBG program allowed this). Its rules for the IV-A Transitional Child Care program required even poor parents to contribute a portion of their child care fees (although the CCDBG program, aimed at similar parents, did not). Its rules for the CCDBG program prohibited states from reimbursing licensed family day care providers at significantly higher rates than unlicensed family day care providers (even though the IV-A programs allowed this). These restrictions made seamless services more difficult to achieve.

A rule recently proposed by HHS would reverse many of these policies.[84] Among other changes, HHS would allow states to reimburse licensed providers within a generic category (such as family day care homes) at significantly higher rates; allow states to exceed the 75 percent of market rate ceiling on federal financial participation; and allow states to waive the Transitional Child Care fee requirement for an impoverished family. The general rule of thumb is that HHS now seeks to eliminate any federal restrictions that make it difficult for states to improve child care quality across the board. When seamless services, quality, and federalism point in the same direction, HHS now supports state discretion.[85] Such steps should promote vertical coordination (across governments) and horizontal coordination (across federal programs) as well.

Despite the progress, much remains to be done if the goal of seamless services is to be attained. In several states, IV-A programs and the CCDBG program are administered by different departments, which presents obvious barriers to coordination.[86] These barriers can be overcome through interagency agreements, interagency task forces, and similar devices. But such linkage mechanisms require considerable patience, dedication, and good will, commodities that are sometimes in short supply.

Even if the same department is responsible for all major child care programs, and even if federal restrictions are relaxed, coordination can be problematic. Separate divisions within the same department often represent different political cultures. One, for example, may stress child care quality, while the other stresses parental self-reliance. Reconciling these cultures is challenging. Integrating data bases, funding streams, and standard operating procedures is also challenging. As an Indiana official puts it, "Even being in the same building and in the same division, we still have coordination problems!"[87]

Programs that require outreach to numerous organizations and constituencies face special implementation difficulties. JOBS, which attempts to integrate employment, education, welfare, and child care, is one such program. According to a GAO study, state welfare agencies have been much more assiduous in reaching out to job training and employment agencies than they have been in reaching out to the child care community.[88] Child care, regarded as an ancillary service, seems to have fallen through the cracks. But the problem is deeper than that. According to Jennings, little progress has been made in developing one-stop eligibility offices for JOBS clients, in sharing electronic data, in developing common application forms, or in achieving integrated case management.[89] Efforts at coordination have been both narrow and superficial.

In short, coordination across federal programs is a necessary but not a sufficient condition for seamless services. It is equally important that there be coordination between child care and welfare agencies, between child care and schools, between child care and health organizations, between child care and the wider society.

## Conclusion

If one considers the evolution of child care policies over the past decade, several developments stand out. There has been a trend towards tougher regulations, especially at the state level, where most of the regulations are formulated and implemented. There has been a trend towards more spending, especially at the federal level, where most of the spending has originated. There has also been a trend towards the use of vouchers in disbursing child care funds. Vouchers have proven contagious and have spread quickly to programs where they were not literally required, such as the IV-A programs.

Despite all of this movement, dissatisfaction with the child care system remains intense and widespread. It is also justifiable. Regulations have gotten tougher, but enforcement remains weak and largely ineffectual. Seamless services have received some attention at the federal and state levels, but most efforts have focused on removing obvious inconsistencies in child care program requirements, as opposed to building bridges with health, education, and welfare programs. Parents have greater choice, but they are handicapped by inadequate information and advice. Although governments have intervened on many fronts, much more remains to be done.

Perhaps the problem is that we have often selected the wrong tool for the task at hand. Or perhaps we have forgotten that one tool is not always enough. Regulatory and spending programs, for example, must be considered simultaneously. We have seen how easy it is for well-intentioned regulatory reforms to scare family day care providers underground or out of business. We have also seen, in Houston, how a timely subsidy helped to cushion the family day care community against the shock of new regulations. Although new rules dampened the supply of family day care homes, prior community interventions created a more forgiving system by expanding supply. By combining policy instruments, we can package carrots and sticks creatively so that we encourage quality without reducing availability.

It is also essential to draw distinctions between good and bad providers. Vermont and Texas have used such distinctions to determine the frequency of inspections. Other states have applied the same principle, with modifications, to the length of inspections. Additional possibilities would be to use such distinctions to determine eligibility for subsidies. A center with a poor track record, for example, might be deemed ineligible for funding under the Social Services Block Grant or the Child Care and Development Block Grant. Some providers would object to this, and statutory revisions would probably be necessary. But such a policy would enhance the ability of regulators to encourage compliance and discourage noncompliance.

Finally, it is important to look beyond the child care community and child care programs, narrowly defined, as we seek to promote comprehensive, seamless services. A holistic perspective involves more than the reconciliation of federal child care programs enacted at different points in time. A holistic perspective requires us to recognize that some market failures cannot be corrected by government intervention alone. When government initiatives fail to promote efficiency, justice, and choice, then it is time to consider societal initiatives that harness the creative energies of schools, corporations, hospitals, and families. That is the subject of chapter 6.

# 6

# Do-Gooders,
# Go-Getters, and
# Go-Betweens

SOCIETY'S ROLE IN addressing child care problems can be described in two ways. First, it might be
said that society establishes a foundation (shaky or firm) upon which the
child care industry and various governments must build. From this vantage point, society is the primary force that determines the extent of our
reliance on child care markets and government interventions to correct
these market failures.

Second, however, it might be said that society fills the gaps left by
inadequate markets and inadequate policies. From this vantage point,
society steps in when other actors have failed. Thus societal institutions
may be viewed as "fixers" whose timely interventions save us from the
market's inability to ensure quality and the government's inability to
ensure economy.

If these perspectives seem diametrically opposed, that is only because
society—a code word for numerous important institutions—is such a
gross category. If one disaggregates societal institutions, one begins to see
how society matters at the beginning and at the end of a long chain of
events. The family, for example, has struggled and evolved through
turbulent times, creating a need for child care markets and for government interventions to correct market failures. These markets and policies

133

have in turn developed in suboptimal ways, generating some interest in schools, churches, and businesses as supportive institutions with the capacity to help forge family-friendly child care arrangements.

This inelegant sequence is not the only one imaginable. In western Germany, for example, it is a well-established principle that churches shall have the first opportunity to establish day care centers (or *Kindergärten*, in German parlance). Only if they decline to do so does the government provide such services. This is a tangible way of saying that society (or, specifically, the religious part of society) shall come first and that government shall come second. On the other hand, well-established government subsidies for the churches make religious initiatives to establish day care centers possible in the first place. Thus even in Germany, it is difficult to say with certainty that society does indeed come first.

Whatever the timing of societal interventions, they are desperately needed in the United States. Budget deficits, a growing underclass, an aging population, rapidly decaying roads and bridges, a threatened environment, and substantial international responsibilities make it difficult for governments to give child care the attention it deserves. A large for-profit sector (for center-based care), a large underground sector (for family day care), poorly trained and poorly paid providers, frazzled parents, and dramatic changes in the work force severely tax self-correcting market forces. Thus intermediary institutions should be encouraged to provide child care, to improve child care, to subsidize child care, or to further develop the child care infrastructure. Such institutions might include schools, churches, hospitals, and other businesses, whether nonprofit or for-profit.

## Schools

The public school is a classic symbol of community. It represents some citizens' noblest aspirations and most cherished dreams. It also epitomizes some deep frustrations. Through public schools, children from different races, creeds, and incomes come together in a setting that should stimulate them, protect them, and help them grow intellectually, socially, and emotionally. With such a vision as a starting point, it is galling to observe widespread boredom, massive discipline problems, and personal failure in many public schools.

Because public schools have often failed to fulfill their basic missions, it may not make sense to encourage them to take on additional tasks, such as immunizing young children, counseling troubled teenagers, or offering school-age child care programs. One argument for doing so, however, is that these activities, if successful, can strengthen the schools' ability to educate and nurture young children. Instead of detracting from education, they can enhance it. In addition, public schools possess valuable expertise that enables them, in principle, to offer better programs than those offered elsewhere. The same can be said of private schools, which currently serve about one-eighth of the school-age population. Much depends, however, on how programs are designed and how they are integrated into school administration.

Elementary schools, whether public or private, are unusually well suited to provide child care services on site or to arrange for their provision. They are already in the business of caring for young children. They are familiar, accessible, and trustworthy. They possess playgrounds, gymnasia, libraries, and cafeterias. They are highly visible and likely to remain in business for a long time. They are also exceptionally convenient, particularly to parents with two or more young children. The presence of a sibling nearby may be reassuring to younger children, and the presence of numerous adults bustling about may be reassuring to parents. The use of school space for child care offers a range of benefits to parents, children, and society as a whole.

## School-Age Child Care

The case for locating school-age child care (SACC) programs at elementary schools is especially strong. When classes end, huge amounts of indoor and outdoor space suddenly become available. By allowing children to remain behind for another two or three hours, SACC programs at elementary schools eliminate the need for parental transportation from the school to a different child care site. This is both convenient for busy parents and less disruptive to children. Moreover, young children may find it comforting to remain in a familiar environment, surrounded by children they already know. In principle, these same advantages also apply to middle schools and high schools. But demand for SACC programs declines precipitously after fifth grade.[1] Thus elementary schools are most directly relevant to school-age child care.

Because they can take advantage of a preexisting physical plant, SACC programs located at elementary schools ought to be able to offer higher wages, lower fees, or both. After all, they probably pay little or nothing for space and utilities. They may also be able to use custodial services already provided to the school. If so, their operating costs should be substantially reduced.

What, exactly, does the evidence suggest? According to a nationwide study, SACC programs offered by public sponsors (mainly public schools) do indeed pay higher wages to employees.[2] Staff turnover is therefore somewhat lower.[3] Staff education is also somewhat better.[4] On the other hand, child/ staff ratios are somewhat higher at publicly sponsored SACC programs.[5] This may be because such programs are unusually attractive to parents.

Public schools—and other public sponsors—are able to keep wages relatively high and turnover relatively low in part because they have lower expenses for rent, utilities, and insurance.[6] They do not, however, charge particularly low fees. Rather, their fees fall somewhere between those charged by for-profits (the highest fees overall) and nonprofits (the lowest fees overall). Thus public schools seem to have appealed to consumers by offering a higher-quality product rather than a cheaper product.

Nationwide, approximately 18 percent of all SACC programs are sponsored by public schools.[7] In contrast, approximately 28 percent of all SACC programs are located in public schools.[8] Naturally, the question arises: if SACC programs are to be available at public schools, should they be managed by the public schools themselves or by outside contractors?

There is no compelling reason why public schools should provide the services themselves. The key benefit to parents and children is that the services are available *at* the public school, not that the services are provided *by* the public school. When public agencies know what they are shopping for, know which suppliers are capable of meeting their needs, and know how to judge performance, they may appropriately purchase services from an outside contractor.[9] School-age child care bears a close enough resemblance to elementary education that "smart buying" would seem eminently possible. Also, if something goes wrong, public schools can always select a different contractor or provide the services themselves.

On the other hand, there is no compelling reason why public schools should not provide the services themselves, either temporarily or over a long period of time, if they wish to do so. Such an arrangement may result in liability insurance savings, if the school's existing coverage applies to activities that take place after regular school hours. Direct provision also gives schools greater control over service delivery, which some principals crave. Finally, direct provision may be desirable if available contractors lack a strong commitment to quality.

*Troubleshooting.* Establishing—and sustaining—a school-based SACC program, however, is seldom a trouble-free experience, regardless of whether contracting occurs. Principals sometimes object to increased paperwork, administrative headaches, and new legal responsibilities. Teachers get angry and upset if their classrooms are in disarray when they return to school in the morning. Janitors resent substantial increases in their workload or altered working hours to accommodate SACC programs. Such problems have discouraged some public school districts from launching or expanding SACC initiatives.

Although these ticking time bombs are indeed worrisome, creative troubleshooters have found ways to defuse them. In Mt. Lebanon, Pennsylvania, the school district's child care coordinator developed written rules of conduct acceptable to the custodial staff. In Denver, Colorado, a SACC program director uses classrooms with the friendliest teachers and avoids messy activities inside those classrooms. Other Denver SACC program directors eschew classrooms altogether. In Raleigh, North Carolina, SACC program directors take pictures of classrooms and multimedia centers in a pristine (pre-SACC) condition so that SACC teachers will have no difficulty restoring the status quo.

The most successful SACC programs are managed not by principals but by a district coordinator, who assumes responsibility for hiring, firing, and other personnel decisions. The SACC program budget is separate from the school budget. Inquiries and complaints are directed to the coordinator, and parental fees are determined by the coordinator or by the school board. Even if public schools run SACC programs themselves, there is no need for principals to assume any new responsibilities.

In short, schools—both public and private—can play a vital role in addressing a critical child care need by providing or arranging for on-site school-age child care. If schools do not meet this challenge, many thousands of children will continue to care for themselves, with all the dangers that entails. As Zigler and Lang explain, latchkey children pose risks to themselves and to their community.[10] They may feel resentment and alienation as a result of their isolation; they may be more susceptible to crimes and accidents than are other children; they may adapt poorly in school and in society; and they may engage in acts of deliquency or vandalism because they are unsupervised. Well-managed SACC programs help prevent these problems.

*Variations in Availability.* Despite the need for school-age child care, many communities lack it. The availability of SACC programs varies

138     DO-GOODERS, GO-GETTERS, AND GO-BETWEENS

TABLE 6-1.  Availability of SACC Programs in Public Schools by
State: Multiple Regression Analysis

| Independent variable | Unstandardized $B^a$ |
|---|---|
| Female employment | 0.181 |
| | (0.403) |
| Per capita spending, elementary and secondary education | 1.616 |
| | (1.652) |
| Percent of school-age children attending Catholic schools | 0.074* |
| | (0.030) |
| Number of school-age children | 0.003 |
| | (0.002) |
| State legislature passed significant SACC law | 27.443** |
| | (6.419) |
| State human services agency regulates SACC programs | −4.322 |
| | (3.749) |
| Constant = −4.076 | |
| Adjusted $R^2$ = .34 | |
| N = 51 | |

a. Standard errors are in parentheses.
*Significant at the .05 level.
**Significant at the .001 level.

sharply from community to community and from state to state (even
more sharply than preschool programs). In a recent report, the U.S.
Department of Education revealed that students attending public schools
in Florida, Hawaii, Kentucky, and North Carolina are much more likely
to have access to an after-school program at their school than students
attending public schools in Idaho, North Dakota, South Dakota, or West
Virginia.[11] The range is extraordinary—from a low of 5.5 percent in
North Dakota to a high of 69.3 percent in Hawaii.

What variables help to explain these sharp differences in the availability of school-age child care? In table 6-1, I report the results of a multiple
regression analysis, in which the percentage of students attending public
schools with extended day programs is the dependent variable.[12] Independent variables include: female employment, per capita spending on elementary and secondary education, the number of school-age children in
the state, the percentage of school-age children in Catholic schools, the
passage of significant school-age child care legislation by the state legislature, and direct state regulation of school-age child care programs run by
public schools.[13]

As table 6-1 reveals, the single best predictor of SACC program
availability at public schools is the passage of strong school-age child care

legislation by the state legislature. Only three states (Indiana, Kentucky, and Hawaii) had passed such legislation by the end of 1990; two of the three states (Kentucky and Hawaii) were far above average in school-age child care availability.[14]

Also important is the extent to which children have enrolled in Catholic schools.[15] Catholic schools are nearly twice as likely to sponsor school-age child care programs as public schools.[16] In states where Catholic schools have made significant inroads, public schools respond by offering more school-age child care programs as an inducement to prospective students. Competition between the public and private sectors encourages the provision of school-age child care at public schools.

Other policy-relevant variables have much more limited effects. Although there is a positive relationship between per capita state spending on elementary and secondary education and the availability of school-age child care, that relationship is not statistically significant at an acceptable level. The relationship between state child care spending and school-age child care availability is weaker still.[17] Nor does state regulation by the human services agency discourage the provision of school-age child care. Although there is a negative relationship between such regulation and the availability of school-age child care in public schools, it is not statistically significant either.

Demographic variables also turn out to be relatively unimportant. As expected, female employment is positively related to the provision of school-age child care at public schools, but the relationship is quite weak, perhaps because female employment levels do not vary much by state. The relationship between the number of children and the provision of school-age child care, also positive, is stronger but not quite statistically significant at an acceptable level.[18]

Overall, these findings suggest that states can improve access to school-age child care by enacting strong legislation, as Indiana, Kentucky, and Hawaii have done. Regardless of what states choose to do, however, public schools react sharply and positively to competition from the private sector. If private schools offer school-age child care programs, public schools will often follow suit.

Of course, these findings say nothing about the quality of school-age child care in public schools, in private schools, or in other settings. When a state mandates school-sponsored school-age child care programs in every public school district, as Indiana has, quality may suffer, especially when school districts have little time to comply. The Kentucky approach, in which schools compete for state funds to establish SACC programs, is more likely to ensure that participating schools will be both motivated enough and competent enough to guarantee quality.

## Other Schools, Other Challenges

Although I have focused on elementary schools and SACC programs, other schools have considerable potential to satisfy our child care needs in other ways. As discussed in chapter 5, many community colleges now offer courses in child care, leading to an associate's degree in early childhood education. It is particularly important that such courses be offered in the evenings, so that child care workers from family day care homes and small centers can take advantage of them.

Four-year colleges and universities can also contribute by developing "articulation agreements" with community colleges so that course credits obtained at a community college count toward a bachelor's degree at the four-year college or university. The University of North Carolina at Greensboro, for example, has such an agreement with Guilford County Community College, and Central Washington University has developed a collaborative degree program with Yakima Valley Community College and Heritage College. Under the latter arrangement, students pursue an associate's degree through the community college and then take upper-division courses from Heritage College and Central Washington University culminating in a bachelor's degree in early childhood education. For the sake of convenience, all of the courses are offered on the community college campus. Tuition discounts help to keep the program affordable.

Colleges and universities can also guarantee on-site child care, discounts for child care purchased elsewhere, generous maternity leave and sick leave policies, flextime for employees, and other family-friendly opportunities. They can establish and support model centers or preschool laboratories for scholarly research. With a little imagination and effort, they too can help to meet the need for better child care and a better understanding of child care's effects on children.

## Churches

Like schools, churches are vital community institutions with the capacity to transform isolated profit-maximizers into members of a common enterprise. Historically, churches have played a major role in delivering a wide range of social services, such as foster homes, soup kitchens, hospices, halfway houses, community health clinics, child care facilities, shelters for battered women, hospitals, and nursing homes.

Because church basements and recreation halls are often vacant on weekdays, it is possible for many churches to offer full-time child care without infringing upon other church activities. The use of such space for child care is good for the church if it raises money or generates parental support for the congregation, good for parents and children if it enables the church to offer care of a higher quality or at a lower price. But when a church is not just a landlord but a provider of child care, some delicate issues arise.

## Funding Dilemmas

The First Amendment to the U.S. Constitution guarantees a separation of church and state that precludes some forms of government funding for church-sponsored activities. Nevertheless, federal courts have held that some forms of government support are constitutionally permissible. For example, the U.S. Supreme Court has approved loans of secular textbooks to children enrolled in parochial schools, reimbursements for administering state-prepared tests, funding for interpreters for deaf students, and funding for busing to and from parochial schools.[19] Tax credits for educational activities sponsored by churches have also occasionally won approval from federal courts, provided that they have a secular purpose and that they are available for both public and private educational expenses.

When designing the Child Care and Development Block Grant program, Congress took these precedents into account and adopted criteria that sought to maximize parental choice without running afoul of the First Amendment. Under this program, vouchers—but not grants—may be used to purchase child care services that include religious worship among other activities. Grants may be used to assist only church-run day care programs that do not include religious worship. The basic premise is that as the religious mission intensifies, the justification for direct government support diminishes.

This arrangement has worked reasonably well and has enabled church-run centers to benefit from new federal aid programs. If church-run centers had been ineligible for federal financial support, some of these programs would have lost vital political support. Also, for-profit centers might have grown at the expense of church-run centers. Given the findings reported in chapter 4, that would have been unfortunate for children, because church-run centers are generally better than for-profit centers. On the other hand, government funding of church-run day care centers presents some difficult public policy dilemmas when those centers are exempt or partially exempt from regulations that apply to purely secular centers.

## Regulatory Dilemmas

In most states, church-run day care centers are subject to the same rules and regulations as other centers. These rules include child/staff ratios, training requirements, health and safety practices, and other requirements. Although many church leaders are comfortable with these requirements, some have contested the applicability of child care regulations to church-run centers. Some Christian ministers object to particular rules, such as corporal punishment bans, which are said to violate religious tenets. Others object to the presence of any government regulation, arguing that to accept government licensing is to imply that the state, and not Christ, is head of their church.

Numerous court cases have made it abundantly clear that states are free to apply the full set of regulations to secular and religious centers alike. For example, a federal appeals court upheld the constitutionality of California's Child Care Facilities Act, which applied child/staff ratios and a corporal punishment ban to both secular and religious centers.[20] Similarly, courts in Kansas, New Mexico, and Michigan have rejected arguments by Baptist churches that their centers should be exempt from state regulation.[21] Esbeck summarizes the case law to date: "The courts have for the most part sustained the licensure of social service ministries pursuant to state police power. . . . In the few cases where religious organizations have successfully challenged state regulation, it has been because regulations are found void for vagueness and thus violative of procedural due process rights."[22]

These court rulings are particularly important because some states roll over and play dead when church-run centers balk at being licensed. In Pennsylvania, for example, dozens of church-run centers, usually under Roman Catholic auspices, remain unlicensed, despite the state's official position that they are supposed to be licensed. The Pennsylvania Catholic

Conference has objected to licensing of church-run centers, and the state's attorneys have refused to challenge that view in court.[23] Thus when state inspectors encounter a recalcitrant director, they are told by supervisors to "back off."[24] Given the pertinent case law, this timidity would seem unwarranted. Although a fierce legal battle might result from an enforcement crackdown, Pennsylvania, like other states, is on firm legal ground in asserting that it has the authority under its police power to apply licensing requirements to church-run facilities, provided that the requirements are not unduly vague.

On the other hand, the U.S. Constitution permits states to grant full or partial exemptions to church-run facilities if they wish to do so. The definitive ruling on this issue comes from the U.S. Supreme Court, which held that a legislative body can, consistent with the Establishment Clause of the First Amendment, exempt a religious organization from regulatory burdens shared by secular organizations otherwise similarly situated.[25] Subsequent federal court rulings have built on that decision.[26]

Of course, states must adhere not only to the U.S. Constitution but also to their respective state constitutions. And state court interpretations of state constitutional rights sometimes differ from federal court interpretations of identical language in the U.S. Constitution. Nonetheless, state courts have generally upheld state exemptions for church-run social service programs.[27]

Thus the question is not whether states have the right to apply all regulations to church-run day care centers (they do), or whether they have the right to exempt church-run day care centers (they do), but whether it is wise to do so. Answering that question requires shifting from legal arguments to policy arguments. Policy analysts might ask, What are the consequences for young children?

First of all, a key role of government regulation is to guarantee the health and safety of children. Measures requiring child immunizations, securely anchored playground equipment, well-balanced meals, and proper storage of cleansers do not interfere with anyone's religious freedom. At the same time, they protect children from long-term and short-term hazards. They also provide a reality check to center directors who may think they are providing adequate care but who are actually putting children in harm's way through carelessness or negligence.

Also, regulations requiring staff members to receive training or education in child care or early childhood education are neither intrusive nor unreasonable. In principle, they actually reduce the need for government monitoring and supervision. Such regulations in the American states are quite modest, especially compared with those in other industrialized countries. Also, they do not prevent churches from emphasizing religious training and education. They constitute a floor, not a ceiling. If a Catholic center believes that a teacher should know CPR, first aid, and the Baltimore catechism, that is still its prerogative.

Another fact is that exemptions and partial exemptions may undermine the quality of care offered by church-run centers. In other policy arenas, where church-run facilities are fully regulated, church-run facilities are often superior to other nonprofits. That is true, for example, of church-run nursing homes.[28] As chapter 4 showed, however, that is not true of child care. Indeed, the quality of care offered by church-run centers is not quite as good as that offered by nonprofits with other sponsors (state and local government agencies, community agencies, private schools, social service agencies, employers).[29] For example, church-run centers have a higher percentage of poorly educated staff members than any other type of nonprofit facility.[30] This may be due to the exemptions discussed above.

Exemptions and partial exemptions also limit opportunities for church-run centers to receive federal and state subsidies. For example, unlicensed facilities are ineligible to participate in the Child and Adult Care Food Program, which reduces center costs and improves the diet of center children. And partially exempt centers are sometimes ineligible for reimbursement rates that fully regulated centers may enjoy. Church-based facilities in North Carolina need not meet the same staff education, training, and curriculum requirements as other facilities, if that is their wish.[31] However, several North Carolina counties, funded by the state Smart Start program, reimburse centers with more-qualified staff members at higher rates.[32] By opting for partial exemption, church-based centers in these counties effectively limit their reimbursement opportunities.

Church-run centers are actually less likely than other centers to care for disadvantaged children. They are much less likely than secular nonprofits to care for children whose parents receive public assistance, and they are even less likely than for-profits to care for such children.[33] Somewhere along the way, churches seem to have lost sight of their obligation to serve the less fortunate members of their community. Exemptions and partial exemptions send precisely the wrong signal to such churches. Instead of encouraging churches to distance themselves from the wider society, the state should encourage them to reach out to society's most vulnerable citizens.

## The Business Community

Unlike schools and churches, manufacturers and retailers are not in business to do good deeds and serve the community. They are in business to make money. The proverbial bottom line encourages them to maximize profits, in the long run or in the short run. To expect companies to behave altruistically is naive. To encourage them to think strategically about connections between child care and traditional business goals is, however, both appropriate and realistic.

Some large corporations, such as IBM and Johnson & Johnson, have been aggressive and imaginative in devising strategies to improve child care for their employees and the community at large. But most companies have taken baby steps, if any. As a result, few parents get significant child care support from their employer. For example, in 1990 only 10 percent of parents report that on-site child care is available at their place of work or their spouse's place of work, and only 8 percent report having access to a flexible spending account, which allows employees to use pretax dollars to purchase child care.[34]

In thinking about family-friendly policies that businesses might adopt, Galinsky draws a useful distinction between *family support* and *work support* policies.[35] Family support policies, which enable the employee to spend more time at home, include such options as flextime, part-time work, work at home, and parental leave. Work support policies, which enable the employee to be at work without distraction from family responsibilities, include such options as on-site child care, resource and referral services, and dependent care assistance plans (or flexible spending accounts). According to Galinsky, companies have embraced family support policies much more enthusiastically than work support policies. Perhaps that is because work support policies usually carry a higher price tag.

## Family Support Policies

For many companies, family support policies have been easier to justify than other family-friendly strategies. For example, among firms with ten or more employees, 61 percent offer flextime, 43 percent offer part-time work, and 16 percent offer work at home as employee op-tions.[36] A number of firms also offer parental leave opportunities, some-times even with pay for a few weeks. Approximately half of all working mothers took a leave of absence from work after the birth of their youngest child, and 28 percent of this group report that their leave was paid.[37]

These policies have been relatively attractive to many firms because they share two characteristics: They make employees happier (and per-haps more productive as a result); and they are usually not very costly to establish or administer (and thus no threat to the bottom line). Flextime, for example, simply juggles employee work hours. In most instances, this works no hardship whatever on employers or supervisors.

Although family support policies are worthwhile and important, they suffer from several serious drawbacks. They are not very generous com-pared with such policies in other countries. Unpaid parental leave seems a remarkably minor concession when one recognizes that paid parental leave for a year or more is the norm in other industrialized countries, such as France, Sweden, and Germany. To offer maternity leave (or paternity leave) without the financial wherewithal to take advantage of it creates the illusion of corporate sensitivity but does not provide meaningful relief to families struggling to make ends meet. And even unpaid parental leave is not universally available in the United States, despite the passage of federal parental leave legislation in 1993.[38]

Also, the ability of employees to take advantage of family support policies depends not only on financial resources but also on supportive managers. Unfortunately, enlightened policies do not guarantee enlight-ened managers. For example, an electrical engineer at Wisconsin Electric Power Company was delighted to read in her company magazine about flexible schedules and work-at-home options. When she asked for part-time work or work at home to care for her ailing child, her supervisor refused.[39] Similarly, U S West employees have encountered managers whose indifference to work-family dilemmas belied public relations puffery about a family-friendly workplace.[40] Even at Johnson & Johnson, a remarkably pro-family company, managers were less than enthusiastic about allowing employees to take advantage of family support options until a supervisor training program resulted in a more family-friendly culture.[41]

Further, family-friendly benefits are least available to those who need them the most. Studies show that persons with lower incomes are less likely to work at companies which offer such benefits.[42] And within a given company, persons with lower salaries have less bargaining power to demand such options without jeopardizing their job, or future pay hikes, or promotion opportunities. At Chevron, for example, blue-collar workers do not enjoy the same family support privileges available to white-collar employees.[43]

Even at the more sensitive companies, family support policies look better on paper than in practice. Work support policies, though less common, do not suffer from false advertising to the same degree. If a firm offers a dependent care assistance plan, for example, there is no incentive, financial or otherwise, to withhold that plan from employees. The problem with many work support policies is not that they are shams but that they are not offered in the first place. On-site child care is a classic example.

## On-Site Child Care

The overwhelming majority of firms do not provide on-site child care. Even large companies with large numbers of female employees usually decide not to do so. A substantial minority of hospitals, however, have established on-site centers to help them recruit and retain nurses and other essential personnel. The case for on-site child care is particularly compelling at hospitals, because hospital personnel must give patients their undivided attention. A family emergency across town could present excruciating difficulties if a work emergency were also in progress. Shift work at hospitals poses additional logistical problems that help to justify on-site child care. According to a 1992 survey by Deloitte and Touche, 21 percent of all hospitals provide on-site child care to their employees.[44]

Among hospitals, nonprofits are more likely than for-profits to offer on-site child care. Once again, it appears that nonprofits repay society for generous tax exemptions by plowing benefits back into the community in the form of child care centers. Religious nonprofits are especially likely to offer on-site child care (see table 6-2). This could reflect altruistic impulses or it could reflect sharply honed competitive sensibilities. Religious hospitals, like religious schools, may believe that family-friendly services enhance their market appeal.

Does an on-site child care center aid a hospital in its efforts to recruit and retain employees? Two separate surveys on hospital employee benefits and personnel experiences permit tentative answers to these questions.

TABLE 6-2. On-Site Day Care Center by Hospital Type

Percent

| Sponsorship | Hospitals with on-site center |
|---|---|
| Government | 9.8 |
| Nonprofit, secular | 24.1 |
| Nonprofit, religious | 37.0 |
| For-profit | 5.3 |
| | |
| Chi square = 68.96 | |
| $p < .00001$ | |
| $N = 1,160$ | |

SOURCE: Deloitte & Touche, "Hospital Human Resource Survey" (Chicago, 1992).

The first, Deloitte & Touche's 1992 survey, included a question on nurse recruitment.[45] The second, conducted by the Springhouse Corporation in January 1993, included a question on nurse turnover.[46] Both surveys asked about various employee benefits, including on-site child care.

The Deloitte and Touche survey suggests that on-site child care is a magnet to potential recruits (see table 6-3). Of hospitals with on-site child care, 67.4 percent say recruiting nurses has been less difficult over the past two years. Of hospitals without on-site child care, 51.3 percent say recruiting nurses has been less difficult over the past two years. This difference is statistically significant at the .001 level.

Of course, if employee benefits cluster together, these results could disguise the effects of some other benefit with which on-site child care is closely associated. To test that proposition, I included several family-friendly benefits from the Deloitte and Touche survey in a multivariate model: flextime, flexible hours, parental leave, a dependent care account, and on-site child care.[47] I also included several other variables in the model: the number of hospital employees (in terms of FTEs); the state's child/staff ratio ceiling (for three-year-olds); and the change in the state's unemployment rate (from 1990 to 1992).[48]

As table 6-4 indicates, four of the five family-friendly benefit coefficients are in the expected direction. Although none of the effects is strong, the on-site child care variable comes very close to being statistically significant at the widely accepted .05 level. Hospitals find it easier to recruit nurses if they have larger work forces (greater visibility may enhance recruitment; economies of scale may permit higher wages), and if the unemployment rate is worsening. More lenient child/staff ratio requirements make it more difficult to recruit nurses, however, even though they reduce child care costs.[49]

TABLE 6-3. Ease of Recruiting Nurses by Presence of On-Site
Child Care Center[a]

Percent

| Difficulty level | Without on-site center | With on-site center |
|---|---|---|
| Much more difficult | 8.8 | 3.7 |
| Slightly more difficult | 14.6 | 12.4 |
| Equally difficult | 25.3 | 16.5 |
| Slightly less difficult | 38.8 | 50.0 |
| Much less difficult | 12.5 | 17.4 |

Chi square = 22.4
$p < .001$
$N = 1,154$

SOURCE: Deloitte & Touche, "Hospital Human Resource Survey."
a. Hospital managers were asked whether recruiting nurses is more or less difficult than two years earlier.

In short, family-friendly benefits for employees result in benefits for employers as well. Hospitals that make a stronger effort to meet the needs of employees with young children report that it is easier to recruit nurses. On-site child care seems to be the most formidable of the family-friendly benefits available to hospitals. Its effects on recruitment are marginally greater than those of other variables.

Retention, however, is another matter. Although the Springhouse survey included several questions on employee turnover (including one on nurse turnover), the relationship between employee benefits and employee turnover may be reciprocal. If hospitals with serious turnover problems upgrade their benefits (including a child care center) as a response, then recursive models (which imply no feedback loop) are insufficient for analysis. This suggests the advisability of two-stage least squares as an estimating technique.[50]

An examination of simple correlation coefficients reveals two variables that influence turnover without influencing the decision to establish a child care center. The minimum wage offered RNs has a negative impact on turnover (companies that pay more to nurses are less likely to see them leave). Similarly, companies that offer relocation expenses to nurses experience lower turnover. Clearly, direct cash payments make a difference. Because neither of these variables has an impact on the establishment of a child care center, they can both serve as instrumental variables in a turnover equation.

It is more difficult to identify variables that influence the decision to provide a child care center but do not influence turnover. Ultimately, I

TABLE 6-4. Factors Affecting Ease of Recruitment of Nurses:
Multiple Regression Analysis

| Independent variable | Unstandardized $B^a$ |
|---|---|
| Number of employees | 2.219E-04**** |
| | (4.134E-05) |
| Child/staff ratio ceiling (3-year-olds) | –.035** |
| | (.015) |
| Change in unemployment rate (1992–90) | .111*** |
| | (.034) |
| Flextime | –.041 |
| | (.074) |
| Flexible hours | .100 |
| | (.073) |
| On-site child care | .169* |
| | (.091) |
| Parental leave | .092 |
| | (.076) |
| Dependent care account | .108 |
| | (.074) |
| Constant = 3.287 | |
| $R^2$ = .08 | |
| N = 1,001 | |

a. Standard errors are in parentheses.
*Significant at the .10 level.
**Significant at the .05 level.
***Significant at the .01 level.
****Significant at the .0001 level.

settled upon the provision of dental insurance and the provision of a pharmacy discount to employees. Each of these variables is related (positively) to the provision of a child care center; neither is related to turnover. My assumption is that these employee benefit decisions were made prior to the decision to establish (or not to establish) a child care center. If so, one can argue that they capture a hospital's predisposition to provide (or not to provide) generous employee benefits.

The results of the two-stage least squares analysis are reported in tables A-3 and A-4 of the appendix. They confirm that higher wages and relocation expenses reduce turnover. Both relationships are statistically significant at acceptable levels. In contrast, a child care center variable purged of the reciprocal influence of turnover has no impact on turnover itself.[51]

The recruitment and retention findings should be viewed with caution. The dependent variable in the recruitment analysis is a perceptual measure and not a behavioral indicator. Perceptions are sometimes mistaken.

Also, I have treated a five-category ordinal-level variable (ease of nursing recruitment) as if it were an interval-level variable, so that OLS multiple regression analysis might be used. As for the retention analysis, model specification opportunities were limited due to the confidentiality of survey responses (for example, I could not control for local wage rates or unemployment rates, because I did not know the identity of individual hospitals). And this analysis says nothing about employees other than RNs or employee outcomes other than turnover.

Nevertheless, these findings are roughly consistent with other research on this subject. In summarizing the literature, Marquart concluded that the presence of an on-site child care center had more of an effect on recruitment and morale than on absenteeism and turnover.[52] She also found that the presence of a center had a greater impact on employees' intentions to remain with their current employer than on their actually doing so when a better job came along.

## Other Strategies

An on-site day care center is not the only work support strategy of interest to parents with young children. Frequently, it is not even highest on the wish list. Many parents prefer a family day care home, or a center closer to home, or a provider who has won the trust of friends and neighbors. For them, an on-site center symbolizes not just corporate empathy but corporate paternalism as well. Aware of this, and aware of the high costs of running a center, many companies have pursued other strategies to demonstrate their commitment to a family-friendly workplace.

One popular approach is to offer the services of a resource and referral agency. In return for a subsidy, a resource and referral agency agrees to provide personalized assistance to employees from Company X who are looking for child care. IBM pioneered this approach by forging an agreement with Work/Family Directions of Watertown, Massachusetts, which in turn works through a network of 250 community-based resource and referral agencies and consultants.[53] Since 1984 more than 60,000 IBM families have used this resource and referral service.[54] Other companies have followed suit, often contracting directly with a resource and referral agency in their community.

Another fruitful strategy has been to set aside money for the recruitment and training of family day care providers. The premise is that this will expand the supply and improve the quality of child care available to employees and, incidentally or not, other members of the community. The biggest initiative of this kind was launched by the Dayton Hudson Corporation of Minneapolis, whose Family-to-Family program has trained more than 8,000 providers in thirty-five cities.[55] As chapter 5 noted, that program contributed to a substantial increase in the number of regulated family day care homes in the Houston metropolitan area. Another approach has been to offer employees discounts that may be used at designated child care facilities in the community (that is, all regulated facilities or facilities that have been approved in advance by the company). For example, the University of Minnesota offers employees a 10 percent discount at specified centers. Some companies, like NationsBank and Lotus, offer generous discounts for off-site child care, but only if employees' income is less than a certain threshold. In this fashion, companies can use scarce resources where they are needed most.

One of the toughest child care problems for parents and employers is care for sick children. As we indicated in chapter 3, seriously ill children should not—and, in most states, may not—be left with their regular child care provider. Work-Family Directions, a Massachusetts firm that assists other firms in meeting the family needs of their employees, has addressed this problem squarely by offering up to twelve paid days a year to care for a sick child.[56] Time Insurance of Milwaukee has used another approach. For a $30 fee, parents secure the right to purchase sick-child care as needed from a medically trained caregiver who can consult with a registered nurse throughout the day.[57] To keep rates low, the company pays half the daily charges.[58] This arrangement offers peace of mind to parents and enables the child to rest at home in his or her bed, supervised by a trained caregiver.

Although each of these strategies is different, they all exemplify what might be called an infrastructure-building approach to child care. Instead of establishing its own separate child care enclave, a company can build on—and contribute to—the existing child care infrastructure in its community. This approach has two advantages: It benefits members of the community, and not just company employees, by strengthening child care institutions that serve the wider society; and it expands employees' freedom of choice by acknowledging that child care at the workplace is not what every parent prefers.

The latter is important, because employees' child care needs—and preferences—do differ. For example, several years ago, Ben and Jerry's of

Waterbury, Vermont, decided to do something bold about child care. Fresh from the triumph of having invented Rain Forest Crunch ice cream, the company conducted an employee survey to help decide what to do. The survey revealed that about half the work force liked the idea of an on-site (or near-site) center, but about half preferred some other option (primarily, a subsidy for some other child care choice). True to its reputation as a progressive company, Ben and Jerry's built a lovely center within easy walking distance of the company's plant—an impressive gesture, but one that does not address every employee's child care needs. Those employees who prefer family day care or a center close to home are out of luck.[59] And the costs of running the center are substantial. If Ben and Jerry's had it to do over again, they might well have pursued a different approach.

## Corporate Quandaries

In wrestling with child care issues, companies face a number of difficult decisions. The most basic of all is whether to do anything. The case for doing something is strong. Hard-headed corporate executives with their eyes on the bottom line recognize that corporate support for child care can be viewed as one or more of the following:
—An investment in the community;
—An investment in a future work force;
—A recruitment and retention device;
—A productivity enhancer;
—An image enhancer; or
—Some combination of the above.
Smith puts it succinctly: "Kin care . . . is not a 'good deed' that companies do for their employees but a *business strategy* for corporate success. Who needs kin care? America's companies do."[60] Although the effects of kin care programs should not be exaggerated, most studies show that positive consequences flow from corporate child care initiatives.[61]
But what exactly should companies do? On-site child care often makes sense for companies with relatively large work forces that include relatively large numbers of women with young children. Hospitals exemplify this. And some hospital-based centers are truly magnificent. For example, the Baptist Medical Center in Oklahoma City features a delightful day care center (The Children's Place), with well-equipped, separate play-

grounds for children of different ages. The center is open from 6 a.m. to midnight, is accredited by the National Association for the Education of Young Children (NAEYC), and boasts an unusually well-educated staff (all teachers and almost all assistant teachers have bachelor's degrees in early childhood education or child development).

But on-site care is not a viable solution for many companies. Even if demand is strong, heavy subsidies may be necessary to keep rates low and quality high. For example, the Baptist Medical Center pays one-fourth of the operating costs of The Children's Place, and Ben and Jerry's picks up approximately half of the annual operating costs of its near-site center. Even with generous subsidies, some company-based centers have difficulty staying afloat. For example, St. Paul's Children's Hospital in Minnesota closed its on-site center after employee interest waned and supervisors grew impatient with the flow of red ink.

On-site child care is also out of the question for small businesses, which lack a critical mass of employees to sustain such an enterprise. Small businesses with highly transitory work forces are especially reluctant to offer substantial benefits to employees who will be working elsewhere the following year. For them, the best strategy may be to prop up the community's child care infrastructure, perhaps in combination with other small businesses. Retailers at a shopping mall could pool their resources to help recruit family day care providers; merchants in a downtown business district could band together to help sustain nearby day care centers.

The idea of business collaboration is not a new one, but it has been confined mostly to large companies, which have been the leading work-support innovators within the business community. For example, the American Business Collaboration for Quality Dependent Care, launched in 1992, involves a series of child care initiatives in forty-four cities. Although a few local governments, nonprofits, and smaller businesses have joined the partnership, the effort is spearheaded by eleven corporate titans: Allstate Insurance Co., American Express, Amoco, AT&T, Eastman Kodak, Exxon, IBM, Johnson & Johnson, Motorola, Travelers, and Xerox.[62]

Despite these promising initiatives, most companies have done very little to enhance the supply or quality of child care in their communities. Under such circumstances, governments may need to stimulate private sector activity through tax incentives. For example, Oregon offers employers a 50 percent tax credit for such child care expenditures as on-site care, child care purchased elsewhere, and resource and referral services.[63] This strategy is especially well suited to small business, because it permits a wide range of approaches that can fit almost any firm's budget.

Separate initiatives, patched together, however, do not necessarily add up to a viable child care system. For a loosely coupled system to work, the connective tissue linking separate institutions must be supple and strong. Resource and referral agencies in particular must be sources of information, wisdom, and advice. They must connect parents to providers, and they must offer parents information worth having. They should also connect parents to regulators and the vital information they possess. They should bring together those who are knowledge-rich and those who are knowledge-poor. If they do this, parents will be better shoppers, and children will receive better care.

## Resource and Referral Agencies

When consumers purchase an automobile or a washing machine or a video-cassette recorder, they can pick up *Consumer Reports* for helpful tips on price and quality. Many consumers have used this information to good advantage, although they receive no personal counseling from the popular magazine. When purchasing child care services, most parents have access to what in principle is an even better source of information and advice—a child care resource and referral agency (R&R) that answers specific questions about what to look for and how to look for it. Resource and referral agencies have grown dramatically in recent years, thanks to corporate contributions, government subsidies, and parental interest. As noted earlier, many large corporations have purchased "enhanced" referral services from R&Rs for their employees. And many state governments have earmarked substantial amounts of federal CCDBG money to assist established R&Rs and start up new ones. In 1994 there were approximately 500 R&Rs in the United States, about four-fifths of which belong to the National Association of Child Care Resource and Referral Agencies (NACCRRA).

Approximately two-thirds of all R&Rs use a software package called "Carefinder." This enables them to store large amounts of useful information about particular day care centers and family day care homes, retrieve it quickly, disseminate it quickly, and update it easily. Most R&Rs field inquiries about regulated facilities only, which helps to promote quality. Most of them charge a nominal fee, which is sometimes waived. Most divulge information over the telephone, which greatly assists busy parents and poor parents in particular. Most of them also offer general advice along with specific information.

The R&R is a marvelous invention, with tremendous potential to assist parents who are trying to do right by their children. It is unfortunate that few R&Rs are living up to that potential. Many R&Rs, regrettably, know about particular child care facilities but do not reveal what they know to parents. Others do not seek out all the facts, for fear that it would place them in an awkward predicament. Still others have sought the facts, only to discover that state officials do not make it easy for them to obtain them. The ultimate losers, of course, are children, who wind up in child care arrangements that parents would not have chosen if they had known of a facility's shaky history.

## See No Evil, Hear No Evil, Speak No Evil

R&Rs reveal a great deal of information about particular child care facilities to parents, but there are many questions that they cannot or will not answer: Is Little Rascals on Elm Street better or worse than Little Beginnings on Maple Street? Have child care inspectors identified staffing problems at either facility? Have child care inspectors identified health or safety problems at either facility? Have any complaints been lodged against either facility? Have any complaints been substantiated against either facility? The sad truth is this: The more important the question, the less likely an R&R is to answer it.

To find out how far R&Rs will go in disseminating useful information to parents, I contacted R&Rs in two states where the potential for meaningful disclosure is particularly high: Texas and Vermont.[64] In these two states, licensors adjust the frequency of center inspections to fit the center's past performance. Thus R&Rs, in principle, could tell parents something extremely useful about licensed centers in their state. For example, if a Vermont center has a three-year license, or a Texas center has a Plan III license (only one inspection per year), it means that that center has been judged by regulators to be above average in quality. Conversely, if a Vermont center has a one-year license or a Texas center has a Plan I license (three or more inspections per year), that center has been deemed below average in quality (unless it is brand new).

TABLE 6-5. Disclosure Policies of Resource and Referral Agencies in Texas and Vermont[a]

| Disclosures | Never | Sometimes | Always |
|---|---|---|---|
| Inspection schedule | | | |
| Texas | 9 | 0 | 0 |
| Vermont | 12 | 0 | 0 |
| Substantiated complaints | | | |
| Texas | 8 | 0 | 1 |
| Vermont | 12 | 0 | 0 |
| Staff with CDA certificates | | | |
| Texas | 2 | 7 | 0 |
| Vermont | 5 | 1 | 6 |
| Staff with college degrees | | | |
| Texas | 2 | 7 | 0 |
| Vermont | 10 | 0 | 2 |

a. The Vermont interviews were conducted in March 1994; the Texas interviews were conducted in April 1994.

As table 6-5 reveals, none of the R&Rs contacted in Texas or Vermont lets parents in on these secrets. Indeed, parents seldom learn that there is such a thing as an extended licensing plan in Vermont or a differential monitoring system in Texas. Other valuable information is also unavailable to parents. Most R&Rs do not tell parents if a complaint against a particular center has been substantiated.[65] And many R&Rs do not tell parents how well trained the staff members are. Typically, R&Rs do not have that information in their files. Some will seek out the information if asked about it; others will not. In some instances, R&Rs actually have the information but refuse to disclose it, referring parents to the state licensing agency instead.

In defense of such buck-passing, one might argue that it is better to get (sensitive) information from the proverbial horse's mouth. But consider several facts: (1) Busy parents don't have the time or the inclination to make additional phone calls to state officials; (2) state child care inspectors, who have access to the pertinent files, are notoriously difficult to reach, because they are out in the field so much of the time; and (3) state licensing agencies sometimes take the same position as R&Rs—they refuse to divulge information over the telephone. Instead they suggest an office visit or perhaps a written request. Few parents will take the search for truth that far. Once they've been rebuffed by an organization that supposedly exists to help them, most parents make do with the information they already have, even if it is a poor guide to quality.

## Legal Nightmares

When asked why they do not provide more quality-relevant information to inquisitive parents, resource and referral agency directors often reply that they are concerned about lawsuits. Two types of lawsuits might materialize, they argue. The first would be a negligence suit by a parent whose child was injured or mistreated at a facility "recommended" by the R&R. The second would be a slander suit by a provider whose facility was badmouthed and thus "not recommended" by the R&R. In both instances, a plaintiff might allege that the R&R had committed a tort and that damages should be paid to compensate for the harm to the child or to the provider's reputation.

How legitimate is the fear of a negligence suit? In some states, R&Rs have a legal statutory duty to compile and distribute current child care information and to provide parents with a single point of access.[66] Seldom, however, do R&Rs have a statutory duty to investigate, supervise, license, or certify child care providers.[67] Instead, state legislatures have typically imposed such a duty on the state's department of human services. Thus in the overwhelming majority of states, R&Rs have no statutory duty whatever to regulate or monitor child care providers. The agencies could get into legal difficulties if they were to misrepresent themselves and a tragedy were to occur at a facility chosen because of that misrepresentation.[68] In the absence of such misrepresentation, however, a claim of direct negligence would probably be unsuccessful.

Another area of torts that is relevant here is that of "imputed negligence" in cases involving "vicarious liability." Researchers explain this concept succinctly: "Imputed negligence means that, by reason of some relation existing between A and B, the negligence of A is to be charged against B, although B has played no part in it, has done nothing whatever to aid or encourage it, or indeed has done all that he possibly can to prevent it."[69]

Imputed negligence cases have arisen most commonly in situations involving employees or independent contractors, where some sort of principal-agent relationship can be said to exist. A resource and referral agency, however, does not hire a child care facility to provide services, nor does it contract out with a child care facility to provide services. Thus neither situation seems applicable.

The most pertinent cases are medical malpractice cases where one physician refers a patient to another physician, who then causes some irreparable harm to the patient. Fortunately for R&Rs, these "vicarious liability" cases strongly suggest that professionals who refer clients to other professionals have little to fear if they behave responsibly. For example, physicians who arrange for patients to see another physician when they are out of the office usually are not liable for negligence if they exercised "due care" in choosing the substitute physician.[70] Similarly, physicians who refer patients to specialists usually are not liable for negligence unless the patient can demonstrate that the specialist was unqualified or incompetent and that the first physician knew or should have known this.[71]

If an R&R were to provide quality-relevant information on individual child care facilities to parents, it would not be placing itself on a fragile legal limb. In fact, reputable organizations routinely refer consumers to service providers who have met some quality threshold established by other reputable organizations. For example, the American Cancer Society regularly refers women seeking mammograms to centers accredited by the American College of Radiology, which employs rigorous criteria for assessing the quality of mammograms offered by different facilities.

If fuller disclosure would not invite successful negligence suits, what about slander suits? Could providers miffed by negative disclosures sue an R&R for slander? Anyone can file a suit, of course, but not everyone can win one. And libel suits are extremely difficult to win, because the courts have long sought to encourage robust freedom of expression. Slander suits are even more difficult to win, because the law assumes that oral defamation leaves a less permanent blot on a person's reputation than written defamation.[72]

In striking a balance between freedom of speech and protection from scurrilous falsehoods, the U.S. Supreme Court has typically asked whether the plaintiff is a public figure (and hence fair game) and whether the speech is of public concern, thus deserving greater protection.[73] A child care provider would probably be regarded as a private figure (and thus in a better position to sue), but a child care facility's performance might well be regarded as a matter of public concern, given that these are community facilities with the capacity to benefit or harm a highly vulnerable population.[74] Under such circumstances, even a false assertion might be protected, so long as "actual malice" was not present.[75]

The easiest way to avoid a slander or libel suit in delicate situations would be to rely on public documents, which government reports of substantiated complaints and inspection results surely are. In numerous cases, the courts have held that "fair reports" of official government proceedings or activities enjoy a "qualified privilege" that immunizes parties who simply "republish" that information, in writing or orally.[76] Moreover, the courts have held that the public filing of a report or communication by an officer or agency of the government brings statements about that report or communication within the scope of the privilege. Thus as soon as a child care inspector writes up an inspection or a complaint visit, the "republication" of that information by a R&R would be privileged.

## The Roots of Reticence

Fear of lawsuits is but one reason for the cautious posture of many R&Rs. Reluctance to alienate providers is another. Most R&Rs believe that they have a dual obligation: to parents and to providers. With two sets of clients, R&Rs straddle a fence. Although they try to help parents, they avoid giving parents information or advice that could damage their standing in the provider community. Often, that means that factual information on inspections and complaints is withheld or not sought out in the first place.

Some R&Rs go to great lengths to avoid upsetting providers. For example, the Denver-based Work and Family Resource Center does not even disclose the full name and address of licensed family day care providers. Instead they divulge a provider's first name, telephone number, and neighborhood. After a telephone conversation with a parent, the provider then decides whether to reveal more. The official rationale for this extraordinary secrecy is that it protects providers from kooks and cranks. Unintentionally, however, it insulates providers from parents who simply do not make a good impression over the telephone, which may include parents of limited means, a limited education, or a different race.

Another reason for limited disclosure is that R&Rs see themselves as "honest brokers." To many, this implies neutrality, which may in turn imply saying as little as possible about the relative merits of different facilities. Some R&Rs have been accused of tilting toward a particular subset of providers, such as family day care providers or nonprofit centers.[77] If the information they divulge is bland and antiseptic, they need not worry about the appearance or the reality of favoritism.

Some R&Rs would like to be more informative, but they are hamstrung by state officials whose own norms discourage disclosure. For

TABLE 6-6. Inspectors' Beliefs about Notifying Resource and
Referral Agencies[a]
Percent

Statement: Resource and referral agencies should be notified if a group day care center
has a poor performance record.[b]

| State | Disagree | Not sure | Agree |
|---|---|---|---|
| Colorado | 15.8 | 5.3 | 78.9 |
| (N) | (3) | (1) | (15) |
| North Carolina | 3.6 | 3.6 | 92.9 |
| (N) | (1) | (1) | (26) |
| Oklahoma | 23.1 | 11.5 | 65.4 |
| (N) | (6) | (3) | (17) |
| Pennsylvania | 20.0 | 8.0 | 72.0 |
| (N) | (5) | (2) | (18) |

a. Numbers in parentheses are totals.

b. This statement was one of several read to child care inspectors in four states, as part of a broader study of child care regulatory enforcement. The interviews were conducted during May, June, August, and September 1994.

example, when North Carolina begins an abuse and neglect investigation at a center or family day care home, the relevant R&R is routinely told that an investigation is under way but is not automatically informed of the outcome of the investigation. Citing time constraints, the abuse and neglect unit has refused to take the additional step of informing the relevant R&R when the investigation is complete. When state officials are not forthcoming and cooperative, R&Rs often make do with innocuous information that tells parents next to nothing about quality.

## Breakthroughs

Most child care inspectors would like to reveal more hard data to R&Rs. When I asked child care inspectors in four states whether R&Rs should be notified when a center has a poor performance record, the overwhelming majority of inspectors in all four states agreed (see table 6-6). A much smaller minority would take the additional step of informing the mass media when a center has a poor performance record.

Straitjacketed by restrictive departmental policies and norms, some child care inspectors have launched their own personal campaigns to keep R&Rs informed. For example, Nancy Fowler, who inspects child care facilities in Alamance County, North Carolina, meets monthly with Kathy Hykes of the Child Care Resource and Referral of Alamance. At these meetings, they discuss outcomes of complaint investigations, interpretations of departmental rules, and other matters.

According to Hykes, who heads the state's R&R network, approximately 30 percent of North Carolina's child care inspectors meet regularly with their R&R counterparts. In effect, these inspectors have set out to reconnect broken circuits. As Rogers and Rogers have argued, every organization has a small percentage of "liaison workers," but we need to get all workers to think of themselves as potential go-betweens with other organizations.[78] A number of North Carolina's child care inspectors have taken on this liaison role, even though it is not in their official job description.

Another approach taken by state licensing officials is to urge parents to contact them directly, thus bypassing the R&R middleperson. Usually, this idea is a rhetorical flourish aimed at justifying poor communication with the R&R. Some states, however, do seem to take this function seriously. In Colorado, for example, the state Office of Child Care Services has issued press releases announcing that child care files are available for public inspection in Denver. Media publicity, solicited and unsolicited, has triggered a substantial flow of file viewers, parents, and others. In July 1994, for example, outsiders reviewed 204 files.[79] If parents could not come to Denver, the state mailed copies of inspection reports at 50 cents per page.

Colorado has also taken the lead in making basic child care information available to parents at kiosks located at shopping malls throughout the state.[80] Consider, for example, the In-Touch Colorado kiosk at the Chapel Hills Mall in Colorado Springs. Situated between a huge bubble gum machine (Goodies Galore) and the Beauty Express (no appointment necessary), the kiosk features a touch-propelled computer system with a menu that covers legal and business issues, games of chance, recreation, and child care.[81] In an introduction, Governor Roy Romer offers the rationale: "No longer will citizens need to rush to distant government offices before closing time, search and pay for parking, end up in a long line for information they need."

In-Touch Colorado's child care questions include the following: What child care is available in my community? How can I find out more about a specific child care facility? What documents do I need to enroll my child in a child care program? What should I look for when selecting child care? Information is also available on income assistance programs (who is eligible and how to apply) and complaint reporting (how to report suspected child abuse and how to file a complaint about a particular facility).

These are basic questions, none of which gets at the quality of individual facilities. But the Colorado Office of Child Care Services is moving in that direction, thanks to a new program announced by Governor Romer in September 1994.[82] By 1996 the office hopes to be able to offer parents information on particular child care facilities through computers located at R&Rs, public libraries, social service agencies, and other sites. Data on the number of substantiated complaints against a particular facility and the types of code violations that inspectors detected during recent visits would be included. Whatever the specific arrangements, the information superhighway could equip consumers to make well-informed child care choices.

## Conclusion

There is much talk these days about the rediscovery of community. Communitarian theorists urge a revival of old-fashioned norms of community solidarity that predated the emergence of a welfare state. They recommend a "moral commonwealth" in which public and private institutions collaborate to meet human needs, an "active society" with stronger families, churches, and schools, and a "strong democracy" in which citizen participation leads to citizen governance.[83] Some observers perceive a shift in this direction.[84]

Given the incidence of both market failure and government failure in child care, it is natural for families to turn to other institutions in the community for relief and support. Schools, churches, and local businesses have much to offer, if their resources, imagination, and good will can be tapped. Other community institutions with a primary focus on child care, such as R&Rs, can contribute a great deal too.

Thus far, however, community institutions have not lived up to their potential in child care. Many public schools close up shop when classes end, while latchkey children spend tedious (and sometimes dangerous) hours home alone. Many churches seek to evade regulatory requirements, instead of working with regulators to improve child care quality. Many companies vie for family-friendly reputations, while supervisors refuse to grant family benefits already on the books. Even R&Rs, which exist to connect parents and providers, do not aggressively seek out good information for their customers the way that fish merchants routinely seek out the catch of the day.

A key reason for these missed opportunities is the persistence of norms inimical to child care. For example, workers commonly have a tendency to define their jobs in narrow, restricted, conventional terms. Teachers educate students, so why allow outsiders to disrupt their classrooms with extraneous activities? Ministers attend to the needs of their congregation, so why permit government inspectors to tell them how to run babysitting programs on church property? Managers produce widgets as efficiently as possible, so why allow family difficulties to slow down next month's widget output?

Some of the barriers to improvement are more imaginary than real. There is no reason for R&Rs not to release quality-relevant information to parents. Neither negligence suits nor slander suits are likely to materialize if R&Rs furnish parents with information that has already been "published" by state child care inspectors. There is also no reason for state officials to keep such information from R&Rs. Nor is there any reason for state officials not to regulate church-based centers as they would any other type of facility. Religious affiliation does not absolve directors of the need to provide a safe and healthy environment for children.

Other barriers, though real, are surmountable. School-age child care programs cannot succeed without the support of principals, teachers, and custodians. But such people can be won over through earnest conversation, sensitive behavior, and creative program design. Corporate initiatives to help families with young children cannot succeed without the support of frontline supervisors. But they too can be won over through training sessions and assurances from CEOs.

Removing barriers to child care in the community is hard work, but forces are at work that can make things much easier. One of them is competition, for both customers and employees. There is reason to believe that competition between public and private schools improves the availability of SACC programs; that competition between hospitals for nurses improves the availability of on-site centers; and that competition between large companies for family-friendly reputations improves the availability of family-support and work-support benefits.

Another bright spot is the quest for economic productivity. Companies get energized and excited about child care when they recognize that a skilled, happy, and productive work force depends upon it. Large companies with large numbers of female employees have begun to recognize that a strong child care infrastructure and a strong corporate performance go hand in hand. Hospitals have been far ahead of the pack, but other large companies have also joined the ranks. Even small businesses might be induced to take small steps, if, for example, they received tax breaks in return.

A final mysterious but positive force is civic duty. Nonprofit centers place greater emphasis on quality than for-profit centers do and nonprofit hospitals offer on-site child care more often. Nonprofits serve a wide variety of diverse goals, but they share a common commitment to community service. By tapping that reservoir of good will, we can help to build a strong child care infrastructure for the future.

# 7 | Reinventing Child Care

I HAVE ESTABLISHED, I hope, that child care problems are widespread and acute. Obviously, they cause
considerable anxiety, concern, and guilt, especially among mothers of
young children. Less obviously, they pose threats to the health and safety
of young children, to their cognitive and emotional development, and to
their comfort and security. Some child care is exemplary; some is terrible;
much falls in between.

So long as these conditions persist, child care will engender a lively
debate in American living rooms. That debate will be muted, however, if
child care remains a semi-public issue. Child care, like the weather, is
something that people discuss a lot. Unlike the weather, it is well within
our collective control. But is it a public problem? And has it reached the
crisis stage?

Consider the following facts:

—The overwhelming majority of young children are placed in child
care arrangements for a considerable period of time. Many of these
children are exposed to facilities where the providers are poorly trained
and educated, where monitoring is infrequent, and where their health and
safety are in jeopardy. The problems are particularly severe in for-profit
centers and unregulated family day care homes.

166

—The child care industry is characterized by low wages, low self-esteem, low professionalism, and high turnover. It is also characterized by weak political lobbying. The child care industry has been largely unsuccessful in looking out for itself. As a result, these conditions are unlikely to change without strong intervention by other parties.

—Parents find it difficult to locate and pay for high-quality child care. They lose time at work and have trouble concentrating on their jobs because of child care problems. They make major personal sacrifices when they cannot find suitable child care for their children. Some parents stay at home when they would rather be working; others work, reluctantly, because they have no real choice.

—Businesses, which routinely oppose government regulations, seem to be waiting for government subsidies to solve the child care problems that their employees face. While acknowledging that such problems affect corporate productivity, business firms wonder why they should be expected to solve problems that affect most Americans at some point in their lives.

—Politicians react sporadically to child care scandals and flaps that generate mass media attention. They impose requirements on bureaucrats that often contradict requirements imposed by politicians from other levels of government. In designing child care solutions, they seldom have the big picture in mind.

—Bureaucrats with child care responsibilities make fitful efforts to coordinate with other bureaucrats and with private sector organizations that play key roles in delivering child care services. But child care bureaucracies remain isolated from one another, even within the same level of government. And child care bureaucrats often "go by the book" when implementing rules and regulations.

—Schools and churches have trouble reconciling child care with other missions they are expected to perform. As a result, many shun child care services or provide them grudgingly. Principals, teachers, and custodians often object to inconveniences that school-based child care presents; ministers and priests often oppose any government regulation of church-based centers.

—Resource and referral agencies dispense information of limited use to limited numbers of parents. Fearful of alienating providers by appearing to take sides, they avoid quality judgments. They also refrain from ferreting out information that could assist parents in making quality judgments. Much of the information that they fail to provide is actually in the public record.

168    REINVENTING CHILD CARE

These conditions have not won universal recognition as a public policy crisis for three reasons. First, young children cannot speak for themselves in a public arena. Unlike other vulnerable populations, they must rely entirely upon others to articulate their interests. The Children's Defense Fund has spoken out vigorously on behalf of children but has focused almost exclusively on policymaking at the national level, though many key decisions are made by state governments, local governments, schools, churches, and firms. In this respect, CDF differs from some early twentieth century interest groups that achieved significant gains for women and children at the state level before turning their attention to Washington, D.C.[1] Other children's advocacy groups have also lobbied primarily at the national level.

Second, the parents of young children, who might be expected to mobilize in support of a stronger child care infrastructure, are unable to cope with the demands of citizenship because they lack time, money, and sleep. Their reserves—financial and emotional—are largely spent. As a result, their frustration, though deep, remains largely private in nature. An Arlington County, Virginia, child care director puts it this way: "The parents of small children don't have the time or the inclination to set up a grassroots organization like Mothers Against Drunk Driving. . . . Even my most knowledgeable parents see child care as a discrete phase. . . . By the time their children are three years old, they're already anticipating the school years."

Third, other issues compete for scarce agenda space in legislative and administrative institutions. Child care remains a semipublic issue in part because health, education, and welfare issues have not been successfully resolved. These issues take priority not just because of their intrinsic importance but also because we are accustomed to thinking of them as collective problems. We are also accustomed to dealing with one issue at a time, in order to make problem-solving more manageable.

Yet it is dangerous to view the world as consisting of so many separate policy domains. Unless we address child care problems head on, poor children will arrive at public schools unprepared to learn. Unless we insist that children in day care centers and family day care homes are properly immunized, health care costs for children will escalate. Unless we ensure that single mothers who participate in work and training programs enjoy reliable child care arrangements, workfare programs will fail. Unless we assist all employees in reconciling the competing demands of work and family, corporate productivity will suffer. Child care is not a remote policy island; it is part of an archipelago with numerous connections and interdependencies that need to be understood.

## Reform Models

Occasionally, the opportunity arises to redesign a policy system. Child care today is on the threshold of such an opportunity. The current system, if one can call it that, evolved haphazardly as a response to changing economic conditions, the decline of the nuclear family, geographic mobility, and the rapid influx of women into the work force. In contrast to other policy systems, such as health and education, the rules of the game have not yet hardened—unions have not transformed informal norms into contractual requirements; professional standards have not become universal; consumers have not mobilized to demand new institutional practices and public policies. The only advantage of years of neglect is that the system is loose enough to be changed.

What, then, should a child care system look like in a country characterized by democracy, federalism, and capitalism? What should a child care system look like in a country characterized, for the most part, by loosely coupled systems? What should a child care system look like in a country marked by extraordinary wealth and huge pockets of poverty? What should a child care system look like in a country where child care itself is sometimes viewed with suspicion and concern?

In constructing a building, a dam, or a child care system, it is critical to employ good design principles. I have already argued that substantive decisions should seek to promote efficiency, justice, and choice. I have also argued that procedural decisions should seek to advance coordination, discretion, and responsiveness. But system design also requires a more specific blueprint or perhaps a series of blueprints. That is where reform strategies come in.

If we are to reinvent our child care system, at least four models are worth considering: a mediating structures model; an informed consumer model; a regulatory bargaining model; and a safety net model (see table 7-1). Strictly speaking, these models are neither mutually exclusive nor exhaustive. But they help to narrow the focus and to consider courses of action in concrete terms. In Wildavsky's words, they permit us to "speak truth to power."[2]

TABLE 7-1.  Reform Models

| Model | Vision | Key values | Key instruments | Examples |
|---|---|---|---|---|
| Mediating structures | Nurturing community | Democracy Responsiveness Empathy | Voluntary associations Good neighbors | Community-based partnerships Family resource centers |
| Informed consumer | Well-ordered market | Choice Empowerment Efficiency | Information Competition | Data banks for parents Better publicity |
| Regulatory bargaining | Judgmental elites | Discretion Flexibility Excellence | Carrots Sticks | Differential monitoring Indicator checklists |
| Safety net | Just welfare state | Equity Quality Protection | Money Mandates | Substantial aid to low-income parents Paid parental leave |

## Mediating Structures Model

A mediating structures model relies upon community-based institutions to achieve meaningful systemic reform. Such institutions include churches, schools, and the family itself. The image that drives this model is that of a caring community in which one person's problem is everyone's problem. Self-help, neighborliness, volunteerism, and civic action are the engines that propel this model. The premise is that those institutions that historically have united people in times of crisis and brought out their better instincts need to be strengthened. But those institutions, as everyone knows, are in trouble today.

A mediating structures model implies that everybody pitches in to help out, but no one runs the show. The government's role, if there is one, must be supportive rather than coercive. Otherwise, government intervention will extinguish the fires of generosity and creativity that burn within any community. Tax incentives and technical assistance, yes. Direct government provision and mandates, no.

In recent years, sociologists have increasingly emphasized the importance of mediating structures and their potential to transform an anomic mass society into a strong vibrant community. The communitarian movement reflects that approach.[3] Its premise is that strong families, churches, and schools are needed to solve fundamental social problems.

A mediating structures approach has several advantages. One is that it could be relatively cheap. By enlisting the creative energies of several institutions—and not just government—it greatly reduces burdens on taxpayers. By enlisting volunteers, it slashes labor costs. By using the physical plants of churches and schools, when they lie fallow, it slashes capital costs as well.

It also strengthens institutions that most people agree are worth strengthening in any event. Thus it combines transcendental and instrumental goals. By equipping families, churches, and schools to cope with child care problems, it helps these same institutions to cope with other problems as well—drug abuse, homelessness, the AIDS epidemic, and so forth. More than other strategies, it has positive spillover effects.

Third, it builds upon and reinforces two of the most notable characteristics of the current system—looseness and diversity. It treats these features not as vices but as virtues. Instead of trying to tighten a loosely coupled system or standardize a heterogeneous system, it preserves and refines both features. At the same time, it strives to improve the availability, affordability, and quality of child care offered under a variety of auspices.

Because of its emphasis on nonprofit organizations, a mediating structures model is likely to strengthen those institutions more than others. It is likely to encourage greater provision of child care services by churches and schools. It is also likely to endorse and emphasize some of the following:

—Organized confederations of family day care providers, who are often isolated today;

—Community-based partnerships that bring local governments, local firms, churches, schools, YMCAs, community action agencies, and children's groups together;

—Businesses allowing parents to spend some time every month at their child's day care center or family day care home;

—Family resource centers that include flexible arrangements for emergency child care services; and

—Strategies that permit parents to stay at home with their children until they are at least one year old.

## Informed Consumer Model

An informed consumer model supplies parents with enough good information to make wise child care choices on behalf of their children.

The presumption is that producers of goods and services respond to pressure from customers and competitors. As consumers become more informed, service providers cut costs or improve quality to remain competitive.

Although economists frequently use an informed consumer model, they use it more than they confirm it. But it is possible to identify some markets that work reasonably well, precisely because consumers are relatively well informed. The market for new automobiles, for example, functions effectively, partly because *Consumer Reports* and other magazines enable savvy consumers to protect themselves—and their pocketbooks—when they shop. The market for colleges and universities also works rather well, thanks to high school guidance counselors and published ratings of institutions of higher learning.[4]

An informed consumer model has several positive features. One is that it recognizes that parents have different tastes and preferences in child care. Parents differ in their emphasis on availability, affordability, and quality, they differ in how they define quality, and they differ in their constraints—how much they can pay, when they can pick up their children, and so forth. By informing parents with different preference functions about varied market opportunities, an informed consumer model permits parents to seek out the best care for their family or their child.

Information about child care is not difficult to produce, at least in principle. Much of the relevant information already exists, in state filing cabinets; the trick is to get that information to parents. This requires breaking old habits, but it does not require large expenditures. The problems here are attitudinal, not financial. When regulators and information brokers become convinced that it is safe and desirable to share really good information with parents, it will happen.

Technologies for information storage and retrieval are improving rapidly. As personal computers and modems have proliferated, it has become possible to transfer information instantaneously from state computer banks (or resource and referral databases) to libraries, firms, or homes. The potential for an information revolution in child care is enormous.

Information contributes to empowerment, which is especially important for poor parents. Many welfare policy specialists believe that disadvantaged adults need to be taught coping skills, for making child care and other decisions. Expectancy models, for example, link dependency to a loss of control and self-esteem.[5] From this perspective, information helps poor parents to function independently, by increasing confidence and control.

If an informed consumer model were to become popular, resource and referral agencies might receive greater financial support. Some of the following might also occur:

—State requirements that day care centers (and perhaps family day care homes) post notices of violations from their last inspection so that parents can view them;

—Mechanisms for transferring state data banks on inspection results and substantiated complaints to resource and referral agencies and ultimately to parents;

—New administrative safeguards so that state agencies can divulge information on abuse and neglect incidents without violating privacy statutes;

—Explicit ratings of child care facilities by state agencies or children's advocacy groups;

—Stronger efforts by the mass media to publicize child care successes and failures; and

—Invitations by state officials to have parents accompany them when they inspect a child care facility.

## Regulatory Bargaining Model

Because children cannot speak for themselves, parents represent them. But when parents lack the time and the expertise to represent children effectively, who will? The principal answer to that question, at least in child care, has been government regulators. A key purpose of government regulation is to protect persons who cannot protect themselves.

A regulatory bargaining model begins with this premise but builds upon it. Instead of stressing command-and-control techniques, it stresses incentives. Instead of emphasizing standard-setting, it emphasizes regulatory enforcement. Instead of encouraging regulators to go by the book, it encourages them to improvise, strike bargains, make deals, reward good performers, and punish bad performers. Its hallmark is not equal treatment for all but unequal treatment of unequals.

This strategy has worked in other policy contexts. Parole boards routinely release prisoners ahead of time, to reward them for good behavior and to make room in prison for other less contrite offenders. Although this practice has its critics, it does ease the burden of an over-loaded law enforcement system. Also, new techniques, such as house arrest plus, permit parole officers to monitor parolees with greater frequency, greater certainty, and greater success.[6] If differential monitoring can work for convicted criminals, surely it can work in other less ominous contexts. Indeed, one can argue that it already works in academia, where scrutiny of unproven (untenured) scholars exceeds scrutiny of (tenured) scholars with established track records.

A regulatory bargaining model has several advantages. It recognizes that providers differ greatly. Some providers are trying to do their best, others are trying to make money. Some providers are highly professional in their orientation, others are slipshod. Some providers have enviable track records, others have skeletons in their closet. Uniform strategies to deal with outstanding and deplorable facilities simply make no sense.

A regulatory bargaining model reallocates the government's attention and shifts resources to problem facilities and problem providers. It redeploys inspectors so that they can concentrate on the hardest cases. In this respect, it encourages the efficient use of scarce resources.

It also facilitates the use of hortatory controls to achieve results. Hortatory controls require two preconditions: (1) regulators must be able to devote enough time to difficult cases that they can establish a working relationship with the regulated firm (or person); (2) regulators must be able to choose a punishment that fits the crime, to select a tailor-made remedy. In the absence of these preconditions, inspectors have little choice but to go by the book.

Finally, a regulatory bargaining model opens up new possibilities for redefining compliance with regulatory standards. In environmental policy, for example, polluters may comply with clean air standards by trading pollution permits, so that air quality improves overall, even if particular polluters violate particular standards. A regulatory bargaining approach could permit similar experiments in child care, as in relaxed child/staff ratio requirements for well-trained providers. If the quality improvement attributable to better training exceeds the quality decline due to higher ratios, we are all better off.

If regulatory bargaining were to become widespread, some of the following initiatives might occur:

—State regulatory agencies would inspect some child care facilities more frequently than others, not just in response to complaints but as part of the license renewal process;

—Some state regulatory agencies would do away with the renewal process altogether (though not regulatory monitoring), thus reducing paperwork requirements;

—State regulatory agencies would use different review instruments under different circumstances, instead of a cookie-cutter, one-size-fits-all approach;

—The federal government would allow state regulatory agencies to withhold federal funding from child care providers who put children at risk;

—Resource and referral agencies would publicize and disseminate regulatory inspection results in an effort to discourage poor performances;

—Insurance companies would offer lower premiums as an inducement or reward to child care providers whose inputs (staff, physical plant) or outputs (code violations, substantiated complaints) are superior.

## Safety Net Model

A safety net model seeks to protect children through all possible means, but especially through national government action. The goal is social justice, across social strata, across generations, and across genders; the instrument is a strong welfare state, with redistributive, regulatory, and distributive functions. The assumption is not only that markets will fail to provide essential collective goods, but that endless tinkering around the margins will only make matters worse.

Like the mediating structures model, a safety net model is fairly comprehensive. Unlike the mediating structures model, it is also fairly coercive. Thus it envisions a tightly coupled system, in which the national government imposes relatively high tax burdens on the rich to accommodate the needs of the poor. It also imposes restrictions on the business community and on state governments that the other models would not contemplate.

The safety net model has been institutionalized in Europe for some time. In Sweden, paid parental leave enables a parent to stay at home until a child is eighteen months old; afterward, parents pay only 12 percent of the costs at government-run day care centers.[7] In France, parents enjoy a family allowance and have access to a highly praised child care system. Parents pay 20 percent of the costs, and employers pay 5 percent of the costs at day care centers. The government picks up the rest of the tab.

Although both Sweden and France are unitary states, the safety net model can also be found in federal systems (with less emphasis on uniformity, of course). In Germany, for example, parents enjoy 18 months of paid parental leave (the payment rate is somewhat lower than in Sweden), plus access to government-funded day care centers. Approximately one-third of the centers in western Germany and a larger percentage of the centers in eastern Germany are actually run by local governments. Although regulations are determined by state governments (or Länder), they are relatively strict, especially with regard to education and training requirements for providers.[8] They are also supplemented by church-run regulatory oversight systems.

The safety net model has several positive features. It has worked rather well in other countries. Child poverty is much lower in France, Sweden, and Germany than in the United States, thanks to family allowances, paid parental leave, and heavily subsidized child care. Indeed, child poverty is higher in the United States than in any other industrialized nation, except perhaps Australia.[9] Throughout Europe, the safety net model has reduced the costs of caring for children. Work-family conflicts have also been reduced, with a concomitant reduction in maternal stress. This is most evident in Sweden.[10]

The safety net model has also worked well in the United States, to the extent that it has been tried. Despite some exaggerated claims, Head Start programs have helped disadvantaged children to cope, to persevere, and to graduate from high school.[11] Preschool programs generally have had positive impacts on children's cognitive development, especially in the short run.[12] And some compensatory education programs, such as the Perry Preschool Program, have scored impressive results over an extended period of time.[13] Child care assistance has also enabled welfare-to-work programs to succeed.[14]

The safety net model reduces risks to children by leaving little to chance. Instead of hoping that businesses will rise to the occasion, it requires paid parental leave. Instead of hoping that state governments will adopt and enforce stringent regulations, it establishes a national regulatory floor (France) or auxiliary regulatory systems (Germany). Instead of hoping that community-based institutions will meet child care needs, it subsidizes them generously to ensure that they will.

If implemented in the United States, a safety net model would undoubtedly differ from its European counterparts. Of necessity, it would recognize that state governments are not satrapies of the central government. It would also recognize that budget constraints and cultural dispositions preclude guarantees of government-sponsored child care programs to all citizens. It might include some of the following features:

—The federal government would provide substantial financial assistance to all poor parents who need child care subsidies in order to work, attend classes, or participate in a job training program.

—The federal government would require businesses (or large businesses) to offer paid parental leave for one year (or six months) to full-time employees who have worked for one year or more (or two years or more).

—The federal government would establish a regulatory floor for all day care centers and all family day care homes, below which state regulations could not fall.

—The federal government would require states to consider and determine the merits of regulatory provisions not encompassed in the national regulatory floor (an agenda-forcing approach).

—State governments would regulate all day care centers and all family day care homes.

—State and local governments would take full advantage of federal child care programs with matching funds requirements, such as Head Start and the IV-A programs.

## Combining Models

In addressing any public policy problem, it is necessary to make choices. But that does not necessarily mean that we must limit ourselves to one or two of the above strategies. Indeed, when confronted by uncertainty and resource constraints, there is much to be said for pursuing multiple strategies, provided, of course, that they are not contradictory. We cannot be certain how a particular strategy will turn out, and the successful pursuit of low-cost alternatives may reduce the time and money required to implement more resource-intensive strategies.

That is not to say, however, that both the public and private sectors should pursue all four models. Nor is it to say that all three levels of government should pursue all four models. A better approach would be to allocate functions to fit the strengths and weaknesses of the federal government, state governments, local governments, and the wider society. Some division of labor, based on the respective strengths and weaknesses of particular institutions, is needed.

It is also important to recognize that each model has a different time line. The Informed Consumer Model and the Regulatory Bargaining Model can be implemented very quickly, with relatively modest resources, and without a wrenching national debate. Quality-relevant data on individual child care facilities are already available in fifty state capitals; all that is needed is the will to disseminate that information to parents. Child care inspectors are also in place in all fifty states; what is needed there is the imagination to redeploy them in more efficient ways and to hire more of them when caseloads are unreasonable.

It is tempting to dismiss changes that can be achieved so quickly as trivial or incremental in nature. The measure of any reform, however, is what it can accomplish, not how many barriers stand in its way. A serious effort to get good information into the hands of parents could revolutionize the child care system by empowering parents to protect their children through making judicious choices. A creative effort to redeploy regulatory resources could rationalize the child care system by rewarding and punishing providers according to their track records. In both instances, incentives would change dramatically. Instead of encouraging providers to cut costs and cut corners, we would encourage them to upgrade quality because that would lead to more customers and fewer (or shorter) regulatory visits.

Both changes would benefit from greater emphasis on performance and performance standards. Both would also benefit from greater emphasis on provider professionalism. The quid pro quo for accomplishment ought to be recognition (higher wages, higher status). And the quid pro quo for professionalization ought to be deregulation (fewer rules, fewer inspections).

Precedents exist in other policy domains for such approaches. For example, nursing homes in several states have been graded or evaluated by state officials or consumer groups. In Florida, nursing homes receive a rating from the state's Department of Health and Rehabilitative Services (superior, standard, conditional) after their annual inspection. That information is disseminated to the public. In southeastern Michigan, a consumer group has published a 688-page guide to the performance of 188 nursing homes, using data from state and federal inspections.[15] In Minnesota, the Minnesota Alliance for Health Care Consumers publishes profiles of nursing homes in the Twin Cities area, including information on ownership, financing practices, and complaints.

Numerous precedents also exist for professionalization and the linking to deregulation. In education, for example, most states upgraded their teacher training and education requirements during the 1980s. These steps enabled the next generation of reformers to argue in favor of site-based management. Now that teachers are better qualified, the argument goes, they deserve to be given a chance to run schools with a minimum of government interference and control. Although decentralization has not proved a panacea, it has liberated many schools from oppressive red tape.[16]

The implementation of other models would be more challenging. A Mediating Structures Model, for example, would require us to revitalize families, churches, and schools. We would have to integrate them in new social networks that include varied but reliable child care arrangements. We would have to design back-up systems to cope with occasional system failures. We would have to recreate a spirit of community comparable to that evoked so vividly in old Frank Capra movies.

There is much to be said for doing all of this. But it would require coalition-building and community-building efforts in thousands of neighborhoods across the nation. It would require institutions that have jealously guarded their autonomy over the decades to reach out to those in need instead of encasing themselves in protective cocoons. It would require a cultural shift away from individualism and toward communitarianism. In the words of some researchers, it would require new "habits of the heart."[17]

A Safety Net Model, in contrast, would require new habits of the purse. It implies, among other things, a strong welfare state, an activist national government, and higher taxes. For example, if an additional 400,000 AFDC recipients were to enroll in welfare-to-work programs in 1999, federal, state, and local governments would have to spend an additional $1.8 billion per year.[18] If an additional one million children of working poor parents were to receive child care support under expanded CCDBG and At-Risk programs in 1999, federal and state governments would have to spend another $1.7 billion per year.[19] The United States would still lag behind social democratic welfare states and corporatist welfare states in per capita government spending for child care but might pull ahead of other liberal market states in both spending and achievement.

In an era of tight budgets and deficit reduction, it is difficult to generate enthusiasm for new social initiatives, even if the target groups seem deserving. Political feasibility aside, it would be risky to increase federal child care spending rapidly. In other policy domains, such as health care, the sudden infusion of substantial federal funding has encouraged the for-profit sector, and especially for-profit chains, to increase their market share. This has happened in home health care, for example. Between 1977 and 1987, as expenditures on home health and outpatient clinics skyrocketed, the for-profit sector's market share increased dramatically, to 68 percent of all establishments.[20] Nursing home trends are somewhat more complex. During the 1970s, as medicaid spending surged, the for-profit sector increased its market share; during the 1980s, as cost-cutting became more prevalent, the for-profit sector's market share declined.[21] In short, the for-profit sector's share of the health care market seems to parallel government spending trends. In child care, where one-third of all centers are currently for-profit, a sharp increase in federal spending could lead to a system where two-thirds of all centers or two-thirds of all center enrollments are for-profit.[22] Child care would be more affordable, but it would also be more mediocre. Such a trend may already be under way. According to a recent study of day care centers in four states, for-profit enrollments have increased more rapidly than non-profit enrollments in all four states.[23]

These concerns would not apply to paid parental leave, which would enable parents to bypass child care outside the home for a period of six months or longer. But paid parental leave could be quite expensive, even if limited to children under the age of one. According to one now-dated estimate, fully paid parental leave for six months would have cost $5 billion per year in 1983, which means that twelve months would have cost approximately $10 billion per year.[24] Paid parental leave would be much more costly today and in the near future, even if wages were not fully replaced. For example, if all women who worked while pregnant received the minimum wage while staying home for one year after the birth of a child, this could cost the government as much as $27 billion per year in 1999.[25] Even if payments to mothers in intact families were half the minimum wage, the annual cost would be approximately $18 billion per year.[26] Governmental expenditures could be trimmed substantially by requiring employers to contribute 40 or 50 percent of the total cost. Studies show that when the government mandates worker benefits, employers pass along the overwhelming majority of the incremental costs to employees in the form of lower wages.[27] Substantial increases in unemployment are highly unlikely. Nevertheless, some low-income wage earners might pay for this benefit with their job, while others paid through lower wages.

If there are difficulties associated with both the Safety Net Model and the Mediating Structures Model, should we pursue neither? Both? Can we invent a Safety Net Model that fits a pluralistic culture, a federal system, and a pinched national treasury? Can we invent a Mediating Structures Model that does not depend on the whims of mayors, ministers, school boards, and community activists? How far can we go in adapting a model without doing violence to its core values? And how can we ensure that the interests of children receive primary consideration? These are difficult but answerable questions.

Support for a Safety Net Model may be stronger than the current national mood suggests. As the welfare system changes from a dole approach to a social contract approach characterized by mutual obligations, support for transfer payments to the poor, including child care assistance, is likely to grow. Social security, which exemplifies the social contract approach, is one of the most popular government programs in America—more popular than highway projects, sewer grants, and farm subsidies. Children as a group are vulnerable and most people agree that children's issues deserve public consideration. As for public concern about government spending, that seems to diminish when "value for money" is high.[28] Thus well-designed programs to shore up the child care system could command broad public support.

The building blocks for a Mediating Structures Model are already in place in many communities. Indeed, they have been in place for at least two centuries. As Tocqueville observed, ours is a nation of joiners. Most Americans belong to a church, for starters.[29] And many Americans belong to other voluntary associations as well. Regardless of memberships, many Americans volunteer time for worthy causes and donate money to others.[30] All that is needed in some communities is a spark; that spark could come from a local firm, a voluntary association, or a new federal program.

The burdens imposed on a Mediating Structures Model and a Safety Net Model will be lessened considerably if an Informed Consumer Model and a Regulatory Bargaining Model are already in place. Child care providers would have ample incentives to improve their performance, because both regulators and parents would take notice. Therefore, the need for national regulations and herculean community initiatives would diminish. A combination of tougher training requirements and higher child/staff ratios would also reduce pressure on community institutions by bolstering professionalism and boosting wages among providers. Instead of having to recruit a new cohort of providers every two to three years, communities could concentrate on nurturing provider networks and sharpening professional skills. The federal government in turn could focus its financial assistance on parental supports rather than provider subsidies.

The models, in short, should be viewed as complementary rather than mutually exclusive. Two of them can be implemented almost immediately and at little cost. The other two will require greater patience (time) and commitment (money). But they should also be part of the package. In a loosely coupled system, every level of government and every major institution has an important role to play. Specifying those roles is a difficult but not impossible task.

## Allocating Functions

Several general principles apply when sorting out appropriate roles for federal, state, and local officials.

First, the federal government excels at redistributing income. When social justice requires a shift of financial resources to poor children and poor parents (including the working poor), the federal government ought to play the lead role. Second, state governments are appropriate choices to regulate industries when interstate externalities are minimal. Even in policy domains where interstate externalities exist, such as environmental protection, we have found it convenient to rely upon state governments to do most of the regulating. Without such externalities, the case for federal regulation, or even federal oversight, is weak. Third, local governments can play valuable roles in disseminating information, in mobilizing citizens, and in forging partnerships with the business community. Local governments should take advantage of their principal strength (proximity to the people) without putting pressure on their Achilles' heel (a weak financial base).

These principles, of course, need to be augmented and refined. The federal government has special responsibilities to the poor, but it should also help middle-class parents to take a sabbatical from work to care for an infant at home. State governments should regulate vigorously enough to promote quality but not so vigorously that they undermine availability or efficiency. Local governments should disseminate information, perhaps, but that does not necessarily mean that they must produce the information.

Table 7-2 outlines some of the key roles that federal, state, and local officials should perform. The tasks include all of those associated with the

Informed Consumer Model and the Regulatory Bargaining Model and some of those associated with the other two models. This division of labor should be viewed as illustrative and provisional. One advantage of a loosely coupled system is that actors can rethink their roles as they learn from experience.

To begin with, the federal government should provide full financial assistance to poor children; collaborate with others to assist near-poor and middle-class children; and eliminate tax benefits to upper-class children. In concrete terms, this means that the federal government should expand CCDBG, the IV-A programs, and Head Start so that all poor children have access to one of these programs; offer inducements to states, businesses, and parents to meet the child care needs of near-poor and middle-class children; and eliminate unnecessary tax breaks to upper-class children by capping the Child and Dependent Care Tax Credit.

Federal support for poor and near-poor children is especially critical if child poverty is to be reduced from its current level of 22 percent. In most states, only a fraction of disadvantaged children nominally eligible for federal child care assistance are actually receiving such assistance. According to recent estimates, approximately one-sixth of eligible children are receiving subsidized care through the CCDBG, the SSBG, and the IV-A programs.[31] Few programs ever reach 100 percent utilization, but child care levels are unusually low.

The federal government can also play a constructive role by offering financial inducements to others to collaborate in assisting middle-class children. For example, the federal government should match (dollar for dollar) businesses that provide paid parental leave for parents with infants. A firm would contribute 40 percent of the minimum wage, the federal government would contribute 40 percent, and the employee would absorb the rest—for exactly one year. The cost of such a program would be considerably less than the figures cited earlier if it were voluntary, with employers participating or not as they wish. For example, if 10 percent of all employers offered such benefits and 10 percent of all mothers with infants claimed them, the cost to the federal government would be approximately $1.7 billion and the cost to employers would be approximately $1.7 billion in 1999.[32] Of course, a voluntary program would also benefit families with infants less. Positive spillover effects are possible, however, if employers who declined to offer paid parental leave were motivated to do something else instead (for example, provide part-time work opportunities or an on-site day care center for infants).

TABLE 7-2. Child Care Functions for Government

| Function | Federal | State | Local |
|---|---|---|---|
| Funding | Match firms that offer paid leave for parents with infants; expand federal child care support to cover all poor children; assist middle class through infrastructure grants to the states | Use dedicated funds to support child care programs; reimburse high-quality providers at higher rates; contribute matching funds to receive federal aid | Assist hospitals and businesses in caring for sick children; contribute matching funds to receive federal aid; assist parents through home visits |
| Regulation | Allow states to terminate funds to provider if children at risk; require training for all funded providers; revise eligibility requirements for CACFP | Tighten training requirements, loosen ratio requirements; reallocate regulatory resources; use intermediate sanctions; regulate all FDCs | Eliminate zoning barriers to FDCs; eliminate restrictive covenants; award bonuses to firms that build or fund child care facilities |
| Information | Support R&D on child care quality; obtain good data on policy implementation | Release information on inspections and substantiated complaints to R&Rs; grade child care facilities | Train caseworkers to advise JOBS clients on child care; enlist R&Rs to offer in-depth advice; encourage parental activism |

For older children, the federal government should offer low-interest loans, roughly comparable to subsidized Stafford loans in higher education, thus permitting middle-class parents to purchase high-quality child care when they need it. The federal government should also provide matching grants to states that choose to invest in child care infrastructure. At the moment, states are not expected to contribute anything for quality improvement funds under the CCDBG. The risk that states will stint on quality by declining federal matches can be reduced by establishing a relatively generous match.

These initiatives would require increased federal spending—for example, an additional $1.8 billion per year by 1999 to fund welfare-to-work programs and an additional $1.7 billion per year by 1999 to assist the working poor. The federal government could save approximately $1 billion per year, however, by eliminating the Child and Dependent Care Tax Credit for families with adjusted gross incomes above $50,000.[33] The federal government could save approximately $1.4 billion per year by gradually phasing out the Child and Dependent Care Tax Credit for families with adjusted gross incomes above $30,000.[34] The federal government could also save at least $195 million per year by 1999 by means-testing payments to family day care homes under the Child and Adult Care Food Program.[35] And some child care spending today actually saves money in the long run. Welfare-to-work programs, which depend heavily on child care spending, generally have favorable benefit/cost ratios, as do well-designed preschool programs aimed at disadvantaged children.[36]

The primary child care mission for state governments should be to regulate all child care providers efficiently and effectively. That means all providers (other than relatives) who care for children outside the child's home. To induce unregulated family day care providers to accept licensing or certification requirements, state governments should streamline the regulatory process, eliminate unnecessarily burdensome regulations, and offer free training at conveniently located sites.

State governments should also take decisive steps to boost the wages of center-based teachers by increasing child/staff ratio requirements for preschoolers at group day care centers. If every state were to raise its ratios to Ohio's level (12:1 for three-year olds, 14:1 for four-year olds), thirty-one states would effectively reduce center staffing requirements. This would enable centers in those thirty-one states to raise wages for teachers without raising parental fees. States must, however, upgrade their training and education requirements as they relax their ratios. Well-trained and well-educated teachers can cope with higher ratios and the challenges they present; poorly trained and poorly educated teachers cannot. In effect, these changes would move us closer to the European model, where teachers are well educated, well trained, and well paid, but where ratios are relatively high.[37] It would also be a giant step in the quest for professionalization of the child care work force.

Beyond these measures, state governments should act to implement the Regulatory Bargaining and Informed Consumer Models. In particular, states should alter their regulatory processes to reward superior performances (with shorter inspections or fewer paperwork requirements) and to punish poor performances (with monetary fines or other sanctions). It is also essential that states provide detailed, current information about provider track records to R&Rs and to parents. Data on inspection results and substantiated complaints should not simply gather dust in state filing cabinets. Such information should be posted on the premises of centers and family day care homes for at least thirty days. It should also be accessible through R&Rs.

Local governments lack the federal government's financial resources and the state governments' child care expertise. They can, however, play a constructive role by stimulating local demonstration projects, fostering community-based networks and partnerships, and bolstering the child care infrastructure. The key point, in Osborne and Gaebler's words, is that they should steer, not row.[38] They can do more to encourage high-quality child care by harnessing the energies of community-based institutions than by providing child care themselves. For example, some local governments have offered developers "bonuses"—partial waivers of the usual floor space or square footage requirements—in return for promises to build a day care center on the premises. Local governments should also work closely with state governments to ensure that information on child care quality is available through local libraries or public schools. Counties, which administer JOBS programs, have a special responsibility to ensure that caseworkers are equipped to answer client questions about child care arrangements or to refer the client to an R&R for immediate assistance.

Local governments can also play a constructive role by eliminating unnecessary regulatory hurdles. It is especially important that local governments eliminate zoning obstacles, such as conditional use permit requirements, for family day care homes. Such requirements, widespread throughout America, discourage family day care providers from accepting government regulation.[39] Local governments should also work with state governments to consolidate building inspections. There is no reason for state and local building inspectors to visit the same center or family day care home. That is precisely the wrong kind of redundancy—duplication rather than backup. Far from contributing to reliability, it encourages family day care providers to remain underground.

If governments have vital roles to play in improving child care, so too do societal institutions (see table 7-3). A number of schools and churches already provide child care services or make their facilities available to organizations that do. Yet much more could be done. For example, less than 7 percent of all black churches operate a day care center.[40] A comparable study of white churches would probably reveal similar numbers. Both churches (black and white) and schools (public and private) should sponsor child care programs or donate space to other nonprofit organizations when direct sponsorship is infeasible. Churches, the first point of entry for many new arrivals in a strange community, can be especially useful in addressing the needs of infants, toddlers, and preschoolers. Schools, which already serve school-age children in many communities, should expand these functions and market them accordingly. As competition between public and private schools heats up, SACC programs will increase and may improve in quality as well.

Although schools and churches can do a great deal to assist parents in meeting their immediate child care needs, they cannot remain indifferent to what goes on at home. Parents-as-teachers programs, literacy programs, and family resource centers can help to sustain developmental gains made in preschool programs. Churches and schools are unusually well-situated to conduct such programs in an effective and nonthreatening manner. Churches and schools must also do more to meet the special needs of the poor. Although publicly sponsored SACC programs, such as those run by public schools, are more likely to offer sliding-scale fees than other SACC programs, sliding-scale fees are still the exception, not the rule.[41] And church-sponsored day care centers are actually less likely than other centers to care for disadvantaged children, the Sermon on the Mount notwithstanding.[42]

The business community represents an underutilized reservoir of creative energy for family support. Some businesses, such as hospitals, should consider on-site day care for their employees. But most businesses should undertake other initiatives. They should assist their employees in

TABLE 7-3. Child Care Functions for Society

| Function | Schools | Churches | Businesses | R&Rs |
|---|---|---|---|---|
| Direct provision | Yes | Yes | Maybe | No |
| Family support | Parents as teachers programs, literacy programs | Parents as teachers programs, pastoral counseling | Paid parental leave, flex-time, part-time work, sick leave for sick children | Information and advice |
| Support for poor clients | Sliding-scale fee schedules | More disadvantaged clients | Sliding-scale fee schedules, charitable contributions | Special assistance to JOBS clients |
| Infrastructure support | Parent associations | Volunteers | FDC recruitment and training, enhanced R&R services | Computerized access to state data banks, FDC recruitment and training |

reconciling the competing needs of work and family by offering paid parental leave, flextime, part-time work, and other arrangements. A paid parental leave program for employees with infants would not be cheap, but expenses could be reduced by matching contributions from the federal government and employee contributions of 20 percent of the cost. Other strategies require creative juggling of work schedules and need not increase employers' expenses. Indeed, the broader consequence of family-friendly reforms at work is that they should yield a more productive, more loyal, and more stable workforce. If so, the investment will have been both socially and commercially responsible.

A key role of business initiatives should be to reduce family stress caused by work-family role conflicts. Studies show that part-time work reduces stress among mothers with young children.[43] Studies also show that less problematic child care enhances the mental and physical health of working mothers with young children.[44] Fathers may also be affected, though the impact is more subtle. Ultimately, children benefit from such initiatives.

The functions of R&Rs are relatively straightforward in theory, surprisingly problematic in practice. The R&R system serves providers (by finding clients) better than it serves parents (by finding good providers). Resource and referral agencies need to demonstrate more vigor, more gumption, and a stronger consumer orientation. They need to supply parents—and especially poor parents—with information worth having. It is not necessary for R&Rs to distinguish between good and bad providers in offering advice. But it is necessary for R&Rs to provide parents with sufficient information so that they can draw such distinctions themselves. This is not a matter of obtaining new data; it is rather a matter of disseminating data already in the public domain.

These are not the only roles that schools, churches, businesses, and R&Rs can play. Nor are they the only institutions that can play constructive roles in reinventing child care. Voluntary associations can mobilize parents and generate support for child care initiatives. Citizens' groups that represent various vulnerable populations can form coalitions and share experiences. Sports clubs, professional associations, colleges and universities, health clinics, and homeless shelters can demonstrate greater sensitivity to child care issues. As Putnam has argued after extensive research in Italy, civic associations can create "norms of generalized reciprocity and networks of civic engagement," which in turn promote trust, cooperation, and progress.[45] Timely government assistance can help, but communities flourish, in the long run, when community institutions are strong.

## Conclusion

Child care is not a new phenomenon, but it has fairly recently become an integral part of American life. Instead of attempting to put the genie back in the bottle, I have asked how we might improve the availability, affordability, and quality of child care. I have asked how we might reduce work-family tensions. Above all, I have asked how we might create a safer, better world for children.

The problems are formidable, because they involve informal norms inside government bureaucracies, the child care industry, and society. Informal norms are not easily identified, much less changed. Yet some of the solutions are easy to justify and easy enough to achieve—better information (to enhance the ability of parents to make good choices) and greater flexibility (to permit regulators to do their jobs more efficiently), for example. Other solutions, though more difficult to achieve, are also easy to justify: greater professionalism (to elevate the esteem and self-esteem of child care providers) and better coordination (across programs, across governments, between the public and private sectors), for example.

Other choices are more difficult. Are the definitions of quality offered by experts or by parents preferable? Should we pursue quality at the expense of availability or affordability? Should we pick winners and losers within the child care industry or adopt a neutral stance? Is federalism up to the challenges we face? Should states sacrifice lower child/staff ratios for higher wages? Should we ask the federal government to do more? If so, how do we pay for it? Should we ask churches, schools, and firms to do more? If so, what happens to their other missions? Do we reinvent child care from the top down or from the bottom up? If we try to do both, do we achieve justice and democracy or inefficiency and lethargy?

In wrestling with these questions, I have relied upon two explicit normative frameworks, focusing on substantive values (efficiency, justice, choice) and procedural values (discretion, coordination, responsiveness). Those frameworks point, unambiguously in my opinion, to the merits of an Informed Consumer Model and a Regulatory Bargaining Model. They do not, however, tell us to what extent we should rely upon either a Safety Net Model or a Mediating Structures Model.

That choice depends in part on how we define each model. In broader terms, it is a choice between a European-style and an American-style approach to child care. The view I have endorsed is a pragmatic one—a hybrid system makes the most sense. The essential features of such a hybrid system are:

—European-style entitlements to help the poor, American-style incentives to help the middle class;

—A European-style emphasis on education and training, an American-style emphasis on safety from fires, disease, and physical abuse;

—A European-style insistence on decent wages, an American-style aversion to exorbitant taxes;

—A European-style view that child care is a public issue, an American-style view that public service delivery is not absolutely necessary;

—A European-style skepticism toward the for-profit sector, an American-style preference for diversity; and

—A European-style view that families need help, an American-style view that parents should be free to choose.

If we look around, we see numerous examples of American-European hybrids. Some of them—lotteries, punk haircuts, Jerry Lewis movies with subtitles—are not particularly edifying. Others—the social security system, the music of Stephane Grapelli, kindergartens—are much more impressive.

A hybrid system is not tidy. But that is to be expected in a democracy characterized by federalism, third-party government, and separate institutions that share powers. The cure for a loosely coupled system that is not working is not necessarily a tightly coupled system that extinguishes diversity, but could be a loosely coupled system with the right incentives. With the right incentives, we can institutionalize coordination, discretion, and responsiveness; we can achieve justice, efficiency, and choice; and we can create a better world for our children.

# Appendix

194    APPENDIX

TABLE A-1. Child Care Quality: Reduced-Form Equations,
Two-Stage Least Squares

| Independent variable | Staff size (N = 717) | Inspections (N = 702) |
|---|---|---|
| For-profit sponsorship | −1.763*** | .616* |
| | (.437) | (.301) |
| Church sponsorship | −.688 | .153 |
| | (.628) | (.431) |
| Public school sponsorship | −1.016 | −1.900* |
| | (1.319) | (.928) |
| Number of children | .129**** | .006* |
| | (.004) | (.003) |
| Mean age of children | −2.813**** | −.211 |
| | (.354) | (.245) |
| Allowed ratio, 3-year-olds | −.326*** | −.053 |
| | (.087) | (.060) |
| Percent of children, parents on AFDC | .006 | .008 |
| | (.009) | (.006) |
| Number of inspections required by state law | .048 | 1.413**** |
| | (.190) | (.131) |
| Licensing trouble in past | .632 | 2.032** |
| | (.986) | (.685) |
| Percent of women in work force | .023 | −.068** |
| | (.031) | (.021) |
| Population per square mile | −3.038E-05 | 5.655E-05 |
| | (4.767E-05) | (3.284E-05) |
| State subsidies | .005 | −.003 |
| | (.007) | (.005) |
| Parental involvement | .567 | .149 |
| | (.497) | (.341) |
| $R^2$ | .62 | .20 |

*Significant at the .05 level.
**Significant at the .01 level.
***Significant at the .001 level.
****Significant at the .0001 level.

TABLE A-2. Child-Care Quality: Final Equations, Two-Stage Least Squares

| Independent variable | Staff size (N = 717) | Inspections (N = 702) |
|---|---|---|
| Mean age of children | –2.828**** | |
| | (.356) | |
| Allowed ratio, 3-year olds | –.304*** | |
| | (.081) | |
| Inspections instrument | –.023 | |
| | (.125) | |
| Number of children | .129**** | –.005 |
| | (.004) | (.011) |
| For-profit sponsorship | –1.756*** | .758* |
| | (.446) | (.322) |
| Church sponsorship | –.659 | .204 |
| | (.630) | (.420) |
| Public school sponsorship | –1.038 | –1.809* |
| | (1.360) | (.905) |
| Percent of children, parents on AFDC | .006 | .007 |
| | (.010) | (.006) |
| State subsidies | .005 | –.003 |
| | (.007) | (.005) |
| Parental involvement | .562 | .098 |
| | (.496) | (.333) |
| Inspections required | | 1.391**** |
| | | (.121) |
| Licensing trouble in past | | 1.981** |
| | | (.666) |
| Percent of women in work force | | –.071*** |
| | | (.020) |
| Population per square mile | | 6.332E-05* |
| | | (3.048E-05) |
| Staff size instrument | | .087 |
| | | (.080) |
| $R^2$ | .62 | .20 |

a. The standard errors in the final equations were corrected, as is customary, by multiplying the standard error for each coefficient by a ratio that corrects for the presence of the instrumental variable. Thus, in the case of the staff size equation, each standard error was multiplied by the ratio of the standard error of the full untransformed equation (with the original version of the inspections variable) to the standard error of the full transformed equation (with the purged version of the inspections variable).

*Significant at the .05 level.

**Significant at the .01 level.

***Significant at the .001 level.

****Significant at the .0001 level.

TABLE A-3. Nursing Retention: Reduced-Form Equations, Two-Stage Least Squares

| Independent variable | Staff turnover | On-site center |
|---|---|---|
| Staff size (FTEs) | −.002 | −2.747E-04* |
| | (.001) | (−.156) |
| Minimum salary (RNs) | −2.436E-04* | 8.364 |
| | (8.194E-05) | (6.418E-06 |
| Dental insurance provided | −1.182 | .343* |
| | (1.605) | (.125) |
| Pharmacy discount provided | 1.086 | .258** |
| | (.894) | (.069) |
| Relocation expenses provided | −2.805** | −.039 |
| | (.749) | (.058) |
| Constant | 24.408 | .766 |
| $R^2$ | .10 | .11 |

*Significant at the .01 level.
**Significant at the .001 level.

TABLE A-4. Nursing Retention: Final Equations, Two-Stage Least Squares

| Independent variable | Staff turnover | On-site center |
|---|---|---|
| Minimum salary (RNs) | −2.521E-04** | |
| | (8.490E-05) | |
| Relocation expenses provided | −2.697*** | |
| | (.748) | |
| Center instrument | 1.358 | |
| | (2.565) | |
| Staff size (FTEs) | −9.922E-04 | −2.507E-04* |
| | (.001) | (1.066E-04) |
| Constant | 22.269**** | .999*** |
| | (4.388) | (.259) |
| Dental insurance provided | | .335** |
| | | (.126) |
| Pharmacy discount provided | | .265*** |
| | | (.069) |
| Turnover instrument | | −.005 |
| | | (.015) |
| $R^2$ | .10 | .10 |

*Significant at the .05 level.
**Significant at the .01 level.
***Significant at the .001 level.
****Significant at the .0001 level.

# Notes

## Chapter One

1. Catherine E. Ross and John Mirowsky, "Child Care and Emotional Adjustment to Wives' Employment," *Journal of Health and Social Behavior*, vol. 9 (June 1988), pp. 127–38.

2. Ellen Greenberger and Robin O'Neil, "Parents' Concerns about Their Child's Development: Implications for Fathers and Mothers' Well-Being and Attitudes toward Work," *Journal of Marriage and the Family*, vol. 52 (August 1990), pp. 621–35.

3. Ibid.

4. Sandra L. Hofferth and others, *National Child Care Survey, 1990* (Washington: Urban Institute, 1991), p. 234.

5. Catherine Johnson, "Save the Children," *New Woman*, vol. 22 (February 1992), p. 61.

6. Karen Oppenheimer Mason and Karen Kuhlthau, "The Perceived Impact of Child Care Costs on Women's Labor Supply and Fertility," *Demography*, vol. 29 (November 1992), p. 527.

7. David M. Blau and Philip K. Robins, "Child-Care Costs and Family Labor Supply," *Review of Economics and Statistics*, vol. 70 (August 1988), pp. 374–81; David C. Ribar, "Child Care and the Labor Supply of Married Women," *Journal of Human Resources*, vol. 27 (Winter 1992), pp. 134–65.

8. Committee on Ways and Means, U.S. House of Representatives, *Overview of Entitlement Programs, The Green Book 1994* (Government Printing Office, 1994), p. 1148.

9. According to the Committee on Ways and Means, the poverty rate for children under the age of six in 1992 was 26 percent. Ibid., p. 1151.

10. Carolee Howes and Judith Rubenstein, "Determinants of Toddlers' Experiences in Day Care: Age of Entry and Quality of Setting," *Child Care Quarterly,* vol. 14 (1985), pp. 140–51; Carolee Howes and others, "Attachment and Child Care: Relationships with Mother and Caregiver," *Early Childhood Research Quarterly,* vol. 3 (December 1988), pp. 403–16; Marcy Whitebook, Deborah A. Phillips, and Carolee Howes, *Who Cares? Child Care Teachers and the Quality of Care in America* (Oakland, Calif.: Child Care Employee Project, 1989); National Research Council, *Who Cares for America's Children?* (Washington: National Academy Press, 1990), p. 92.

11. Richard Ruopp and others, *Children at the Center: Summary Findings and Their Implications* (Cambridge, Mass.: Abt Associates, 1979); Deborah A. Phillips, ed., *Quality in Child Care: What Does Research Tell Us?* (Washington: National Association for the Education of Young Children, 1987); Deborah Lowe Vandell, "A Longitudinal Study of Children with Day-Care Experiences of Varying Quality," *Child Development,* vol. 59 (October 1988), pp. 1286–92; Whitebook and others, *Who Cares?;* National Research Council, *Who Cares for America's Children?,* pp. 66–70.

12. Robert Haveman and Barbara Wolfe, *Succeeding Generations: On the Effects of Investments in Children* (New York: Russell Sage Foundation, 1994), p. 248.

13. Victor R. Fuchs, *Women's Quest for Economic Equality* (Harvard University Press, 1988), p. 147.

14. James Walker, "Public Policy and the Supply of Child Care Services," in David M. Blau, ed., *The Economics of Child Care* (New York: Russell Sage Foundation, 1991), p. 68.

15. Ellen Eliason Kisker and others, *A Profile of Child Care Settings: Early Education and Care in 1990, Vol. 1* (Princeton, N.J.: Mathematica Policy Research Inc., 1991), p. 22; Barbara Willer and others, *The Demand and Supply of Child Care in 1990* (Washington: National Association for the Education of Young Children, 1991), p. 60.

16. Kisker and others, *A Profile of Child Care Settings,* p. 50.

17. Ibid., p. 53.

18. Without paid child care, many AFDC recipients cannot afford to work. See Christopher Jencks and Kathryn Edin, "Do Poor Women Have a Right to Bear Children?" *The American Prospect,* no. 20 (Winter 1995), pp. 43–52. Furthermore, the success of welfare-to-work programs depends on the quality, stability, and convenience of child care arrangements. For example, in a study of California's welfare-to-work program, known as GAIN, Meyers found higher attrition when parental satisfaction with the child care arrangement was lower, when the parent found it necessary to change child care more often, and when the distance between the child care setting and GAIN program activities was greater. See Marcia K. Meyers, "Child Care in JOBS Employment and Training Programs: What Difference Does Quality Make?" *Journal of Marriage and the Family,*

vol. 55 (August 1993), pp. 767–83. Attrition is a serious problem in such programs. In this particular study, over one-fourth of the women participants had dropped out within one year.

19. Judith M. Gueron, Edward Pauly, and Cameron M. Lougy, *From Welfare to Work* (New York: Russell Sage Foundation, 1991), pp. 162–64.

20. Carnegie Task Force on Meeting the Needs of Young Children, *Starting Points: Meeting the Needs of Our Youngest Children* (New York: Carnegie Corporation, 1994).

21. Ibid., p. 4.

22. U.S. General Accounting Office, "Childhood Immunization: Opportunities to Improve Immunization Rates at Lower Cost," GAO/HRD-93-41 (GAO, March 1993), p. 2.

23. Lawrence Schweinhart and David Weikart, "The Effects of the Perry Preschool Program on Youths through Age 15—A Summary," in The Consortium for Longitudinal Studies, *As the Twig is Bent: Lasting Effects of Preschool Programs* (Hillsdale, N.J.: Lawrence Erlbaum Associates, 1983), pp. 71–101; Martin Woodhead, "When Psychology Informs Public Policy: The Case of Early Childhood Intervention," *American Psychologist*, vol. 43 (June 1988), pp. 443–54; Ron Haskins, "Beyond Metaphor: The Efficacy of Early Childhood Education," *American Psychologist*, vol. 44 (February 1989), pp. 274–82; Valerie Lee and others, "Are Head Start Effects Sustained? A Longitudinal Follow-up Comparison of Disadvantaged Children Attending Head Start, No Preschool and Other Preschool Programs," *Child Development*, vol. 61 (April 1990), pp. 495–507; W. Steven Barnett, "Benefits of Compensatory Preschool Education," *Journal of Human Resources*, vol. 27 (Spring 1992), pp. 279–312; Edward Zigler and Susan Muenchow, *Head Start: The Inside Story of America's Most Successful Educational Experiment* (Basic Books, 1992); Douglas J. Besharov, "Fresh Start: What Works and What Doesn't Work in Head Start?", *New Republic*, June 14, 1993, pp. 14–16.

24. William T. Gormley, Jr., "State Regulations and the Availability of Child-Care Services," *Journal of Policy Analysis and Management*, vol. 10 (Winter 1991), pp. 78–95; Margaret K. Nelson, "A Study of Family Day Care Providers: Attitudes Toward Regulation," *Child and Youth Care Forum*, vol. 20 (August 1991), pp. 225–42; Sandra L. Hofferth, Duncan D. Chaplin, and Douglas A. Wissoker, "State Regulations and Child Care Choices," unpublished manuscript, Urban Institute, Washington, May 4, 1994.

25. Richard Louv, *Childhood's Future* (Boston: Houghton Mifflin, 1990); Sharon Lynn Kagan, "Examining Profit and Non-profit Child Care: An Odyssey of Quality and Auspices," *Journal of Social Issues*, vol. 47 (Summer 1991), pp. 87–104; Edward F. Zigler and Mary E. Lang, *Child Care Choices: Balancing the Needs of Children, Families, and Society* (Free Press, 1991); Susan Kontos, *Family Day Care: Out of the Shadows and Into the Limelight* (Washington: National Association for the Education of Young Children, 1992).

26. K. Alison Clarke-Stewart, *Daycare* (Harvard University Press, 1982); Schweinhart and Weikart, "The Effects of the Perry Preschool Program on Youths

through Age 15," pp. 71–101; Jay Belsky, "Infant Day Care: A Cause for Concern?", *Zero to Three*, vol. 7 (September 1986), pp. 1–7; Deborah A. Phillips ed., *Quality in Child Care*. Nazli Baydar and Jeanne Brooks-Gunn, "Effects of Maternal Employment and Child-Care Arrangements on Preschoolers' Cognitive and Behavioral Outcomes: Evidence from the Children of the National Longitudinal Survey of Youth," *Developmental Psychology*, vol. 27 (November 1991), pp. 932–45.

27. Gosta Esping-Andersen, *The Three Worlds of Welfare Capitalism* (Cambridge, England: Polity Press, 1990).

28. Esping-Andersen does not discuss Japan in detail, and there is no scholarly consensus on how it should be classified. Some scholars believe that Japan shares much in common with corporatist welfare states. See Steven R. Reed, *Making Common Sense of Japan* (University of Pittsburgh Press, 1993), p. 24. Other scholars believe that Japan shares more in common with liberal market states. See Francis Castles and Deborah Mitchell, "Identifying Welfare State Regimes: The Links Between Politics, Instruments, and Outcomes," *Governance*, vol. 5 (January 1992), pp. 1–26.

29. Siv Gustafson and Frank P. Stafford, "Three Regimes of Child Care: the United States, the Netherlands, and Sweden," in Rebecca M. Blank, ed., *Social Protection versus Economic Flexibility: Is There a Trade-Off?* (University of Chicago Press, 1994), p. 345.

30. For a discussion of ratios in Sweden, see William T. Gormley, Jr., and B. Guy Peters, "National Styles of Regulation: Child Care in Three Countries," *Policy Sciences*, vol. 25 (November 1992), p. 386. For a study of Finland, see Alfred J. Kahn and Sheila B. Kamerman, *Social Policy and the Under-3s: Six Country Case Studies* (Columbia University School of Social Work, 1994), p. FI32.

31. Bengt-Erik Andersson, "Effects of Public Day-Care: A Longitudinal Study," *Child Development*, vol. 60 (August 1989), pp. 857–66. See also Kahn and Kamerman, *Social Policy*, p. D52.

32. A typical compensation rate, for one year or so, is 80 percent of forgone wages.

33. Kahn and Kamerman, *Social Policy*, table A-15.

34. Ibid., pp. FR53, IT17.

35. Ibid., p. G50.

36. Italy is an exception. Family day care homes constitute a tiny fraction of the Italian child care market. Ibid., p. IT12.

37. Gail Richardson and Elisabeth Marx, *A Welcome for Every Child: How France Achieves Quality in Child Care* (New York: French-American Foundation, 1989), p. 18.

38. Kahn and Kamerman, *Social Policy*, pp. IT10–11.

39. Gormley and Peters, "National Styles of Regulation," p. 385.

40. In Italy, staff members are well educated and well paid but not necessarily well trained in early childhood education. See Kahn and Kamerman, *Social Policy*, p. IT18.

41. France is a possible exception. Single mothers with two children are eligible for a family benefits package equal to 64 percent of the median wage. See Kahn and Kamerman, *Social Policy,* p. FR19.

42. Childcare Resource and Research Unit, *Child Care in Canada: Provinces and Territories 1993* (University of Toronto, 1993), p. 87.

43. Although federal rules determine whether payments under the Canada Assistance Plan may be used at for-profit centers, the provinces are free to decide whether other subsidies are available to for-profit centers.

44. In New Zealand, a unitary state, regulations are promulgated by the national government. In the United Kingdom, the central government and the local authorities share regulatory responsibilities.

45. Katherine Teghtsoonian, "Institutions and Ideology: Sources of Opposition to Federal Regulation of Child Care Services in Canada and the U.S.," *Governance,* vol. 5 (April 1992), p. 203; Gormley and Peters, "National Styles of Regulation: Child Care in Three Countries," pp. 381-99; Deborah Brennan, "Australia," in Moncrieff Cochran, ed., *International Handbook of Child Care Policies and Programs* (Westport, Conn.: Greenwood Press, 1993), p. 25.

46. Childcare Resource and Research Unit, *Child Care in Canada,* p. 97.

47. Kahn and Kamerman, *Social Policy,* Tables A8, A9.

48. On the relative level of child poverty in the United States, see Timothy Smeeding, Barbara Boyle Torrey, and Martin Rein, "Patterns of Income and Poverty: The Economic Status of Children and the Elderly in Eight Countries," in John L. Palmer, Timothy Smeeding, and Barbara Boyle Torrey, eds., *The Vulnerable* (Washington: Urban Institute, 1988), p. 97. For further information on single mothers as heads of households, see Irwin Garfinkel and Sara McLanahan, "Single-Mother Families, Economic Insecurity, and Government Policy," in Sheldon H. Danziger, Gary D. Sandefur, and Daniel H. Weinberg, eds., *Confronting Poverty: Prescriptions for Change* (Harvard University Press, 1994), p. 209.

49. Bronwen Cohen, "The United Kingdom," in Moncrieff Cochran, ed., *International Handbook of Child Care Policies and Programs* (Westport, Conn.: Greenwood Press, 1993), p. 525.

50. William T. Gormley, Jr., "Institutional Policy Analysis: A Critical Review," *Journal of Policy Analysis and Management,* vol. 6 (Winter 1987), pp. 153-69.

## Chapter Two

1. These definitions vary somewhat from study to study. See National Research Council, *Who Cares for America's Children?* (Washington: National Academy Press, 1990), p. 46.

2. Ibid., p. 17.

3. Martin O'Connell, "Where's Papa? Fathers' Role in Child Care" (Washington: Population Reference Bureau, September 1993), p. 14.

4. Stephanie Coontz, *The Way We Never Were: American Families and the Nostalgia Trap* (Basic Books, 1992), pp. 185-86.

5. The U.S. divorce rate increased sharply after 1965 but declined somewhat during the 1980s. See Norval D. Glenn, "The Recent Trend in Marital Success in the United States," *Journal of Marriage and the Family*, vol. 53 (May 1991), pp. 261-70. Thus while a rising divorce rate may have contributed to the initial surge in female employment, other factors seem to have been at work during the 1980s.

6. Bureau of the Census, *Statistical Abstract of the United States, 1993* (U.S. Department of Commerce, 1993), p. 400.

7. National Research Council, *Who Cares for America's Children?*, p. 21; U.S. Committee on Ways and Means, House of Representatives, *Overview of Entitlement Programs: 1991 Green Book* (Government Printing Office, May 7, 1991), p. 1032.

8. National Research Council, *Who Cares for America's Children?*, p. 18.

9. It is somewhat puzzling that the Nelson family has come to epitomize the traditional family. Ozzie never seemed to be at work, nor was it clear what he did for a living. In fact, he always seemed to have time for golf, for a trip to the malt shop with his sons, and for unintended mischief-making.

10. Coontz, *The Way We Never Were*, p. 18.

11. Arlie Hochschild, *The Second Shift: Working Parents and the Revolution at Home* (Viking, 1989).

12. Mitzi Dunn, "Employers' Child Care Policies: Sick Child Care," in Janet Hyde and Marilyn Essex, eds., *Parental Leave and Child Care: Setting a Research and Policy Agenda* (Temple University Press, 1991), p. 246.

13. These problems are more likely with family day care providers and nannies, less likely with group day care centers.

14. Sandra L. Hofferth and others, *National Child Care Survey, 1990* (Washington: Urban Institute, 1991), p. 347.

15. Audrey Light and Manuelita Ureta, "Gender Differences in the Quit Behavior of Young Workers," unpublished manuscript, Unicon Research Corporation, Los Angeles, September 22, 1989, p. vii.

16. Felice N. Schwartz, "Management Women and the New Facts of Life," *Harvard Business Review*, vol. 67 (January/February 1989), p. 65. Unfortunately, Schwartz does not reveal the identity of the corporation. Thus it is difficult to know whether these figures are typical or not.

17. Martin O'Connell, "Maternity Leave Arrangements: 1961-85," in *Work and Family Patterns of American Women*, Current Population Reports, series P-23, no. 165 (GPO, March 1990), p. 23.

18. Hochschild, *The Second Shift*.

19. Frances K. Goldscheider and Linda J. Waite, *New Families, No Families? The Transformation of the American Home* (University of California Press, 1991), p. 11; Barbara Vobejda, "Children Help Less at Home; Dads Do More," *Washington Post*, November 24, 1991, p. 1; Martin O'Connell, "Where's Papa? Fathers' Role in Child Care"; Kathleen Gerson, "A Few Good Men: Overcoming the Barriers to Involved Fatherhood," *American Prospect*, no. 16 (Winter 1994), pp. 78-90.

20. Fathers are also entitled to parental leave, and 40 percent of Swedish fathers have claimed that entitlement for some period of time. Sheila Kamerman, School of Social Work, Columbia University, telephone interview, January 13, 1994.

21. Elisabet Ornerborg, "Nearly 60,000 Children on Day Care Waiting Lists," *Inside Sweden*, no. 4 (November 1989), p. 4.

22. Kamerman, telephone interview.

23. Ibid.

24. Rick Atkinson, "Worried Germany Grapples With Population Shortage," *Washington Post*, March 12, 1994, p. 14.

25. Ellen Galinsky, "Families and Work: The Importance of the Quality of the Work Environment," in Sharon L. Kagan and Bernice Weissbourd, eds., *Putting Families First* (San Francisco: Jossey-Bass, 1994), p. 119.

26. Committee for Economic Development, *Why Child Care Matters: Preparing Young Children for a More Productive America* (New York: CED, 1993), p. 48.

27. Phyllis Moen, *Working Parents: Transformations in Gender Roles and Public Policies in Sweden* (University of Wisconsin Press, 1989), p. 112.

28. In 1992, for example, 25 percent of all women who work in the United States worked part time. That percentage is lower than comparable percentages in the Netherlands (63 percent), the United Kingdom (45 percent), Sweden (41 percent), Japan (35 percent), and Germany (34 percent), though roughly the same as in Canada and France. See Alfred J. Kahn and Sheila B. Kamerman, *Social Policy and the Under-3s: Six Country Case Studies* (Columbia University Press, 1994), table A-8.

29. Sheila B. Kamerman, "Starting Right: What We Owe to Children Under Three," *American Prospect*, no. 4 (Winter 1991), p. 71.

30. Moen, *Working Parents*, p. 65.

31. Schwartz, "Management Women and the New Facts of Life," pp. 65-76.

32. Tamar Lewin, "'Mommy Track' Sets off a Furor," *New York Times*, March 8, 1989, p. 18.

33. Approximately one-third of all mothers of young children fit that description. See Hofferth and others, *National Child Care Survey*, p. 33.

34. Gerson estimates that approximately one-third of all men are "involved fathers" who are full and active participants in child rearing. See Gerson, "A Few Good Men," p. 78. Because Gerson's sample included fatherless men, the percentage of fathers who fit that description may be higher still.

35. National Research Council, *Who Cares for America's Children?*, p. xiii; Edward F. Zigler and Mary E. Lang, *Child Care Choices: Balancing the Needs of Children, Families, and Society* (New York: Free Press, 1991), pp. 1-76; Rachel Connelly, "The Importance of Child Care Costs to Women's Decision Making," in David M. Blau, ed., *The Economics of Child Care* (New York: Russell Sage Foundation, 1991), p. 87.

36. Hofferth and others, *National Child Care Survey, 1990*, p. 223.

37. Ellen Eliason Kisker and others, *A Profile of Child Care Settings: Early Education and Care in 1990, Vol. 1* (Princeton, N.J.: Mathematica Policy Research Inc., 1991), p. 75.

38. Kisker and others, *A Profile of Child Care Settings*, p. 56.

39. National Research Council, *Who Cares for America's Children?*, p. 232.

40. Ibid., p. 29.

41. National Center for Educational Statistics, *The Condition of Education: 1993* (U.S. Department of Education, 1993), p. 373.

42. Author's calculations using data from District of Columbia Department of Human Services, "School Age Child Care in the District of Columbia: Annual Report" (Washington: Office of Early Childhood Development, January 1992), p. 12.

43. Under the Act, "public accommodations" such as group day care centers or even family day care homes cannot refuse admission based on disability alone. A child care establishment could assert, however, that the costs of adapting a site to meet the needs of a disabled person are prohibitive and that handicapped access is not "readily achievable." Family day care homes can probably make such arguments with greater justification than group day care centers.

44. Zigler and Lang, *Child Care Choices*, p. 144.

45. "Late Night Child Care Nearly Non-Existent," *Pittsburgh Press*, April 12, 1991, p. 11.

46. A sick-child care facility in the Tidewater area was forced to close in 1991, due to financial problems. The center, known as the Kids Comfort Station, struggled to break even throughout its relatively brief life span.

47. Committee for Economic Development, *Why Child Care Matters*, p. 49.

48. O'Connell, "Where's Papa?," p. 2; Zigler and Lang, *Child Care Choices*, p. 9.

49. John Morris, "Cost, Revenues, Subsidies: A Descripive Analysis," in Suzanne Helburn, ed., *Cost Quality and Child Outcomes in Child Care Centers*, Technical Report (Economics Department, University of Colorado at Denver, 1995), table 8.5.

50. Sylvia Ann Hewlett, *When the Bough Breaks: The Cost of Neglecting Our Children* (Basic Books, 1991), p. 51.

51. Marcy Whitebook, Carolee Howes, and Deborah A. Phillips, *Who Cares? Child Care Teachers and the Quality of Care in America* (Oakland, Calif.: Child Care Employee Project, 1989), p. 143.

52. Thanks to the Child Care and Development Block Grant and the At-Risk program, both created in 1990, and both aimed at low-income parents, the percentage may have declined somewhat since 1990.

53. GAO, following OMB, defined poor children as those living in families with an annual household income below $12,674 for a family of four. Their figures may slightly understate the extent to which preschool children attend an organized child care facility. See U.S. General Accounting Office, "Poor Pre-school- Aged Children: Numbers Increase but Most Not in Preschool," GAO/HRD-93-111BR (GAO, July 1993), p. 35. There is no reason, however, to doubt the overall conclusion that poor and near-poor preschool children have less access to child care.

54. In 1990 GAO defined near poor children as those living in families with an annual household income between 100 and 133 percent of the poverty level— or between $12,674 and $16,856 for a family of four. Ibid., p. 1.

55. Heather Buttaro, Testimony on Child Care and Development Block Grant, Hearings conducted by the Nebraska Department of Social Services, Lincoln, July 12, 1991.

56. Abt Associates, "National Day Care Study: Preliminary Findings and Their Implications" (Cambridge, Mass.: Abt Associates, January 31, 1978); Carolee Howes and Judith Rubenstein, "Determinants of Toddlers' Experience in Day Care: Age of Entry and Quality of Setting," *Child Care Quarterly*, vol. 14 (Summer 1985), pp. 140–51; Whitebook and others, *Who Cares?*; National Research Council, *Who Cares for America's Children?*, pp. 88–91.

57. Abt Associates, "National Day Care Study"; K. Alison Clarke-Stewart, "In Search of Consistencies in Child Care Research," in Deborah A. Phillips, ed., *Quality in Child Care: What Does Research Tell Us?* (Washington: National Association for the Education of Young Children, 1987), pp. 114–16; Deborah A. Phillips, Kathleen McCartney, and Sandra Scarr, "Child-Care Quality and Children's Social Development," *Developmental Psychology*, vol. 23 (July 1987), pp. 537–43; National Research Council, *Who Cares for America's Children?*, pp. 88–89.

58. Abt Associates, "National Day Care Study," p. 87; Howes and Rubenstein, "Determinants of Toddlers' Experience in Day Care," pp. 140–51; National Research Council, *Who Cares for America's Children?*, p. 87.

59. Abt Associates, "National Day Care Study"; Whitebook and others, *Who Cares?*, p. 112; National Research Council, *Who Cares for America's Children?*, pp. 89–90.

60. J. L. Fischer, "Family Day Care: Factors Influencing the Quality of Caregiving Practices," Ph.D. dissertation, University of Illinois, Urbana, 1989; Kathy Modigliani, "Promoting High-Quality Family Child Care" (Boston: Wheelock College, February 1994), p. 6.

61. Abt Associates, "National Day Care Study"; Whitebook and others, *Who Cares?*, p. 112; National Research Council, *Who Cares for America's Children?*, pp. 89–90.

62. Whitebook and others, *Who Cares?*, p. 112.

63. Sandra Scarr, *Mother Care, Other Care* (Basic Books, 1984), pp. 31–32; National Research Council, *Who Cares for America's Children?*, p. 91.

64. The National Association for the Education of Young Children (NAEYC) has concluded that a ratio no higher than 10:1 is best for children aged thirty-six to forty-seven months. See Kisker and others, *A Profile of Child Care Settings*, p. 128.

65. The NAEYC has concluded that a group size no larger than twenty is best for children aged thirty-six to forty-seven months. Ibid., p. 119.

66. According to Kisker and colleagues, 75 to 76 percent of all centers meet NAEYC child/staff ratio recommendations for three-year-olds and 83 to 84 percent of all centers meet NAEYC group size recommendations for three-year-

olds. Ibid., pp. 121, 129. It should be noted, however, that lower percentages meet NAEYC recommendations for infants and toddlers.

67. William T. Gormley, Jr., and B. Guy Peters, "National Styles of Regulation: Child Care in Three Countries," *Policy Sciences,* vol. 25 (November 1992), p. 386; Gail Richardson and Elisabeth Marx, *A Welcome for Every Child: How France Achieves Quality in Child Care* (New York: French-American Foundation, 1989), p. 18; Joseph J. Tobin, David Y. H. Wu, and Dana H. Davidson, *Preschool in Three Cultures: Japan, China, and the United States* (Yale University Press, 1989), pp. 36–38; Lois Peak, *Learning to Go to School in Japan: The Transition from Home to Preschool Life* (University of California Press, 1991), p. 52.

68. Gormley and Peters, "National Styles of Regulation," p. 388.

69. Peak, *Learning to Go to School in Japan,* p. 52.

70. Whitebook and others, *Who Cares?,* p. 35.

71. Ibid., p. 70.

72. According to the Bureau of National Affairs, the average annual turnover was 8.4 percent in 1992, 9.6 percent in 1991. Bureau of National Affairs, *Job Absence and Turnover* (Washington: BNA, March 1993). These figures were obtained by multiplying the December turnover rate by twelve, as recommended by the BNA staff.

73. Deborah A. Phillips, *Statement before the Committee on Education and Labor,* House of Representatives, Hearings on Child Care, Serial 101-18, 101 Cong. 1 sess. (GPO, February 9, 1989), p. 74.

74. An additional problem is the possibility that teachers were not in fact randomly selected. If center directors deliberately chose one of their better teachers for illustrative purposes, this would, of course, inflate the teacher training figures.

75. Zigler and Lang, *Child Care Choices,* p. 16.

76. Hillel Goelman and Alan Pence, "Effects of Child Care, Family, and Individual Characteristics on Children's Language Development: The Victoria Day Care Research Project," in Deborah A. Phillips, ed., *Quality in Child Care: What Does Research Tell Us?* (Washington: National Association for the Education of Young Children, 1987), pp. 105–120.

77. Patricia Divine-Hawkins, "Family Day Care in the U.S.: Executive Summary" (Washington: Administration for Children, Youth and Families, U.S. Dept. of Health and Human Services, July 1981), p. 31.

78. Danetta Cox and Richard Sherrill, "Traditional and Modernized Characteristics of Registered and Unregistered Family Day Care Providers" (1989), ERIC Document 290-577.

79. Margaret Nelson, "A Study of Family Day Care Providers: Attitudes Toward Regulation," *Child and Youth Care Forum,* vol. 20 (August 1991), p. 230; Barbara Willer and others, *The Demand and Supply of Child Care in 1990* (Washington: National Association for the Education of Young Children, 1991), pp. 18–19.

80. For a good discussion of the advantages and disadvantages of family day care, see K. Alison Clarke-Stewart, *Daycare* (Harvard University Press, 1982).

81. Kontos, *Family Day Care*, p. 55.

82. Willer and others, *The Demand and Supply of Child Care in 1990*, pp. 18–19.

83. Ibid.

84. Modigliani, "Promoting High-Quality Family Child Care," p. 4.

85. Whitebook and others, *Who Cares?*, pp. 49–51.

86. The average annual income of regulated family day care providers, before expenses, was about $10,000 in 1990. If one assumes annual expenses of approximately $3,000, that leaves a net income of $7,000 per year. See Modigliani, "Promoting High-Quality Family Child Care," pp. 21–22.

87. Ellen Galinsky and Judy David, *The Preschool Years: Family Strategies that Work* (New York: Times Books, 1988), p. 424; Phillips, Statement before the Committee on Education and Labor, p. 71; Samuel J. Meisels and L. Steven Sternberg, "Proprietary Child-Care Givers: Is '18 and Warm' Enough?" *Education Digest*, vol. 55 (January 1990), p. 62.

88. Paul E. Peterson, "An Immodest Proposal," *Daedalus*, vol. 121 (Fall 1992), p. 70.

89. Paul Starr, *The Social Transformation of American Medicine* (New York: Basic Books, 1982).

90. Caroline Zinsser, *Raised in East Urban: Child Care Changes in a Working Class Community* (Columbia University Teachers College Press, 1991).

91. According to Weimer and Vining, "A good is congestible if the marginal social cost of consumption can become positive beyond some level of consumption." See David Weimer and Aidan Vining, *Policy Analysis: Concepts and Practice* (Englewood Cliffs, N.J.: Prentice Hall, 1989), pp. 40–41. They cite fishing as an example; after a certain point, additional fishers become a threat to the early arrivals who still hope to catch a fish.

92. Ibid., pp. 45–47.

93. E. S. Savas, *Privatization: The Key to Better Government* (Chatham, N.J.: Chatham House, 1987), p. 53.

94. Although home schooling has attracted some interest in recent years, it is still a fringe movement preferred by a curious mixture of evangelical Christians and democratic reformers.

95. Scarr, *Mother Care, Other Care*; Deborah Fallows, *A Mother's Work* (Boston: Houghton Mifflin, 1985); Jay Belsky, "Infant Day Care: A Cause for Concern?", *Zero to Three*, September 1986, pp. 1–7; K. Alison Clarke-Stewart, "Infant Day Care: Maligned or Malignant?" *American Psychologist*, vol. 44 (February 1989), pp. 266–73.

96. Clarke-Stewart, *Daycare*.

97. Brian E. Vaughn, Frederick Gove, and Byron Egeland, "The Relationship between Out-of-Home Care and the Quality of Infant-Mother Attachment in an Economically Disadvantaged Population," *Child Development*, vol. 51 (December 1980), pp. 1203–14; Jay Belsky, "'The Effects' of Infant Day Care Reconsidered," *Early Childhood Research Quarterly*, vol. 3 (1986), pp. 235–72; National

Research Council, *Who Cares for America's Children?* (Washington: National Academy Press, 1990), p. 60.

98. Clarke-Stewart, "Infant Day Care."

99. Deborah Lowe Vandell, V. Kay Henderson, and Kathy Wilson, "A Longitudinal Study of Children with Day-Care Experiences of Varying Quality," *Child Development*, vol. 59 (October 1988), pp. 1286–92.

100. Richard A. Musgrave and Peggy B. Musgrave, *Public Finance in Theory and Practice* (McGraw-Hill, 1973), pp. 80–81.

101. John Rawls, *A Theory of Justice* (Harvard University Press, 1971), p. 3.

102. Ibid.; Michael Walzer, *Spheres of Justice: A Defense of Pluralism and Equality* (Basic Books, 1983); James S. Fishkin, *Justice, Equal Opportunity, and the Family* (Yale University Press, 1983); Brian Barry, *Theories of Justice* (University of California Press, 1989).

103. Robert H. Haveman and Burton Weisbrod, "Defining Benefits of Public Programs: Some Guidelines for Policy Analysts," in Robert H. Haveman and Julius Margolis, eds., *Public Expenditure and Policy Analysis*, 3d ed. (Boston: Houghton Mifflin, 1983), pp. 80–104; Lee S. Friedman, *Microeconomic Policy Analysis* (McGraw-Hill, 1984); Weimer and Vining, *Policy Analysis*.

104. This is the widely used Kaldor-Hicks principle. In contrast, a pure Pareto criterion states that a policy proposal is efficient only if it leaves some people better off without leaving anyone worse off. The Kaldor-Hicks principle is more widely used because, in practice, few policy proposals leave no one worse off than before.

105. Fishkin, *Justice, Equal Opportunity, and the Family.*

106. William T. Gormley Jr., "State Regulations and the Availability of Child Care Services," *Journal of Policy Analysis and Management*, vol. 10 (Winter 1991), pp. 78–95; Abt Associates, "National Day Care Study."

107. Gormley, "State Regulations," pp. 78–95.

108. Abt Associates, "National Day Care Study."

109. Charles W. Anderson, *Pragmatic Liberalism* (University of Chicago Press, 1990).

# Chapter Three

1. William T. Gormley, Jr., "State Regulations and the Availability of Child-Care Services," *Journal of Policy Analysis and Management*, vol. 10 (Winter 1991), pp. 78–95.

2. William T. Gormley, Jr., "Day Care Regulation in the South," unpublished manuscript, Georgetown University, 1991.

3. The demand for family day care is also greatest in the Midwest. See Sandra L. Hofferth and others, *National Child Care Survey, 1990* (Washington: Urban Institute, 1991), pp. 53–55. The precise relationship between demand and supply is unclear.

4. Hofferth and others, *National Child Care Survey, 1990*, p. 99.

5. Alfred J. Kahn and Sheila B. Kamerman, *Child Care: Facing the Hard Choices* (Dover, Mass.: Auburn House Publishing Company, 1987), p. 101.

6. Laura Jereski, "Heard on the Street: Kinder-Care is a New Toy for the Bulls," *Wall Street Journal,* April 20, 1993, p. C1.

7. Susan Caminiti, "KinderCare Learning Centers: New Lessons in Customer Service," *Fortune,* September 20, 1993, p. 79.

8. Homes with nannies and au pairs are largely unregulated.

9. Under legislation enacted in Virginia in 1993, family day care homes caring for six or more children will not be subject to state licensure until July 1, 1996. In the meantime, family day care homes are free to participate in a voluntary registration program.

10. U.S. General Accounting Office, "Child Care: States Face Difficulties Enforcing Standards and Promoting Quality," GAO/HRD-93-13 (GAO, November 1992), p. 19.

11. William T. Gormley, Jr., "Family-Friendly Regulations for Family Day Care Homes," in Marshall A. Worden and David A. de Kok, eds., *The Family Friendly City: Conflicts in Accommodating the Changing Family* (Tucson: Drachman Institute for Land and Regional Development Studies, University of Arizona, May 1992), p. 5.

12. The Federal Interagency Day Care Requirements were scuttled as part of the transformation of Title XX into the Social Services Block Grant, as codified by the Omnibus Budget and Reconciliation Act of 1981.

13. For example, instead of requiring that children be immunized, states may simply require that providers be informed about the advantages of immunization. See U.S. Department of Health and Human Services, "Final Rule, Child Care and Development Block Grant," *Federal Register* (Government Printing Office, August 4, 1992), pp. 34352–431.

14. Registration or certification of family day care homes, in Wisconsin and in other states that practice registration or certification, is a good deal more significant than the registration of relatives required by the CCDBG program, which is a mere formality. In Dane County, a nonprofit organization registers family day care homes; in Milwaukee County, a nonprofit organization certifies family day care homes. In Wisconsin, registration emphasizes provider training and parental monitoring, while certification emphasizes regular inspections.

15. Gilbert Y. Steiner, *The Children's Cause* (Brookings, 1976), pp. 15–22; Mary Frances Berry, *The Politics of Parenthood: Child Care, Women's Rights, and the Myth of the Good Mother* (Viking, 1993), pp. 106–107.

16. A limited number of group day care centers also have sponsors, though the program neither requires nor encourages this.

17. Committee on Ways and Means, U.S. House of Representatives, *Overview of Entitlement Programs: 1992 Green Book* (GPO, May 15, 1992), pp. 974–75.

18. Sandra L. Hofferth, "The 101st Congress: An Emerging Agenda for Children in Poverty," in Judith A. Chafel, ed., *Child Poverty and Public Policy* (Washington: Urban Institute, 1993), p. 210.

19. Philip K. Robins, "Child Care Policy and Research: An Economist's Perspective," in David M. Blau, ed., *The Economics of Child Care* (New York: Russell Sage Foundation, 1991), p. 26.

20. Gina Adams and Jodi R. Sandfort, "State Investments in Child Care and Early Childhood Education" (Washington: Children's Defense Fund, 1992), p. 1.

21. Catherine E. Born, *Our Future and Our Only Hope* (Washington: National League of Cities, 1989), p. 34.

22. The distinction between preservice and in-service training is not always clear. For example, preservice training is something of a misnomer in some states, which allow providers to complete said preservice training within so many months after beginning employment.

23. Telephone interview with Mary Patrick, Yakima Valley Community College, Yakima, Washington, October 22, 1993.

24. According to the past and current presidents of the National Association of Child Care Resource and Referral Agencies (NACCRA), the number of resource and referral agencies increased from 60 in 1988 to 496 in 1993. Telephone interview with Tutti Sherlock, Rochester, Minn., June 17, 1992; personal interview with Yasmina Vinci, Washington, D.C., February 7, 1994.

25. Edward Zigler and Susan Muenchow, *Head Start: The Inside Story of America's Most Successful Educational Experiment* (Basic Books, 1992), pp. 162–63.

26. Telephone interview with Marilyn Henry, Council of Early Childhood Professional Recognition, Washington, D.C., March 4, 1994.

27. Susan Kontos, *Family Day Care: Out of the Shadows and into the Limelight* (Washington: National Association for the Education of Young Children, 1992) p. 112.

28. Kontos, *Family Day Care*, pp. 119–46.

29. William T. Gormley, Jr., "Regulating Mister Rogers' Neighborhood: The Dilemmas of Day Care Regulation," *Brookings Review,* vol. 8 (Fall 1990), pp. 21–28.

30. Ellen Eliason Kisker and others, *A Profile of Child Care Settings: Early Education and Care in 1990, Vol. 1* (Princeton, N.J.: Mathematica Policy Research Inc., 1991), pp. 51–52.

31. Adams and Sandfort, *State Investments in Child Care*, attachment A.

32. Karl E. Weick, "Educational Organizations as Loosely Coupled Systems," *Administrative Science Quarterly,* vol. 21 (March 1976), pp. 1–19.

33. Weick, "Educational Organizations," pp. 1–19; John W. Meyer and Brian Rowan, "The Structure of Educational Organizations," in John W. Meyer and W. Richard Scott, eds., *Organizational Environments: Ritual and Rationality* (Beverly Hills, Calif.: Sage Publications, 1983), pp. 71–97; Adam Gamoran and Robert Dreeben, "Coupling and Control in Educational Organizations," *Administrative Science Quarterly,* vol. 31 (December 1986), pp. 612–32.

34. For example, no central authority assigns children to a particular day care center, as they are assigned to a particular public school. Indeed, there is nothing

quite comparable in child care to the local school board, which exercises considerable control over the allocation of resources within a school system.

35. John O'Looney, "Beyond Privatization and Service Integration: Organizational Models for Service Delivery," *Social Service Review,* vol. 67 (December 1993), pp. 526–29.

36. Lisa Gerrard, "Day-Care Sanctions Stricter in Other States," *Potomac News,* September 27, 1993, p. 4.

37. Eugene Bardach and Robert A. Kagan, *Going By the Book: The Problem of Regulatory Unreasonableness* (Temple University Press, 1982).

38. Donald C. Baumer and Carl E. Van Horn, *The Politics of Unemployment* (Washington: Congressional Quarterly Press, 1985).

39. Deborah A. Phillips and others, "Child Care for Children in Poverty: Opportunity or Inequity?", *Child Development,* vol. 65 (April 1994), pp. 472–92.

40. William T. Gormley, Jr., and B. Guy Peters, "National Styles of Regulation: Child Care in Three Countries," *Policy Sciences,* vol. 25 (November 1992), pp. 381–99; Gail Richardson and Elisabeth Marx, *A Welcome for Every Child: How France Achieves Quality in Child Care* (New York: French-American Foundation, 1989), p. 25.

41. James R. Walker, "New Evidence on the Supply of Child Care," *Journal of Human Resources,* vol. 27 (Winter 1992), p. 62.

42. Bernard Spodek, keynote address at the annual meeting of the Wisconsin Early Childhood Association, Madison, November 4, 1988.

43. Caroline Zinsser, *Raised in East Urban: Child Care Changes in a Working Class Community* (Columbia University Teachers College Press, 1991).

44. In a study of family day care providers in Milwaukee County, Wisconsin, I found that the average cost of home improvement for compliance with state and local regulations was $936. See William T. Gormley, Jr., "Family Day Care Regulation in Wisconsin: The Bureaucracy Heals Itself" (Madison: Robert La Follette Institute of Public Affairs, University of Wisconsin, 1990), p. 11.

45. Sharon L. Kagan, *United We Stand: Collaboration for Child Care and Early Education Services* (Columbia University Teachers College Press, 1991), p. 3.

46. Michael Lipsky, *Street-Level Bureaucracy: Dilemmas of the Individual in Public Services* (New York: Russell Sage Foundation, 1980).

47. Gary Sykes, "Fostering Teacher Professionalism in Schools," in Richard Elmore, ed., *Restructuring Schools: The Next Generation of Educational Reform* (San Francisco: Jossey-Bass, 1990), p. 84.

48. Gail Richardson and Elisabeth Marx, *A Welcome for Every Child: How France Achieves Quality in Child Care* (New York: French-American Foundation, 1989), p. 15.

49. A quality circle is a management reform that involves workers in the organization and design of workplace tasks.

50. Purposive incentives refer to appealing organizational goals, such as world peace or racial equality. Solidary incentives refer to the joys of interacting with other people in small groups. For a discussion of organizational incentive systems, see Peter

B. Clark and James Q. Wilson, "Incentive Systems: A Theory of Organizations," *Administrative Science Quarterly*, vol. 6 (September 1961), pp. 129–66.

# Chapter Four

1. Ellen Eliason Kisker and others, *A Profile of Child Care Settings: Early Education and Care in 1990, Vol. 1* (Princeton, N.J.: Mathematica Policy Research, 1991); Ellen Galinsky and others, *The Study of Children in Family Child Care and Relative Care* (New York: Families and Work Institute, 1994).

2. Barbara Willer and others, *The Demand and Supply of Child Care in 1990* (Washington: National Association for the Education of Young Children, 1991), pp. 18–19.

3. RMC Research Corporation, *National Study of Before and After School Programs: Final Report* (U.S. Department of Education, Office of Policy and Planning, 1993), p. 38.

4. In London, for example, for-profit nurseries increased by more than 60 percent between 1985 and 1988. See Penelope Leach, *Children First* (Knopf, 1994), p. 81.

5. Willer and others, *The Demand and Supply of Child Care*, p. 31.

6. H. Naci Mocan, "Quality-Adjusted Cost Functions for Child-Care Centers," *American Economic Review (Papers and Proceedings)*, vol. 85 (May 1995), pp. 409–13; Swati Mukerjee and Ann Witte, "Provision of Child Care: Cost Functions for Profit-Making and Not-for-Profit Day Care Centers," *Journal of Productivity Analysis*, vol. 4 (June 1993), pp. 145–63; Anne Preston, "Efficiency, Quality, and Social Externalities in the Provision of Day-Care: Comparisons of Nonprofits and For-Profit Firms," *Journal of Productivity Analysis*, vol. 4 (June 1993), pp. 165–82.

7. Kisker and others, *A Profile of Child Care Settings*, pp. 234–37.

8. RMC Research Corporation, *National Study of Before and After School Programs*. The exception is that child/staff ratios are lower at SACC programs run by for-profit firms. The other findings are as one would expect: for-profits pay SACC staff members less, which increases turnover; for-profits are less likely to offer health insurance, with adverse consequences for recruitment and retention; and for-profit directors are less likely to have a bachelor's degree.

9. Kisker and others, *A Profile of Child Care Settings*, pp. 234–35.

10. For literature on the effects of teacher education, see Marcy Whitebook, Carolee Howes, and Deborah Phillips, *Who Cares?: Child Care Teachers and the Quality of Care in America* (Oakland, Calif.: Child Care Employee Project, 1989), p. 113; Richard Ruopp and others, "Children at the Center: Final Report of the National Day Care Study" (Cambridge, Mass.: Abt Associates, 1979); National Research Council, *Who Cares for America's Children?* (Washington: National Academy Press, 1990), pp. 89–90. On the importance of ratios, see Whitebook and others, *Who Cares?*, pp. 113–14; Carolee Howes and Judith Rubenstein, "Determinants of Toddlers' Experiences in Day Care: Age of Entry and Quality of Setting," *Child Care Quarterly*, vol. 14 (1985), pp. 140–51;

National Research Council, *Who Cares for America's Children?*, pp. 88–89. For research on turnover effects, see Carolee Howes and others, "Attachment and Child Care: Relationships with Mother and Caregiver," *Early Childhood Research Quarterly*, vol. 3 (1988), pp. 403–16; Whitebook and others, *Who Cares?*, pp. 109–111; National Research Council, *Who Cares for America's Children?*, pp. 91–92.

11. Ordinary least squares multiple regression analysis is a technique used to estimate the effects of two or more independent variables on an interval-level dependent variable. It identifies a line (or equation) that minimizes the sum of the squared vertical distances from actual data points. Two stage least squares is a technique used to deal with reciprocal causality. Thus if X causes Y but Y also causes X, the effects of X on Y can be isolated by controlling for the effects of Y on X.

12. Kisker and others, *A Profile of Child Care Settings*, pp. 12–13.

13. Data on state education and training requirements were obtained from a content analysis of state rules and regulations. Data on child/staff ratio requirements were obtained from the authors of the *Profile of Child Care Settings* report. Data on state child care expenditures (or subsidies) were obtained from the Children's Defense Fund report, "State Investments in Child Care and Early Education." See Gina Adams and Jodi R. Sandfort, "State Investments in Child Care and Early Education" (Washington: Children's Defense Fund, March 1992). All of the supplementary variables were from 1990, which is when the *Profile of Child Care Settings* data were gathered.

14. I hypothesized that centers with a conspicuously low number of staff members (controlling for the number of children and the mean age of children) would trigger more inspections. If anything, the opposite seems to be the case.

15. J. Johnston, *Econometric Models*, 2d ed. (McGraw Hill, 1972), pp. 321–423; Jan Kmenta, *Elements of Econometrics*, 2d ed. (Macmillan, 1986), pp. 672–87; Peter Kennedy, *A Guide to Econometrics*, 3d ed. (MIT Press, 1992), pp. 151–75.

16. Vermont has relatively stringent child care standards, including low child/staff ratios, which traditionally have discouraged chains from locating in such states. In addition, Vermont has relatively tough water quality standards, which can increase the costs of starting up and operating a group day care center. More broadly, Vermonters remain unusually suspicious of chains. For example, they have successfully opposed efforts by Wal-Mart to open stores in Williston and St. Albans. See Malcolm Gladwell, "Wal-Mart Encounters a Wall of Resistance in Vermont," *Washington Post*, July 27, 1994, p. 3.

17. Two for-profits ran two centers each, and a nonprofit ran four centers in the Middlebury area as of 1994. These are exceptions to the general rule.

18. I focused on 1991 relicensings for reasons discussed in chapter 5.

19. Before making these comparisons, I considered controlling for center capacity, but that proved unnecessary because there is no relationship between for-profit status and center capacity, at least in Vermont. The simple correlation coefficient between the two variables is .014.

20. For example, an inspector may note that the absence of a full-length mirror makes dress-up play less fulfilling, even though such a mirror is not a legal requirement.

21. In conducting this content analysis, I examined all substantiated complaints filed against centers between 1989 and 1993, not just complaints against centers relicensed in 1991. This permitted me to review a somewhat larger number of cases than would otherwise have been possible.

22. Burton A. Weisbrod, *The Nonprofit Economy* (Harvard University Press, 1988), p. 158.

23. This legal requirement is something of an anachronism. Because of the passage of new federal child care subsidy programs in 1988 and 1990 (especially the IV-A programs), Social Services Block Grant funding now constitutes a relatively small percentage of federal child care funding for disadvantaged children. Thus a for-profit center may be caring for a substantial number of poor children receiving federal funds, only a few of whom are receiving SSBG funds. To get around this problem, some USDA regional offices have taken advantage of the fact that SSBG child care money and Title IV-A child care money are placed in the same pool of funds in some states. If 25 percent or more of a for-profit center's children receive support from that pool of funds, the center is considered to be eligible for the Child and Adult Care Food Program. This creative rule interpretation helps but is an imperfect solution for two reasons: (1) some states have not consolidated their IV-A and SSBG funding streams; and (2) many states keep their IV-A and SSBG funding separate from their Child Care and Development Block Grant funding. Thus even in a state with some pooling, a for-profit center would be ineligible to participate in the Child and Adult Care Food Program if 20 percent of its children received funding from the combined IV-A and SSBG funds, while 10 percent of equally poor children received funding from a separate CCDBG account.

24. A very large chain may even insure itself, as KinderCare does.

25. Barry Bluestone and others, *The Retail Revolution: Market Transformation, Investment, and Labor in the Modern Department Store* (Boston: Auburn House Publishing Co., 1981), p. 62.

26. Not every child care chain is publicly held. La Petite Academy, based in Kansas City, went private in 1992.

27. Kisker and others, *A Profile of Child Care Settings*, p. 53.

28. Suzanne W. Helburn, ed., "Cost, Quality, and Child Outcomes in Child Care Centers, Technical Report," Economics Department, University of Colorado at Denver, January 1995, table 11.16.

29. Return on equity refers to net income (latest year) divided by shareholders equity (previous year). The average for industries as a whole is in the range of 12 to 15 percent. Return on assets refers to net income (latest year) divided by total assets (previous year). The average for industries as a whole tends to be about 10 percent. Return on sales (or profitability) refers to net income (latest year) divided by operating revenue (also latest year). The average for industries as a whole tends to be about 5 percent.

30. This appears to have been because of some spectacularly bad investments in other fields (for example, the savings and loan industry) and not because of the intrinsic unprofitability of child care. See Laura Jereski, "Heard on the Street: Kinder-Care is a New Toy for the Bulls," *Wall Street Journal*, April 20, 1993, p. C1.

31. In fiscal year 1993, group day care centers received $483.1 million in reimbursements, commodities, and cash in lieu of food under the Child and Adult Care Food Program. In September 1993, an illustrative month, 28,500 centers were participating in the program. Thus the average value of participation was $16,951. U.S. Department of Agriculture, Food and Nutrition Division, "Key Data Report," unpublished report, January 1994, pp. 11, 18.

32. In principle, for-profits could always enroll more disadvantaged children. And they would have financial incentives to do so. However, many for-profits have deliberately located in relatively prosperous suburban communities, in an effort to target more affluent clients. This is especially true of the chains. For them, dramatic changes in enrollment patterns are unlikely.

33. Kisker and others, *A Profile of Child Care Settings,* p. 51.

34. A significant increase, however, is unlikely. Even nonprofit day care centers receive only 4 to 11 percent of their revenues from government sources. See Kisker and others, *A Profile of Child Care Settings,* p. 52.

35. Joseph Rees, *Reforming the Workplace: A Study of Self-Regulation in Occupational Safety* (Temple University Press, 1988).

36. William T. Gormley, Jr., and B. Guy Peters, "National Styles of Regulation: Child Care in Three Countries, *Policy Sciences,* vol. 25 (November 1992), pp. 381–99.

37. Ian Ayres and John Braithwaite, *Responsive Regulation: Transcending the Deregulation Debate* (Oxford University Press, 1992), pp. 101–32. Although a full-blown enforced regulation model has yet to be employed in the real world, some prototypes do exist, including mine safety regulation and pharmaceutical regulation in the United States.

38. Another possibility is that nonprofit organizations such as the YMCA, though not chains in the traditional sense, might grow. Additional research is needed to determine whether nonprofit chains are better or worse than other nonprofits.

39. Willer and others, *The Demand and Supply of Child Care,* p. 60.

40. Galinsky and others, *The Study of Children in Family Child Care,* p. 57.

41. Hillel Goelman and Alan Pence, "Effects of Child Care, Family, and Individual Characteristics on Children's Language Development: The Victoria Day Care Research Project," in Deborah A. Phillips, ed., *Quality in Child Care: What Does Research Tell Us?* (Washington: National Association for the Education of Young Children, 1987), pp. 89–104.

42. Goelman and Pence, "Effects of Child Care, Family, and Individual Characteristics," p. 91. It should be noted, however, that licensed homes customarily care for more children than unlicensed homes.

43. Galinsky and others, *The Study of Children in Family Day Care.*

44. Ibid.

45. Mickey Butts, "Day Care Laws: An Essential Guide," *Parenting* (November 1993), p. 131.

46. Ibid.

47. Willer and others, *The Demand and Supply of Child Care*, pp. 18–19; Galinsky and others, *The Study of Children in Family Child Care*, p. 14.

48. Galinsky and others, *The Study of Children in Family Child Care*, p. 90.

49. These findings differ from findings on access to center-based care of high quality. According to some researchers, extremely disadvantaged children often have access to better center-based care than working-class or middle-class children. See Deborah A. Phillips and others, "Child Care for Children in Poverty: Opportunity or Inequity?" *Child Development*, vol. 65 (April 1994), pp. 472–92. This is due in part to the Head Start program, which targets disadvantaged children.

50. Margaret K. Nelson, "A Study of Family Day Care Providers: Attitudes Toward Regulation," *Child and Youth Care Forum*, vol. 20 (August 1991), pp. 225–42.

51. Galinsky and others, *The Study of Children in Family Child Care*, p. 49.

52. William T. Gormley, Jr., "Family Day Care Regulation in Wisconsin: The Bureaucracy Heals Itself" (Madison, Wisc.: Robert La Follette Institute of Public Affairs, 1990).

53. Advisory Commission on Intergovernmental Relations, "Child Care: The Need for Federal-State-Local Coordination" (Washington: ACIR, March 1994), p. 30.

54. Butts, "Day Care Laws," p. 131.

55. William T. Gormley, Jr., "State Regulations and the Availability of Child-Care Services," *Journal of Policy Analysis and Management*, vol. 10 (Winter 1991), pp. 78–95.

56. Margaret K. Nelson, *Negotiated Care: The Experience of Family Day Care Providers* (Temple University Press, 1990), pp. 220–23.

57. The Dayton-Hudson Foundation and the Pew Charitable Trusts are among the foundations that have provided generous support to family day care home initiatives.

58. William T. Gormley, Jr., "Regulating Mister Rogers' Neighborhood: The Dilemmas of Day Care Regulation," *Brookings Review*, vol. 8 (Fall 1990), pp. 21–28.

59. Jeremy Main, "The Curmudgeon Who Talks Tough on Quality," *Fortune*, June 25, 1984, pp. 118–22; Andrea Gabor, *The Man Who Discovered Quality* (New York: Times Books, 1990), pp. 69–100.

60. Gabor, *The Man Who Discovered Quality*, p. 10.

61. For example, parents of children at a center in the state's Department of Education building voted in November 1993 to replace the incumbent licensee (a Harrisburg-based for-profit firm) with another licensee (a Wilkes Barre–based for-profit firm). The new licensee has improved working conditions for staff

members by boosting their salaries and by offering them a better benefits package. According to center director Jennifer Shirk, the new licensee also provides training opportunities that exceed state requirements and is working towards obtaining accreditation by the National Association for the Education of Young Children (NAEYC).

62. The *Profile* database includes several measures of parental involvement. I chose the following: whether parents regularly participate in choosing activities and monitoring (a dichotomous variable).

63. Ordinary least squares (OLS) regression analysis is inappropriate when the dependent variable is dichotomous, because OLS assumes that the dependent variable has an unrestricted range. Through logistic regression analysis, the dependent variable is transformed into a logged probability. See Kennedy, *A Guide to Econometrics*, pp. 234–36. Thus I regress the log odds of each center's offering an examination on the independent variables in each model.

64. Although many technical colleges and community colleges offer courses in health and safety as part of their child care curriculum, these courses are often taught by child development professionals rather than health professionals. Health issues may not be emphasized as a result.

65. In Minneapolis, for example, regular visits by a public health nurse cost approximately $200 per year per center.

66. Mary Walton, *The Deming Management Method* (Perigee, 1986), p. 60.

67. Child care occupied a prominent place in North Carolina's 1992 gubernatorial campaign for two reasons. Former Governor Jim Hunt, having established himself as an "education" governor during his first and second terms, wanted to be known as an "early education" governor during his third term. Also, a lurid, highly publicized child abuse scandal at the Little Rascals Day Care Center in Edenton, North Carolina, riveted voter attention to child care as a pressing public issue. The TEACH program was originally funded by the Child Care and Development Block Grant and private sources. Currently, the program is funded almost exclusively by state legislative appropriations. The program is administered by the Day Care Services Association of Orange County, under contract to the state.

68. The Division of Child Development is in the Department of Human Resources.

69. The state also contributes a $22 travel stipend per provider per quarter to center staff members and family day care providers alike.

70. Program organizers strongly prefer Option 1. They established a second option for two main reasons: (1) some centers felt that they simply could not afford substantial release time; and (2) some centers, such as Head Start programs, are locked into fixed salary structures by law. Option 2 addresses both problems by allowing centers to contribute cash in lieu of release time and by allowing centers to make one-time cash payments rather than permanent salary adjustments. Under Option 2, centers must contribute 50 percent of both tuition and book costs. Teachers, therefore, pay nothing for tuition and books. However, they also get less release time and no permanent pay hike.

71. The state also contributes $22 per quarter for travel and reimburses the provider for the cost of hiring a substitute for 11 hours per quarter.

72. Telephone interview with Margaret Moberley, Day Care Services Association of Orange County, Carrboro, N.C., April 6, 1995.

73. The Delaware First program, for example, established a career ladder that enables entry-level providers to advance steadily to better jobs as they receive more education and training.

74. Elaine Enarson, "Experts and Caregivers: Perspectives on Underground Day Care," in Emily K. Abel and Margaret K. Nelson, eds., *Circles of Care: Work and Identity in Women's Lives* (State University of New York Press, 1990), p. 237.

75. The diversion of some revenues into profits also helps to account for these differences.

## Chapter Five

1. Lester M. Salamon and Michael S. Lund, "The Tools Approach: Basic Analytics," in Lester M. Salamon, ed., *Beyond Privatization: The Tools of Government Action* (Washington: Urban Institute, 1989), pp. 23–49.

2. Christopher Hood, *The Tools of Government* (Chatham, N.J.: Chatham House, 1983), p. 153.

3. Deborah A. Phillips and Debra Mekos, "The Myth of Child Care Regulation: Rates of Compliance in Center-Based Child Care Settings," paper prepared for the 1993 annual research conference of the Association for Public Policy Analysis and Management.

4. To test this proposition, I obtained unpublished data from a U.S. General Accounting Office (GAO) survey of state child care regulators conducted between March 1991 and May 1992. These data indicate which states possess particular enforcement techniques, ranging from being able to establish a corrective action plan to being able to close a facility immediately. I developed a nine-item index as a measure of enforcement clout against centers and compared that index with child/staff ratio requirements and preservice training requirements, also for centers. Simple correlation coefficients were not statistically significant at an acceptable level. They were also consistently in the wrong direction. Thus, if anything, states with higher regulatory standards have somewhat weaker enforcement tools at their disposal. I would like to thank Janet Mascia of GAO for supplying these data in a timely fashion.

5. The ratio for one-year-olds, previously 7:1, is now 5:1.

6. Personal interview with Raymond Smith, North Carolina Division of Child Development, Raleigh, N.C., November 17, 1993.

7. Cheryl D. Hayes, John L. Palmer, and Martha J. Zaslow, eds., *Who Cares for America's Children? Child Care Policy for the 1990s* (Washington: National Academy Press, 1990), pp. 88–89.

8. William T. Gormley, Jr., "State Regulations and the Availability of Child-Care Services," *Journal of Policy Analysis and Management*, vol. 10 (Winter 1991), pp. 78–95.

9. Time-series analysis, as developed by George Box and Gwilym Jenkins, is a technique used to isolate the effects of one or more independent variables on a series with autocorrelated disturbances. By removing the trend from the series through statistical means, as well as any cyclical effects that may be present, it is possible to transform a nonstationary series into a stationary series that can then be analyzed with fairly conventional techniques, such as OLS multiple regression analysis. For a lucid exposition of time-series analysis, see Richard McCleary and Richard A. Hay, Jr., *Applied Time Series Analysis for the Social Sciences* (Beverly Hills, Calif.: Sage Publications, 1980). For an excellent introduction to time-series tests, see Jeff B. Cromwell, Walter C. Labys, and Michel Terraza, *Univariate Tests for Time Series Models* (Beverly Hills, Calif.: Sage Publications, 1994).

10. When a dependent variable (or series) is nonstationary, it cannot be analyzed through least squares regression analysis. Therefore, it is necessary to transform the variable into a stationary series where autocorrelation between disturbances is no longer a problem. First differencing of a monthly series accomplishes this by creating a new series in which each month's observation becomes the difference between that month's observation and the previous month's observation.

11. The FDCS series suggested decay and dampening in the ACF, a single spike at lag one in the PACF. The DFDCS series revealed a reasonably stationary picture, with only one statistically significant spike at lag three. However, the Box-Pierce Q statistic of 40.60 at twenty lags was statistically significant at the .01 level. Therefore, I cannot state with certainty that the model residuals for DFDCS are white noise.

12. There is every reason to believe that an increase in the number of births fuels the demand for child care and results in an increase in the number of family day care homes. The timing of that impact, however, is more difficult to predict than, say, the impact of births on elementary school enrollments, because parents are free to place their children in a child care facility as infants, toddlers, pre-schoolers, or not at all. I used a two-year lag in the model because most family day care providers are willing to accept toddlers. If I had been looking at center-based care, I probably would have used a three-year or four-year lag.

13. The differenced series for homes (DHOMES) is also eminently stationary. An analysis of the ACF and PACF functions at twenty lags reveals a Box-Pierce Q statistic of 26.88, which is not statistically significant at an acceptable level. Therefore, I can state with confidence that the residual ACF does not differ from a white noise ACF. See McCleary and Hay, *Applied Time Series Analysis for the Social Sciences*, p. 99.

14. The FDCS series, at twenty lags, was characterized by decay and dampening in the ACF, a single spike at lag one in the PACF. The DFDCS series, at twenty lags, included no statistically significant spikes and yielded a Box-Pierce Q-statistic of 14.07, which was definitely not statistically significant. I can safely conclude in this instance that the model residuals were no different than white noise.

15. I did not, however, lag the female employment variable, because an unlagged variable produced a better fit.

16. This subsequently became a 30 percent sample.

17. This requirement may not have been fully implemented throughout Texas until 1993. I have verified, however, that the requirement was implemented in the Houston area in January 1992.

18. Statewide data on the number of registered family day care homes were missing for a crucial twelve-month interval. I would like to thank Virginia Hancock and Jan Martin for supplying the Houston data.

19. The autocorrelation and partial autocorrelation functions for FDCS (the original series), at twenty lags, revealed decay and dampening and a single spike at lag one. The autocorrelation and partial autocorrelation functions for the differenced series (DFDCS) revealed no statistically significant spikes, at twenty lags, and a Box-Pierce Q statistic of 28.34, which was not statistically significant at an acceptable level. Therefore, I concluded that the model residuals resemble white noise.

20. It is somewhat puzzling to discover, once again, a negative relationship between the number of births, lagged two years, and the differenced family day care series. One possibility is that the effects of oscillating birth rates within a given state are quickly eclipsed by substantial in-migration and out-migration. Or it could be that as family day care providers give birth a second or third time, their inclination to stay in business diminishes.

21. William T. Gormley, Jr., "Family Day Care Regulation in Wisconsin: The Bureaucracy Heals Itself" (Madison: Robert La Follette Institute of Public Affairs, University of Wisconsin, 1990).

22. Gormley, "State Regulations and the Availability of Child-Care Services," p. 87.

23. Missouri Department of Social Services, "Licensing Rules for Child Day Care Homes in Missouri" (Jefferson City, Mo.: September 1982), p. 16.

24. Missouri Department of Social Services, "Licensing Rules for Family Day Care Homes in Missouri" (Jefferson City, Mo.: September 1991), pp. 16–17.

25. The new rules did grandfather in existing equipment to some extent. Specifically, the six-foot-high rule applies only to new licensees or to new equipment.

26. Gormley, "State Regulations and the Availability of Child-Care Services," pp. 78–95.

27. Sandra L. Hofferth, Duncan D. Chaplin, and Douglas A. Wissoker, "State Regulations and Child Care Choices," unpublished manuscript, Urban Institute, Washington, May 4, 1994.

28. Helen Blank, "Investing in Our Children's Care" (Washington: Children's Defense Fund, June 1993), p. 33.

29. Gormley, "State Regulations and the Availability of Child-Care Services."

30. Ellen Galinsky and others, *The Study of Children in Family Child Care and Relative Care* (New York: Families and Work Institute, 1994), p. 47.

31. Another problem with license revocation is that it does not always guarantee that a facility will cease to operate. This is particularly true of family day care homes. The problem is not unique to child care. For example, Jacobs has

noted that thousands of Americans continue to drive automobiles despite having had their driver's license revoked. See James B. Jacobs, *Drunk Driving: An America Dilemma* (University of Chicago Press, 1989), p. 151.

32. U.S. General Accounting Office, "Child Care: States Face Difficulties Enforcing Standards and Promoting Quality," GAO/HRD-93-13 (GAO, November 1992), p. 19.

33. John Braithwaite, *To Punish or Persuade: Enforcement of Coal Mine Safety* (Albany: State University of New York Press, 1985).

34. Ian Ayres and John Braithwaite, *Responsive Regulation: Transcending the Deregulation Debate* (Oxford University Press, 1992), p. 36.

35. The state government lawyers who make these decisions are usually responsible for a wide variety of social services cases (concerning AFDC and Medicaid payments, for example) and not just child care cases. Child care cases typically constitute a small fraction of their total workload.

36. Wayne B. Gray and John T. Scholz, "Does Regulatory Enforcement Work? A Panel Analysis of OSHA Enforcement," *Law and Society Review*, vol. 27, no. 1 (1993), p. 186.

37. Stephen G. Breyer, *Regulation and its Reform* (Harvard University Press, 1982); Martha Derthick and Paul J. Quirk, *The Politics of Deregulation* (Brookings, 1985).

38. Eugene Bardach and Robert A. Kagan, *Going by the Book: The Problem of Regulatory Unreasonableness* (Temple University Press, 1982), p. 165.

39. The timing was felicitous. The 1989–93 files were relatively complete; earlier files were not.

40. I deliberately recorded problems, rather than rule violations, for two reasons. First, it was not always possible to tell from the case file whether a specific regulation had been violated. Second, from a provider's point of view, a problem as perceived by the state inspector is a matter of concern, regardless of whether it is officially a rule violation. Because the inspector is free to decide the disposition of a license renewal request, anything worthy of the inspector's attention is also worthy of the provider's attention.

41. Although I relied primarily on the Recommendations for Improvement section, I used any and all documents in the center's file, including compliance checklists and conditions specified in the license renewal letter. Indeed, in a few instances, it was necessary to rely exclusively on these items, because the recommendations for improvement were missing.

42. The relevant starting date, I concluded, was the date on which the renewal was granted; the relevant termination date was the expiration date of the renewed license. If the period between the two dates exceeded eighteen months but not thirty months, it was deemed a two-year renewal. If the period exceeded thirty months, it was deemed a three-year renewal.

43. In Vermont, as in most other states, initial licensing consists of a series of increasingly formal visits, in which center personnel are advised on steps that must be taken to meet state (and local) requirements. Center personnel are often

told not to take premature steps to bring their center into compliance, for fear that they might make hasty purchases or construction decisions that subsequently turn out to be inappropriate or unnecessary. Thus, unacceptable conditions during these pre-licensing visits may reflect a center's proper willingness to await further guidance rather than incorrigible behavior.

44. Three-year licenses were excluded from this phase of the analysis because they constituted a relatively small number of cases and because only a handful of them had been renewed as of early 1994.

45. In 1993 inspectors noted an average of 4.75 problems at group day care centers that received a two-year license in 1991, as opposed to 5.47 problems at centers that received one-year licenses in 1991 and 1992.

46. For the purpose of this exercise, I defined cumulative history as the combined problem (or very serious problem) scores for 1991, 1990, and 1989, divided by three. If data for one of these years was missing, I focused on the remaining two years and divided by two. In the overwhelming majority of cases, data for all three years were available.

47. Vivian Cadden, "The State of the States," *Working Mother*, vol. 18 (March 1994), pp. 31–38.

48. Richard Fiene and Mark Nixon, "The Instrument Based Program Monitoring Information System and the Indicator Checklist for Child Care," *Child Care Quarterly*, vol. 14 (Fall 1985), pp. 198–214.

49. For optimal results, the weightings should be obtained through a questionnaire survey of experts, including providers; the statistical comparisons of individual items with overall compliance scores should be made by a trained statistician or policy analyst. In principle, either step may come first. If the weighting comes first (Fiene's preference), the overall compliance score is adjusted to reflect the greater importance of certain items. The inclusion of individual items is then based on their ability to predict the adjusted compliance score. If the compliance prediction measures come first, all regulatory requirements are initially weighted equally. Subsequently, regulatory requirements deemed to be highly risk related are added to the indicator checklist even if they did not predict overall compliance as well as other items.

50. Fiene cites Pennsylvania, Utah, Florida, and Washington State. Personal interview with Richard Fiene, Pennsylvania Bureau of Child Care Services, Harrisburg, October 25, 1993.

51. U.S. General Accounting Office, "Child Care: States Face Difficulties Enforcing Standards and Promoting Quality," p. 22.

52. Fiene and Nixon, "The Instrument Based Program Monitoring Information System and the Indicator Checklist for Child Care," p. 207.

53. The initial policy in West Virginia was for indicator checklists to be used on monitoring visits (once a year), while the full set of regulations would be used on renewal visits (once every two years). Over time, inspectors came to use indicator checklists for renewals as well, if the center's past performance warranted it. Telephone interview with Kay Tilton, West Virginia Office of Social Services, Charleston, July 28, 1994.

54. For example, some North Carolina inspectors report that they use the indicator checklist with every renewal. Others note that the indicator checklist has not been updated since it was first developed in 1990. If so, this increases the chances that providers will simply focus on the previous year's renewal instrument because the odds are that it has not changed. Failure to update may be due in part to technical difficulties that arise when designing an indicator checklist. For example, North Carolina's experts rated so many regulatory requirements a nine or ten on a scale of one to ten that there was little opportunity for differential weighting. Personal interview with Jeanie Marlowe, North Carolina Division of Child Development, Raleigh, June 7, 1994.

55. Richard Pierce, Jr., Sidney Shapiro, and Paul Verkuil, *Administrative Law and Process* (Mineola, N.Y.: Foundation Press, 1985), pp. 360–62.

56. Sheila B. Kamerman, "Starting Right: What We Owe to Children Under Three," *American Prospect*, no. 4 (Winter 1991), pp. 63–73.

57. Sandra L. Hofferth, "The 101st Congress: An Emerging Agenda for Children in Poverty," in Judith A. Chafel, ed., *Child Poverty and Public Policy* (Washington: Urban Institute, 1993), p. 210.

58. In making these estimates, I have relied upon Hofferth's breakdown of federal child care spending for fiscal year 1994 and my own assessment of who benefits primarily from each program. See Hofferth, "The 101st Congress," p. 210. A more fine-grained analysis would dissect each program separately. For example, the Child and Adult Care Food Program primarily benefits the poor, but some middle-class children do receive funding (for example, middle-class children enrolled in participating family day care homes). Conversely, the Child and Dependent Care Tax Credit primarily benefits the middle class, but some working poor parents have taken advantage of it.

59. Hayes and others, *Who Cares for America's Children?*, p. 197.

60. Stephen W. Raudenbush and others, "Can Government Raise Child-Care Quality? The Influence of Family Demand, Poverty, and Policy," *Educational Evaluation and Policy Analysis*, vol. 15 (Fall 1993), p. 275.

61. Valerie Lee and others, "Are Head Start Effects Sustained? A Longitudinal Follow-up Comparison of Disadvantaged Children Attending Head Start, No Preschool, and Other Preschool Programs," *Child Development*, vol. 61 (April 1990), pp. 495–507; Edward Zigler and Susan Muenchow, *Head Start: The Inside Story of America's Most Successful Educational Experiment* (Basic Books, 1992).

62. Ruth McKey and others, "The Impact of Head Start on Children, Families and Communities: Head Start Synthesis Project" (Government Printing Office, 1985); Zigler and Muenchow, *Head Start*.

63. Zigler and Muenchow, *Head Start*, p. 209.

64. Ron Haskins, "Beyond Metaphor: The Efficacy of Early Childhood Education," *American Psychologist*, vol. 44 (February 1989), pp. 274–82.

65. For example, the Perry Preschool Program featured a 5:1 child-to-staff ratio and teachers with postgraduate degrees in early childhood education, which

is not the norm for Head Start programs. Also, the Perry Preschool Program arranged for teachers to visit every child's home once a week. In contrast, Head Start staff members struggle to visit each home twice a year. See Zigler and Muenchow, *Head Start,* p. 213.

66. Julia B. Isaacs, "Participation of Child Care Centers in the Child and Adult Care Food Program," mimeo, Congressional Budget Office, October 1993, table 3.

67. Under current law, children in participating family day care homes are automatically eligible for a full subsidy, unless the children are the provider's own. The provider's own children are eligible for full funding if the family income is lower than 185 percent of the poverty level; otherwise they receive no funding.

68. Deil S. Wright, *Understanding Intergovernmental Relations,* 3rd ed. (Pacific Grove, Calif.: Brooks/Cole, 1988), pp. 212–13.

69. Advisory Commission on Intergovernmental Relations, *Regulatory Federalism: Policy, Process, Impact and Reform* (Washington: ACIR, February 1984).

70. Nancy Ebb, "Child Care Tradeoffs: States Make Painful Choices" (Washington: Children's Defense Fund, January 1994), pp. 12–13.

71. In a survey of twenty-five states, the U.S. Department of Health and Human Services found that twenty-one were using identical reimbursement rates for federally assisted child care. Telephone interview with Mary Ann Higgins, Administration for Children, Youth, and Families, U.S. Department of Health and Human Services, Washington, D.C., July 18, 1994.

72. Ebb, "Child Care Tradeoffs," p. 10.

73. For example, some states report child care disregard payments on their FSA-104 forms (for the JOBS program), while others do not. Similarly, some states carefully avoid double-counting in completing their ACF-700 forms (for the CCDBG program), while others do not. In sifting through various forms, one occasionally notes cells that do not add up to listed totals and other basic problems. The data difficulties are probably due to antiquated computer systems at the state level, diverse record-keeping practices at the state level, limited technical assistance from the federal government, and insufficient lead time from the federal government when distributing new forms. Some of these problems are being addressed.

74. Paul E. Peterson, Barry G. Rabe, and Kenneth K. Wong, *When Federalism Works* (Brookings, 1986).

75. Administration for Children and Families, "Child Care and Development Block Grant: First Annual Report to the Congress on State Program Services and Expenditures" (U.S. Department of Health and Human Services, 1993), table 12.

76. Blank, "Investing in Our Children's Care."

77. In the model, I have used only one regulatory variable (a dichotomous variable for inspections that apply to family day care homes receiving CCDBG funds but not other family day care homes) because of high collinearity between that variable and the training variable. Had I used the training variable instead, the results would have been the same.

78. In the conference report accompanying the bill, the congressional conferees stated that "parents should have the greatest choice possible in selecting child care for their children." See U.S. House of Representatives, "Child Care Statement of Managers," *Congressional Record*, October 26, 1990, p. H12691. The conferees went on to say that a parent assisted under the direct services portion of the CCDBG must have the option of receiving a certificate (or voucher).

79. John E. Chubb and Terry M. Moe, *Politics, Markets, and America's Schools* (Brookings, 1990).

80. John F. Witte and Mark E. Rigdon, "Private School Choice: The Milwaukee Low-Income Voucher Experiment," paper presented at the 1992 annual meeting of the American Political Science Association; Jeffrey R. Henig, *Rethinking School Choice: Limits of the Market Metaphor* (Princeton University Press, 1994).

81. I should note, however, that the National Education Association and the National Council of Jewish Women refused to support the Child Care and Development Block Grant because of their unremitting opposition to funding for church-sponsored child care. See Hofferth, "The 101st Congress," p. 222.

82. John Witte, "The Milwaukee Parental Choice Program: Third Year Report," *La Follette Policy Report*, vol. 6 (Winter 1994), pp. 6–7.

83. Galinsky and others, *The Study of Children in Family Child Care and Relative Care.*

84. U.S. Department of Health and Human Services, "Proposed Rule: Child Care and Development Block Grants and Aid to Families with Dependent Children and Child Care Programs," *Federal Register* (May 11, 1994), pp. 24510–27.

85. Commitment to quality at HHS, however, is now stronger than commitment to either federalism or seamless services. For example, HHS is proposing immunization requirements for all children receiving care under CCDBG, even though this reduces state discretion and could weaken seamless services if states decline to apply such requirements to IV-A programs.

86. In California, for example, the IV-A programs are administered by the Department of Social Services, while the CCDBG program is administered by the Department of Education.

87. Telephone interview with Janet Deal, Indiana Division of Families and Children, Indianapolis, February 4, 1994.

88. U.S. General Accounting Office, "Welfare to Work: States Begin JOBS, but Fiscal and Other Problems May Impede Their Progress," GAO/HRD-91-106 (GAO, September 1991), p. 23.

89. Edward T. Jennings, Jr., "Coordination and Welfare Reform: The Quest for the Philosopher's Stone," *Public Administration Review*, vol. 54 (July/August 1994), pp. 341–48.

## Chapter Six

1. RMC Research Corporation, in collaboration with School-Age Child Care Project at Wellesley College and Mathematica Policy Research Inc., *National*

*Study of Before and After School Programs: Final Report* (U.S. Department of Education, Office of Policy and Planning, 1993), p. 18.

2. Ibid., p. 84.

3. Ibid., p. 90.

4. Ibid., p. 88.

5. Ibid., p. 92.

6. Ibid., p. 52.

7. Ibid., p. 38.

8. Ibid., p. 74.

9. Donald F. Kettl, *Sharing Power: Public Governance and Private Markets* (Brookings, 1993), pp. 179–97.

10. Edward F. Zigler and Mary E. Lang, *Child Care Choices: Balancing the Needs of Children, Families, and Society* (Free Press, 1991), p. 127.

11. National Center for Education Statistics, *The Condition of Education: 1993* (U.S. Department of Education, 1993), p. 373.

12. The source of these data is U.S. Department of Education, National Center for Education Statistics, *The Condition of Education*. The survey was conducted between late December 1990 and early June 1991. Data are also available on the percentage of public schools offering school-age child care programs. To use such data, however, would be to weight small and large schools equally. Data on the percentage of students who have access to programs at their school in effect controls for differences in student enrollment.

13. Data on female employment and the number of school-age children statewide are from the U.S. Bureau of the Census, *Statistical Abstract of the United States* (Government Printing Office, 1991), pp. 23, 144. For information on per capita spending on education, see "Direct General Expenditures of State and Local Governments for All Functions and for Education, by Level and State: 1989–90," *1993 Digest of Education Statistics* (GPO, 1993), p. 40. For data on children in Catholic schools, see Frederick H. Brigham, Jr., "U.S. Catholic Elementary and Secondary Schools, 1989–90: Annual Statistical Report on Schools, Enrollment and Staffing" (Washington: National Catholic Educational Association, 1990), pp. 23–25. The number of Catholic elementary and secondary school children divided by the total number of elementary and secondary school children yielded the ratio used here. The variable for legislation was created by analyzing annual summaries of state child care legislation prepared by the National Conference of State Legislatures in Denver, Colorado. As of 1990, only three states had passed significant school-age child care legislation: Indiana (in 1989), Kentucky (in 1990), and Hawaii (in 1990). Information on direct regulation of SACC programs run by public schools was supplied by Gwen Morgan of Work/Family Directions, Watertown, Massachusetts, in a telephone interview on November 24, 1993. Although Morgan's figures are more current than the data used for other variables in the model, a less precise measure of the same phenomenon from an earlier year yields similar results. The earlier figures, from the Children's

Defense Fund, were not used because they intermix regulation of school-age child care programs and preschool programs run by public schools.

14. Indiana required that every public school district develop a policy concerning the availability of its buildings for school-age child care. Kentucky provided for the establishment of Family Resource Centers, including school-age child care programs, in 25 percent of schools with relatively large populations of disadvantaged children. And Hawaii established an advanced school-age child care program, known as the A+ program, in 170 elementary schools. Indiana subsequently mandated that each school district provide school-age child care or contract out for its provision.

15. The findings might well have been quite similar, if figures for all private schools had been used instead.

16. According to the U.S. Department of Education, only 20.5 percent of our nation's public schools offer after school programs. See National Center for Education Statistics, "Schools and Staffing in the United States: Selected Data for Public and Private Schools, 1990-91" (U.S. Department of Education, June 1993), pp. 9–10. In contrast, 38.3 percent of Catholic schools offer such programs. The survey was conducted between December 1990 and June 1991.

17. The child care spending figures were obtained from Adams and Sandfort. See Gina Adams and Jodi R. Sandfort, "State Investments in Child Care and Early Childhood Education" (Washington: Children's Defense Fund, March 1993), attachment A. The correlation between per capita elementary and secondary education spending and child care spending per child is .61. Because of this high collinearity, I have not included both variables in the same model. The fact that there is a stronger relationship between education spending and school-age child care availability suggests that school-age child care may be perceived more as an educational issue than as a child care issue.

18. The positive relationship suggests that it may take a critical mass of children and parents statewide to generate sufficient interest in school-age child care to provoke a strong policy response. However, this hypothesis is only weakly supported.

19. Elizabeth Samuels, "The Art of Line Drawing: The Establishment Clause and Public Aid to Religiously Affiliated Child Care," *Indiana Law Journal,* vol. 69 (Winter 1993), p. 77.

20. *North Valley Baptist Church* v. *McMahon,* 893 F. 2d 1139 (9th Cir. 1990).

21. *Health Services Division* v. *Temple Baptist Church,* 814 P.2d 130 (N.M. 1991); *State ex rel. Pringle* v. *Heritage Baptist Temple, Inc.,* 696 P.2d 1163 (Kan. 1985); *Michigan Dept. of Social Services* v. *Emanuel Baptist Preschool,* 455 N.W.2d 1 (Mich. 1990). In the Michigan case, the state supreme court held that licensure imposes a "minimal and indirect burden" on the church's exercise of religion. In contrast, the court held, there is a "substantial state interest" in protecting the health and welfare of preschool children receiving care outside the home. The court declined to address the applicability of particular rules to the

# 228    NOTES TO PAGES 142–44

church-based center on the grounds that these issues were not yet "ripe" for adjudication.

22. Carl H. Esbeck, "Government Regulation of Religiously Based Social Services: The First Amendment Considerations," *Hastings Constitutional Law Quarterly*, vol. 19 (Winter 1992), p. 411.

23. The Pennsylvania Catholic Conference objects in particular to regulations that "intrude into program content and staff selection at day care centers." See Henry J. Aschenbrenner, Letter to Mark Ragan, U.S. Department of Health and Human Services, from the Deputy Executive Director of the Pennsylvania Catholic Conference (Harrisburg, Pa.: October 11, 1991), p. 3. More broadly, however, the Conference argues that the state lacks legal authority to license church-run social service programs, such as day care centers. The Conference cites *Commonwealth of Pennsylvania* v. *Ruff Edge Farms*, in which Pennsylvania's commonwealth court ruled that religious instruction conducted by a church-run foster care program is not subject to state regulation but that overnight residential care offered by the same program is. See *Commonwealth of Pennsylvania, Department of Public Welfare* v. *Ruff Edge Farms*, No. 164 C.D., 1985. Despite the Conference's interpretation, this case, if anything, would seem to support the state's authority to regulate church-run social service programs in the usual manner, provided that no attempt is made to regulate the content or the extent of religious instruction.

24. A supervisor explains the process: "You won't find my representatives arguing with the minister that he should be in compliance. We give them the rules. If they read the information and decide to apply [for a license], fine. If we can gain access to assess their facility, we'll do it. If we're denied access, we put that down and forward that information to headquarters. Headquarters forwards it to the attorney general's office and it stays in never-never land." Personal interview (anonymous), Pennsylvania Bureau of Child Care Services, June 14, 1994.

25. *Corporation of the Presiding Bishop of the Church of Jesus Christ of Latter-Day Saints* v. *Amos*, 483 U.S. 327 (1987).

26. See, for example, *Forest Hills Early Learning Center* v. *Grace Baptist Church*, 846 F.2d 260 (4th Cir. 1988). In that case, a federal appeals court rejected the argument made by secular day care centers that Virginia's partial exemption of church-run centers placed them at a competitive disadvantage. Citing the *Amos* decision, the court argued that religious exemptions lessen the risk of entanglement between church and state and are thus justifiable, though not required.

27. As Esbeck notes, the few decisions to the contrary were decided before the Amos decision or on the basis of an issue other than the First Amendment. Esbeck, "Government Regulation of Religiously Based Social Services," p. 396.

28. Burton A. Weisbrod, *The Nonprofit Economy* (Harvard University Press, 1988).

29. The quality of care offered by church-run centers is also worse than that offered by public schools. The quality of care offered by church-run centers, however, does not differ significantly from that offered by independent non-

profits. For relevant comparisons, see Ellen Eliason Kisker and others, *A Profile of Child Care Settings: Early Education and Care in 1990, Vol. 1* (Princeton, N.J.: Mathematica Policy Research, Inc., 1991), pp. 234–37.

30. Ibid., p. 234.

31. By filing a request with the state, church-based centers are designated as 110-106 facilities, which means that they are not technically licensed and that they are exempt from certain regulatory requirements. When inspecting such facilities, state inspectors complete a "notice of compliance" form rather than a license renewal form. According to figures supplied by the Division of Child Development, nearly 50 percent of the church-based centers in North Carolina have elected 110-106 status.

32. These centers, known as AA facilities, must meet other quality requirements as well.

33. Kisker and others, *A Profile of Child Care Settings*, p. 234.

34. Sandra L. Hofferth and others, *National Child Care Survey, 1990* (Washington: Urban Institute, 1991), p. 358.

35. Ellen Galinsky, "Families at Work: The Importance of the Quality of the Work Environment," in Sharon Lynn Kagan and Bernice Weissbourd, eds. *Putting Families First: America's Family Support Movement and the Challenge of Change* (San Francisco: Jossey-Bass, 1994), pp. 112–36.

36. Ibid.

37. Hofferth and others, *National Child Care Survey, 1990*, pp. 371–76.

38. Under that law, companies with fewer than fifty employees are exempt. The law also exempts employees who work less than twenty-five hours per week and employees who have worked less than one year for the company. About half of all U.S. workers are said to be covered by the new law.

39. Sue Shellenbarger, "Work and Family: No Action; So Much Talk, So Little Action: With all the Hype about Family-Friendly Policies, Why is it Business as Usual at Most Companies?", *Wall Street Journal*, June 21, 1993, p. 1.

40. Robert Rose, "Work and Family: On the Job; Small Steps: At U S West, the Culture is Changing; but it isn't Always Smooth—or Easy," *Wall Street Journal*, June 21, 1993, p. 10.

41. Galinsky, "Families at Work," p. 23.

42. Hofferth and others, *National Child Care Survey, 1990*, p. 379; Galinsky, "Families at Work."

43. Shellenbarger, "Work and Family," p. 1.

44. Deloitte and Touche, "Hospital Human Resource Survey," Chicago, 1992. I would like to thank Bill Chafetz of Deloitte & Touche's Chicago office for providing these data in a timely manner and for a reasonable fee.

45. Ibid.

46. The Springhouse survey was conducted for the National Association for Health Care Recruitment. I would like to thank Peg Keeler of the Springhouse Corporation (Springhouse, Pa.) for providing these data in a timely manner and for a reasonable fee.

47. I excluded job-sharing from the model because it is highly correlated with flexible hours.

48. The FTE data come from Deloitte & Touche, *Hospital Human Resource Survey Results—1992* (Chicago: Deloitte & Touche, 1992). The child/staff ratio data come from Gina C. Adams, "Who Knows How Safe? The Status of State Efforts to Ensure Quality Child Care" (Washington: Children's Defense Fund, 1990), pp. 100–101. The unemployment data come from U.S. Bureau of the Census, *Statistical Abstract of the United States* (GPO, 1992), p. 402; and U.S. Bureau of the Census, *Statistical Abstract of the United States* (GPO, 1993), p. 396.

49. Although more lenient (higher) ratios lower center costs and parental fees, they also lower quality. This could give mothers of young children, including nurses, pause before working outside the home. Overworked nurses, as members of a caring profession where personal attention makes a difference, may be especially sensitive to the quality implications of inadequate staffing.

50. J. Johnston, *Econometric Methods,* 2d ed. (McGraw-Hill, 1972), pp. 321–423. Jan Kmenta, *Elements of Econometrics,* 2d ed. (Macmillan, 1986), pp. 672–87. Peter Kennedy, *A Guide to Econometrics,* 3d ed. (MIT Press, 1992), pp. 151–75.

51. Interestingly enough, a turnover variable purged of the reciprocal influence of a child care center also has no impact on the establishment of a child care center.

52. Jules M. Marquart, "How Does the Employer Benefit from Child Care?", in Janet Shibley Hyde and Marilyn J. Essex, eds., *Parental Leave and Child Care: Setting a Research and Policy Agenda* (Temple University Press, 1991), pp. 229–45.

53. Dayle M. Smith, *Kin Care and the American Corporation: Solving the Work/Family Dilemma* (Homewood, Ill.: Business One Irwin, 1991), p. 252.

54. J. T. Childs, Jr., keynote address at the annual meeting of the National Association for Regulatory Administration, Bloomington, Minn., September 19, 1993.

55. Milton Moskowitz and Carol Townsend, "100 Best Companies for Working Mothers," *Working Mother,* vol. 17 (October 1994), p. 36.

56. Ibid., p. 67.

57. The registered nurse has already visited the home in advance and has discussed (and recorded) the child's diet, allergies, and daily habits with the parent in a nonemergency setting. The program is run by Columbia Hospital of Milwaukee in collaboration with Time Insurance.

58. Mitzi Dunn, "Employees' Child Care Policies: Sick Child Care," in Janet Shibley Hyde and Marilyn J. Essex, eds., *Parental Leave and Child Care: Setting a Research and Policy Agenda* (Temple University Press, 1991), pp. 246–51.

59. Employees at other Ben and Jerry's sites, which have no on-site center, also might benefit from an alternative strategy.

60. Smith, *Kin Care and the American Corporation,* p. 32. Kin care includes both children and (elderly) parents.

61. Marquart, "How Does the Employer Benefit from Child Care?"

62. Collaborators include a few not-so-small law firms and two YMCAs.

63. In each instance, the child care must actually be used by employees. Thus the tax credit does not apply to charitable contributions that support child care providers.

64. Most of these particular interviews were conducted by my research assistant, Jennifer Bush. The Vermont interviews were conducted in March 1994; the Texas interviews were conducted in April 1994.

65. In three instances (two in Vermont, one in Texas), R&Rs report that they avoid referrals to centers with substantiated complaints, though they do not explicitly address such matters in conversations with parents.

66. That is probably true, for example, in states where R&Rs or R&R networks were created by the state legislature.

67. Two partial exceptions come to mind. In New Jersey and Wisconsin, some R&Rs have entered into contracts with state or local agencies to certify that certain family day care homes are in compliance with voluntary standards that make them eligible for specific programs, such as the Child and Adult Care Food Program. In both states, however, compliance with mandatory standards is the responsibility of state officials.

68. An example of false representation would be for an R&R to claim that all child care facilities listed on its roster are licensed by the state when that is not the case. To avoid such a possibility, R&Rs should update their files regularly.

69. W. Page Keeton and others, *Prosser and Keeton on the Law of Torts*, 5th ed. (St. Paul: West Publishing Co., 1984), p. 499.

70. *Wilson v. Martin Memorial Hospital*, 61 S.E.2d 102 (N.C. 1950); *Kavanaugh v. Nussbaum*, 523 N.E.2d 284 (N.Y. 1988); *Reed v. Gershweir*, 772 P.2d 26 (Ariz. 1989).

71. *Harwick v. Harris*, 166 So.2d 912 (Fla. 1964); *McCay v. Mitchell*, 463 S.W.2d 710 (Tenn. 1970); *Ross v. Sher*, 483 S.W.2d 297 (Tex. 1972); *Tramutola v. Bortone*, 304 A.2d 197 (N.J. 1973); *Stovall v. Harms*, 522 P.2d 353 (Kans. 1974).

72. Robert D. Sack and Sandra S. Barron, *Libel, Slander, and Related Problems*, 2d ed. (New York: Practising Law Institute, 1994), p. 69.

73. *Philadelphia Newspapers, Inc. v. Hepps*, 475 U.S. 767 (1986); *Dun & Bradstreet Inc. v. Greenmoss Builders, Inc.*, 472 U.S. 749 (1985); *Gertz v. Robert Welch Inc.*, 418 U.S. 323 (1974); *New York Times v. Sullivan*, 376 U.S. 254 (1964).

74. Four dissenters in *Greenmoss*, for example, took the position that a report about a local firm's alleged bankruptcy raised an issue of public concern because a bankruptcy could have economic repercussions and because citizens might reconsider their views of economic regulation if the report were true. The majority did not fully explain its belief that the bankruptcy did not raise an issue of public concern, but the sale of information for profit by Dun & Bradstreet may have been a factor (despite a series of rulings, some judges attach less weight to commercial free speech than to political free speech). If so, the resolution of a slander suit against an R&R might hinge in part on the question of whether the

R&R sells its information for profit. Although some R&Rs charge a nominal fee for their services, many waive that fee, and the overwhelming majority of R&Rs are nonprofit organizations. Thus it should be easier for R&Rs to claim that political—and not commercial—free speech is involved.

75. Actual malice is defined as knowledge of a statement's falsity or reckless disregard of whether or not the statement was false.

76. Sack and Barron, *Libel, Slander, and Related Problems,* pp. 370–83; Keeton and others, *Prosser and Keeton on the Law of Torts,* pp. 825–36.

77. U.S. Advisory Commission on Intergovernmental Relations, "Child Care: The Need for Federal-State-Local Coordination" (Washington: ACIR, March 1994), p. 50.

78. Everett M. Rogers and Rekha A. Rogers, *Communication in Organizations* (Free Press, 1976), p. 137.

79. Sue Conley of the Office of Child Care Services estimates that approximately 120 individuals examined the 204 files.

80. As of 1994, kiosks were located in Colorado Springs, Grand Junction, Fort Collins, and a Denver suburb.

81. Each computer is attached to a printer that prints copies of answers to particular queries free of charge.

82. Jennifer Gavin, "Wider Access to Day-Care Files Gets OK," *Denver Post,* September 7, 1994, p. 20.

83. Philip Selznick, *The Moral Commonwealth: Social Theory and the Promise of Community* (University of California Press, 1992); Amitai Etzioni, *The Spirit of Community: Rights, Responsibilities, and the Communitarian Agenda* (Crown Publishers, 1993); Benjamin R. Barber, *Strong Democracy: Participatory Politics for a New Age* (University of California Press, 1984).

84. Dewitt John, *Civic Environmentalism: Alternatives to Regulation in States and Communities* (Washington: CQ Press, 1994).

## Chapter Seven

1. Theda Skocpol, *Protecting Soldiers and Mothers: The Political Origins of Social Policy in the United States* (Harvard University Press, 1992), pp. 311–524.

2. Aaron B. Wildavsky, *Speaking Truth to Power: The Art and Craft of Policy Analysis* (Boston: Little, Brown, 1979).

3. Philip Selznick, *The Moral Commonwealth: Social Theory and the Promise of Community* (University of California Press, 1992); Amitai Etzioni, *The Spirit of Community: The Reinvention of American Society* (Touchstone Books, 1993).

4. Several organizations publish annual ratings of colleges and universities. *The Fiske Guide to Colleges* evaluates more than 300 schools, based on surveys of school administrators and open-ended surveys of the student body. *The Princeton Review* evaluates nearly 300 schools, based on surveys of independent college counselors and closed-ended surveys of the student body. *U.S. News and World*

*Report* also publishes an annual review, based on a reputational survey and data published by other sources.

5. Mary Jo Bane and David T. Ellwood, *Welfare Realities: From Rhetoric to Reform* (Harvard University Press, 1994), pp. 74–78.

6. John J. DiIulio, Jr., "Punishing Smarter: Penal Reforms for the 1990s," *Brookings Review,* vol. 7 (Summer 1989), p. 9.

7. Stringent regulations, adapted from now defunct national regulations, guarantee high quality at day care centers.

8. William T. Gormley, Jr., and B. Guy Peters, "National Styles of Regulation: Child Care in Three Countries," *Policy Sciences,* vol. 25 (November 1992), pp. 381–99.

9. Timothy Smeeding, Barbara Boyle Torrey, and Martin Rein, "Patterns of Income and Poverty: The Economic Status of Children and the Elderly in Eight Countries," in John L. Palmer, Timothy Smeeding, and Barbara Boyle Torrey, eds., *The Vulnerable* (Washington: Urban Institute, 1988), pp. 89–119.

10. Phyllis Moen, *Working Parents: Transformations in Gender Roles and Public Policies in Sweden* (University of Wisconsin Press, 1989).

11. Martin Woodhead, "When Psychology Informs Public Policy: The Case of Early Childhood Intervention," *American Psychologist,* vol. 43 (June 1988), pp. 443–54; Valerie Lee, Elizabeth Schnur, and Jeanne Brooks-Gunn, "Does Head Start Work? A 1-Year Follow-Up Comparison of Disadvantaged Children Attending Head Start, No Preschool, and Other Preschool Programs," *Developmental Psychology,* vol. 24 (March 1988), pp. 210–22; Ron Haskins, "Beyond Metaphor: The Efficacy of Early Childhood Education," *American Psychologist,* vol. 44 (February 1989), pp. 274–82; Edward F. Zigler and Susan Muenchow, *Head Start: The Inside Story of America's Most Successful Educational Experiment* (Basic Books, 1992), pp. 150–70.

12. W. Steven Barnett, "Benefits of Compensatory Preschool Education," *Journal of Human Resources,* vol. 27 (Spring 1992), pp. 279–312.

13. Lawrence Schweinhart and David Weikart, "The Effects of the Perry Preschool Program on Youths through Age 15—A Summary," in The Consortium for Longitudinal Studies, *As the Twig is Bent: Lasting Effects of Preschool Programs* (Hillsdale, N.J.: Lawrence Erlbaum Associates, 1983), pp. 71–101; Barnett, "Benefits of Compensatory Preschool Education."

14. Judith M. Gueron and Edward Pauly, *From Welfare to Work* (New York: Russell Sage Foundation, 1991), pp. 162–64.

15. Citizens for Better Care, *The Consumer Guide to Nursing Homes in Southeast Michigan* (Detroit: Citizens for Better Care, 1994).

16. Richard Elmore, "School Decentralization: Who Gains? Who Loses?" in Jane Hannaway and Martin Carnoy, eds., *Decentralization and School Improvement* (San Francisco: Jossey-Bass, 1993), pp. 33–54.

17. Robert N. Bellah and others, *Habits of the Heart: Individualism and Commitment in American Life* (University of California Press, 1985).

18. These estimates, from the Congressional Budget Office, are based on the Clinton administration's 1994 welfare reform proposal. See Congressional Budget

Office, "The Administration's Welfare Reform Proposals: A Preliminary Cost Estimate" (CBO, December 1994). The CBO estimates that the federal government would have to spend $1.5 billion in additional dollars in 1999 for welfare-to-work programs alone and that state and local governments would have to spend $420 million in additional dollars in 1999 for welfare-to-work programs and for an expanded At-Risk program. I estimate that $304 million of the $420 million in new state and local expenditures would be devoted to child care for welfare-to-work programs (based on CBO's breakdown of federal spending). Thus $1.5 billion (in federal expenditures) plus $304 million (in state and local expenditures) yields approximately $1.8 billion.

19. According to the Administration for Children and Families, "Fact Sheet: ACF Child Care Programs Serving Children and Families" (Washington: U.S. Department of Health and Human Services, January 1995), the Child Care and Development Block Grant program served 756,000 children and the IV-A At-Risk program served at least 219,000 children during fiscal year 1993. Federal budget outlays for the CCDBG program in fiscal 1993, minus infrastructure expenses aimed at improving quality, amounted to approximately $835 million ($892 million minus 6.25 percent). Federal budget outlays for the At-Risk program amounted to approximately $270 million, and corresponding state government expenditures amounted to approximately $204 million, if one assumes an average 57 percent federal match. Thus the federal government and the state governments spent a combined total of $1.309 billion to serve 975,000 children. To serve an additional million children at the time would have cost approximately $1.343 billion ($1.309 billion x 1.026). If one assumes equally proportionate increases in CCDBG and At-Risk expenditures, no change in matching rates, and new appropriations to cover 4 percent annual increases in the cost of child care, the federal government and the state governments would need to spend an additional $1.699 billion in fiscal year 1999.

20. Lester M. Salamon, *America's Nonprofit Sector: A Primer* (New York: Foundation Center, 1992), p. 63.

21. Salamon, *America's Nonprofit Sector,* p. 67.

22. It is important to note that more than one-third of all children enrolled in group day care centers are enrolled in for-profit centers. For-profit centers enjoy larger average enrollments than other centers, and chain-affiliated for-profit centers enjoy particularly large enrollments. See Barbara Willer and others, *The Demand and Supply of Child Care in 1990* (Washington: National Association for the Education of Young Children, 1991), pp. 18–19. Larger capacities and lower prices may help to explain these differences.

23. Suzanne W. Helburn, ed., "Cost, Quality, and Child Outcomes in Child Care Centers, Technical Report" (Economics Department, University of Colorado at Denver, 1995), table 4.8.

24. Meryl Frank, "Cost, Financing, and Implementation Mechanisms of Parental Leave Policies," in Edward Zigler and Meryl Frank, eds., *The Parental Leave Crisis: Toward a National Policy* (Yale University Press, 1988), pp. 317–

18. Claims might be lower, of course, if women returned to work before the year was up.

25. I assume that there would be 4 million infants in 1999 and that the minimum wage would have increased from $4.25 per hour to $5.00 per hour (or $10,400 per year). I also assume that 65 percent of all mothers with infants would claim benefits. This last assumption is a bit speculative. Sixty-five percent of all pregnant women worked while pregnant during the 1980s, but that percentage could increase if paid parental leave became available. On the other hand, some women would undoubtedly choose to go back to work sooner than required. Multiplying 4 million by $10,400 by .65, one gets $27.0 billion.

26. This assumes that one-third of all mothers of infants will be single mothers in 1999. Thus one multiplies 1.33 million by $10,400 by .65. One then multiplies 2.67 million by $5,200 by .65. Adding the two together yields $18.0 billion.

27. Jonathan Gruber and Alan Krueger, "The Incidence of Mandated Employer-Provided Insurance: Lessons from Workers' Compensation Insurance," in David Bradford, ed., *Tax Policy and the Economy 5* (MIT Press, 1991), pp. 111–43; Jonathan Gruber, "The Incidence of Mandated Maternity Benefits," *American Economic Review*, vol. 84 (June 1994), pp. 622–41.

28. Fay Lomax Cook and Edith J. Barrett, *Support for the American Welfare State: The Views of Congress and the Public* (Columbia University Press, 1992), pp. 121–24.

29. James E. Curtis, Edward G. Grabb, and Douglas E. Baer, "Voluntary Association Membership in Fifteen Countries: A Comparative Analysis," *American Sociological Review*, vol. 57 (April 1992), p. 145.

30. Independent Sector, *Giving and Volunteering in the United States: 1992 Edition* (Washington: Independent Sector, 1992).

31. U.S. Advisory Commission on Intergovernmental Relations, *Child Care: The Need for Federal-State-Local Coordination* (Washington: ACIR, March 1994), p. 39.

32. As in the previous example, I project a minimum wage of $10,400 and 4 million infants. A 10 percent participation rate (as opposed to a 65 percent participation rate) would yield a total cost of $4.16 billion, to be allocated as follows: federal government, 40 percent ($1.66 billion); employers, 40 percent ($1.66 billion); and employees, 20 percent ($0.83 billion).

33. In 1994 the federal government awarded tax credits worth approximately $2.7 billion through the Child and Dependent Care Tax Credit. Of that amount, about 36 percent went to families with adjusted gross incomes above $50,000. See Committee on Ways and Means, U.S. House of Representatives, *Overview of Entitlement Programs: 1994 Green Book* (GPO, 1994), p. 707.

34. National Commission on Children, *Beyond Rhetoric: A New American Agenda for Children and Families* (GPO, 1991), p. 451.

35. See Congressional Budget Office, "The Administration's Welfare Reform Proposals," table A.3. The Congressional Budget Office's estimate (cost savings of $195 million in 1999) assumes that family day care homes could qualify for funds

if (1) the home is located in a low-income area; (2) the provider is low-income; or (3) the children are means-tested (only those with incomes below 185 percent of the poverty level would qualify). Thus a somewhat more austere program (means-testing for all children) would save more than $195 million per year.

36. See Gueron and Pauly, *From Welfare to Work*, for a benefit-cost analysis of welfare-to-work programs. See Barnett, "Benefits of Compensatory Preschool Education," for a benefit-cost analysis of preschool programs.

37. Advisory Commission on Intergovernmental Relations, *Child Care*, pp. 19–21.

38. David Osborne and Ted Gaebler, *Reinventing Government: How the Entrepreneurial Spirit is Transforming the Public Sector* (Reading, Mass.: Addison-Wesley, 1992), pp. 25–48.

39. William T. Gormley, Jr., "Regulating Mister Rogers' Neighborhood: The Dilemmas of Day Care Regulation," *Brookings Review*, vol. 8 (Fall 1990), pp. 21–28.

40. C. Eric Lincoln and Lawrence Mamiya, *The Black Church and the African American Experience* (Duke University Press, 1990), p. 256.

41. RMC Research Corporation, *National Study of Before & After School Programs* (Portsmouth, N.H.: RMC, 1993), p. 55.

42. Ellen Eliason Kisker and others, *A Profile of Child Care Settings: Early Education and Care in 1990, Vol. 1* (Princeton, N.J.: Mathematica Policy Research, 1991), p. 234.

43. Moen, *Working Parents*.

44. Catherine E. Ross and John Mirowsky, "Child Care and Emotional Adjustment to Wives' Employment," *Journal of Health and Social Behavior*, vol. 29 (June 1988), pp. 127–38; Ellen Greenberger and Robin O'Neil, "Parents' Concerns about Their Child's Development: Implications for Fathers' and Mothers' Well-Being and Attitudes toward Work," *Journal of Marriage and the Family*, vol. 52 (August 1990), pp. 621–35.

45. Robert D. Putnam, *Making Democracy Work: Civic Traditions in Modern Italy* (Princeton University Press, 1993), p. 177.

# Index